A Soul Set Free

A Soul Set Free

A Study of the Epistle to the Romans

Dr. Stanford E. Murrell

Stanford E. Murrell, *A Soul Set Free: A Study of the Epistle to the Romans*
Copyright © 2013 by Stanford Murrell.

All right reserved. No part of this publication may be reproduced, stored in a retrieval system, or transmitted in any form by any means, electronic, mechanical, photocopy, recording, or otherwise without prior permission of the author, except as provided by USA copyright law.

ISBN-13: 978-1492200628
ISBN-10: 149220062X

"For therein is the righteousness of God revealed from faith to faith: as it is written, The just shall live by faith."

—Romans 1:17, KJV

Table of Contents

1	Romans 1	7
2	Romans 2	94
3	Romans 3	116
4	Romans 4	145
5	Romans 5	172
6	Romans 6	216
7	Romans 7	224
8	Romans 8	236
9	Romans 9	261
10	Romans 10	275
11	Romans 11	286
12	Romans 12	300
13	Romans 13	314
14	Romans 14	319
15	Romans 15	324
16	Romans 16	332

Appendix I   *General Comments and Practical Application from The Epistle to the Romans*   342

1

Romans 1

c. 57 AD

> *"Spiritual revival in the Church will be connected to a deeper understanding of this book."*
> —Frederick Godet
> 19th Century Swiss Theologian

A Servant of Jesus Christ: Romans 1:1

The apostle Paul was one of the most remarkable men to have walked on planet earth. Brilliant of mind, slow of speech, physically unattractive, his influence upon human history is without question. And yet, not many would ever have heard of him had he not had a crisis of conscience one day that led to a dramatic conversion experience.

According to Acts 9, Paul, initially known as Saul of Tarsus, was part of a religious persecution of the Church in Jerusalem. He had already consented to the death of the Christian named Stephen, the implication being that Saul was in a position of leadership to stop the stoning of this saint. But Saul did not allow Stephen to live, for he was angry, and thirsty for blood. Saul felt threatened by the dynamics of the message of the gospel that proclaimed the Messiah had come and that His name was Jesus. For Saul and many others, that was impossible! Jesus was an impostor. Jesus had been crucified. Jesus had been condemned for crimes against the state.

Good people would not have killed the Messiah if He had really been sent from God. Surely Christ was not the Chosen One of Israel, for He claimed to be the Son of God. He had also blasphemed by claiming to be very God, of very God. Then He claimed that He could forgive sins because He was the Savior of the world! In addition, Jesus taught of a spiritual kingdom within the hearts of men, thereby destroying the political hopes and dreams of the nationalists. Now His followers were teaching that the Law of Moses was no longer effective, and the sacrifices should cease. All of this disruption was just too much for the people of Palestine. Neither Saul nor the other Jewish leaders could handle the moral, social, financial, and religious revolution that was going on. This Christian movement had to be destroyed, and Saul was deemed the proper instrument suited for its demise. His qualifications were impeccable.

- Saul was a Hebrew of the Hebrews, for he was of the purest Hebrew blood. He had been *"circumcised the eighth day, of the stock of Israel, of the tribe of Benjamin"* (Philippians 3:5). Despite the fact that Saul was born in the Gentile city of Tarsus in Cilicea (Acts 21:39), his devout Jewish parents made sure he preserved, and honored his cultural, and racial identity.

- Saul was, like his father, a Pharisee (Acts 23:6). He was not only racially a Jew, but also religiously a conservative Jew.

- Saul was a proficient Jew. Tarsus was celebrated as a school of Greek literature. Here, Saul acquired knowledge of Greek authors and philosophy, which would later qualify him to challenge their thinking, by quoting their own authors: Aratus (Acts 17:18-28), Menander (1 Corinthians 15:33), and Epimendies (Titus 1:12). In addition to a Greek education, Saul's main education was in the race of his people, for he sat at the feet of Gamaliel (Acts 22:3).

- Saul was a hardworking Jew. As a young man, he had learned the Cilician trade of making tents of goat's haircloth (Acts 18:3). Jewish custom required that each child learn a trade regardless of how wealthy the parents might be.

- To add to his advantages of having both a Jewish and Greek cultural upbringing, Saul possessed Roman citizenship from birth, which brought immediate, and important privileges in certain circumstances (Acts 22:28).

All of these natural elements, helped to create in the soul of Saul, a spirit of religious self-righteousness, worldly sophistication, and an unbridled zeal, that led him to violently oppose any threat to his heritage. The growing Christian community possessed just such a threat, and so it was that Saul made *havoc* of the Church. He ravaged the Church, as a wild beast by storming into the houses where worship services were being held, and hauling men and women off to prison (Acts 8:3). Later, with many tears and much sorrow, Saul would confess that he did these horrible things in unbelief (1 Timothy 1:12-16). Though God had mercy upon him, Saul was still at fault for his crimes against Christ, and His Church, for Saul might have known the truth if he had sought for it. Saul did not seek the truth in Christ, and remained dead in trespasses and sin.

Only a supernatural act of sovereign grace could subdue the wild beast that rode Saul's will. Such grace did come to Saul, when the resurrected Christ arrested him, as he was seeking to arrest others. Of this great event, there are three accounts: one by Luke (Acts 9), and the others by Saul (Acts 22; Acts 16). According to Saul's own narrative, he was on his journey to Damascus, with authoritative letters from the High Priest of Israel, empowering him to arrest and bring back to Jerusalem all who were followers of The Way (Acts 7:2). It did not matter if the people involved were men, women, or children. It did not matter if economic hardships were created. It did not matter if fear and terror were unleashed. It did not matter if families were torn apart. The only caution was not to let the Gentile governors become involved in the persecution process. The Christians were to be brought to Jerusalem! And so it was, on a particular day, at noontime, a brilliant light suddenly shone upon Saul and his company, who were committed to executing religious crimes against humanity. The light from heaven was equivalent to the explosion of a nuclear bomb, for it was brighter than the brightness of the sun itself.

Saul was thrown to the earth, as were his companions (Acts 26:14). After a few moments, some of them arose and stood up speechless, wondering what was happening (Acts 9:7). Then they heard the sound of a voice, but did not understand what they were hearing (1

Corinthians 14:2). However Saul understood, for it was the voice of the Son of God, saying in the Hebrew language, *"Saul, Saul, Why persecutest thou Me?"* Jesus had taught His followers that when they were persecuted, He would be wounded with them (Matthew 25:40), and He was. *"Saul, It is hard for thee to kick against the prick"* (Acts 26:14). Saul was acting like an ox being driven. When the animal kicked back, it only made the goad pierce the flesh deeper (Matthew 21:44; Proverbs 8:36). So, when Saul kicked against the Church, he was ultimately hurting himself. When he heard these words, the Bible says that Saul trembled, as a Philippian jailer would later tremble (Acts 16:30-31). And Saul said, *"Lord, what wilt Thou have me to do?"* In these simple words, all the facets of saving faith are manifested.

First, Saul recognized the Lordship of Christ. Jesus is not only the Savior of the soul; He is the Sovereign of all life. The Biblical example of a true conversion experience records that individuals fall before Jesus, and recognize Him as Lord and Savior.

Second, there was submission to the Savior. *"Lord, what wilt Thou have me to do?"* asked Saul. Until now, Saul had been doing all that He wanted to do, with the result that people were afraid of him. Saul was not bringing joy or happiness into the lives of others, but hatred and hardship. Doing things his way had not made Saul, or anyone else happy.

Third, Saul, on that Damascus Road, manifested tremendous faith in the Person of Christ. Saul understood it all. Jesus was alive! Jesus had come back from the dead! Jesus really was who He claimed to be!

Somehow, time managed to pass that day, and the next. Life went on, but Saul was never the same again. He had become a Christian, and he would grow in grace, and in knowledge of our Lord and Savior, Jesus Christ. The Bible tells us that Saul did grow in the graces of life, to the point that he was ready to minister to the Church as an apostle. But that acceptance would not happen suddenly. Time had to pass before Saul was accepted as a true minister of Christ, with a right to speak as an apostle of Jesus Christ (1 Corinthians 14:37). He, who had persecuted the Church, had to prove himself.

Separated unto the Gospel of God: Romans 1:1

In his preface to *St. Paul's Epistle to the Romans,* the great Reformation leader Martin Luther began with these thoughts: *"This Epistle is in truth the principal part of the New Testament and the very purest Gospel. It fully deserves that every Christian should know it by heart, word for word, and should feed upon it every day, as daily bread for his soul. It cannot be read too often nor too deeply pondered, and the more it is studied the more precious and sweet to the taste does it become."*

Harry Ironside said, *"It is the most scientific statement of the divine plan for the redemption of mankind. It is the orderly setting forth of the Gospel that the mind of man craves, the declaration of man's need along with the gracious plan of God's salvation which culminates in His glorification."* With these wonderful words of exhortation, and explanation, the study of Romans continues in verse one. From the hour of his conversion to Christ, Saul realized that he had been separated unto the gospel of God.

First, he had been separated from his life of honors. Saul was a Pharisee, and as a Pharisee he had been a respected member of society. He had been a ruler of the Jews, with sweeping political power; but from the moment he met the Master, Saul became a servant, a *doulos,* separated from the titles of worldly recognition.

Second, Saul, now Paul, had been separated from the works of the Law. All his life Paul had been taught the value and importance of the Law. The Law was holy, just, and good; but the Law was also severe. The Law was critical of the human heart and human conduct, for it judged the individual. The Law was meant to judge this, because in His infinite wisdom the Lord God was making a point: no one can keep the Law. *"There is none righteous, no not one."* The basic commandments are constantly being violated.

One day, on the road to Damascus, Saul of Tarsus realized this simple gospel truth. He too was a violator of the Law. One day, on the road to Damascus, Saul was slain in the spirit, as he realized that he was breaking many facets of that which he wanted so desperately to honor. For example, the Law said, *"Thou shalt have no other gods before me."* Saul had another god, so called, besides the Lord Jesus. His god was religion. Saul of Tarsus was giving his life to Judaism, with all its rules and regulations, with all its ceremonies and rituals. The Law said, *"Thou shalt not kill,"* but Saul had murder in his heart and the blood of the martyred Stephen on his hands. The Law said, *"Thou shalt not covet,"* but Saul wanted what the Christian community had. By being converted to Christ, Saul was separated in his heart from a system of salvation by works under the Law, to loving a precious Savior, and living under grace.

Martin Luther on Faith

Then third, Saul was separated from the works of the flesh, to a life of faith. What is faith?

"...Faith is a divine work in us, which transforms us and begets us anew from God (John 1:13), which crucifies the Old Adam, makes us in heart, temper, disposition, and in all our powers entirely different men, and brings with it the Holy Spirit. O, this faith is a living, busy, active, powerful thing! It is impossible that it should not be ceaselessly doing that which is good. It does not even ask whether good works should be done; but before the question can be asked, it has done them, and it is constantly engaged in doing them. But he who does not do such works is a man without faith. He gropes and casts about himself to find faith and good works, not knowing what either of them is, yet prattles and idly multiplies words about faith and good works. Faith is a living, well-founded confidence in the grace of God; so perfectly certain that it would die a thousand times rather than surrender its conviction. Such confidence and personal knowledge of divine race make its possessor joyful, bold, and full of warm affection toward God and all created things all of which the Holy Spirit works in faith. Hence, such a man becomes without constraint willing and eager to do good to everyone, to serve everyone, to suffer all manner of ills, in order to please and to glorify God, who has shown toward him such grace".

At a meeting in Aldersgate Street, London, on 24 May 1738, *"about a quarter before nine,"* John Wesley heard this extended definition of faith, and felt his heart *strangely warmed.* Wesley prayed that God would grant him the priceless gift of faith, and the Lord was gracious. Like Saul of Tarsus, like every soul that comes to the Savior, John Wesley (1703-1791) was separated unto the gospel that has its origin in God. Having been separated unto the gospel, Saul was immediately made an apostle of the Lord Jesus Christ. In this manner, great honor was added to great grace.

Doctrine of Apostleship

1. The word *"apostle"* refers to a person sent forth on an important and special mission. The word in the Greek, speaks of a person sent forth. The twelve Disciples of Christ were sent out to preach the gospel of redeeming grace.

2. The Biblical list of apostles include the following, (Matthew 10:25; Mark 3:14-19; Luke 6:13-16; Acts 1:13): Andrew, Bartholomew, James the younger and the son of Alphaeus; James the elder; John, a son of Zebedee; Jude (Lebbaeus or Thaddeus); Philip; Simon the Canaanite; Simon, also called Peter; Judas Iscariot; Matthew (Levi); and Thomas (Didymus).

3. Later, Matthias was selected by The Twelve to replace Judas Iscariot (Acts 1:15-26).

   Special Note. It is possible that God never honored the selection of Matthias. It was His will that Paul would be appointed to take the place of Judas as the *Apostle to the Gentiles*.

4. Apostleship required specific qualifications. There were specific qualifications to being an apostle. An Apostle was one who had been with Christ from the beginning of His ministry (Acts 1:21), was an eyewitness of the resurrected Christ, and had to have the ability to confer gifts upon others (1 Corinthians 9:12; 2 Corinthians 12:12; Romans 1:11; 15:18-19).

5. Following the Day of Pentecost, the Apostles were new men, for they received power from on high as Jesus had promised (Luke 24:48,49; Acts 1:8,22; 2:32; 3:15,32; 8:31).

6. In a wider usage, the word may refer to an individual sent on a special commission, such as Barnabas (Acts 14:14).

7. Jesus is called an Apostle in Hebrews 3:1. From the moment of his conversion, Paul was destined to be an Apostle, for sovereign grace had separated him unto the gospel of God. The phrase, *"the gospel of God"* reminds us of the true origin of the gospel. The gospel is not a lie nor is it a dream. The good news of divine grace is not the creation of the fertile imaginations of men. It is of God! Therefore, to Him, is all honor, and glory, and power!

Christ in the Old Testament: Romans 1:2

The apostle Paul argued that the gospel he preached was first declared in the Old Testament so that it can be said that, *"The Old is by the New explained, and The New is in the Old contained; or, The New is in the Old concealed; The Old is in the New revealed."* The good news, which Paul proclaimed, was the same gospel of mercy and truth, which has always been presented to man as the way of salvation. There is only one avenue of redemption and that is by grace through faith in the person of Jesus Christ as He is presented.

No generation has ever been left without knowledge of the Lord. The advent, the character, the work, and the kingdom of the Messiah are predicted in the Old Testament. In the New Testament the discovery is made that Jesus is the promised Messiah. The Lord said that Abraham rejoiced to see His day. Abraham was saved by faith in Christ.

Because the Old Testament consistently teaches salvation in the Person of Christ, these Scriptures are to be viewed as being *holy*, or of Divine origin. Proper respect and reverence must be shown to them. Christ showed proper respect when He appealed to the Scriptures as vindication of His messianic claims (Luke 24:25-32, 44-48; 4:21; 22:37). Paul showed respect by believing what they taught. The apostle then argued his case.

It was God Who promised a Redeemer. It was God who promised a Redeemer by His prophets. It was God who preserved the promise of a Redeemer through His prophets in sacred writing. It was God who gave man His revelation. When Adam and Eve first heard the gospel in Genesis 3:15, it was according to Divine revelation. When

Moses received the instructions for the Tabernacle, it was according to Divine revelation. The gospel is not, and has never been the product of the progressive religious development in the imaginations of men. The gospel is according to Divine promise provided outside man's human understanding. And always, the gospel speaks of Christ.

Perhaps the greatest illustration of the gospel in the Old Testament is found in the Tabernacle. Everything about the Tabernacle spoke of Christ, including where it was built. The Bible teaches that the Tabernacle was built in the wilderness. It was not built in Egypt, but in the wilderness, and for good reason. Egypt was the place of idolatry. God's people had to be delivered from such an environment, prior to participating in pure worship.

After four hundred years of bondage to the Egyptians, the deliverance of Israel came. It came by a double redemption: the sprinkling of blood and the crossing of the Red Sea. In a mighty way God showed Himself strong on behalf of His people. After they had been brought out of Egypt, the Jews were instructed to build a place of worship. The result was the Tabernacle. With Egypt behind them, and Canaan in front; delivered from the one, but not yet entered into rest in the other; ever on the move, while being dependent upon the grace of the Most High; the Jews roamed in the desert, covered by the blood, while feeding on the Lamb, and worshipping in the Tabernacle. In the Tabernacle the gospel was preached. Paul was right. Christ is to be found in the Old Testament. He can be found in the Tabernacle in the wilderness. In fact, on every page, in every verse, the Lord will be discovered to the discerning, spiritual eye that looks for Him.

Where Does the Most High Dwell?

If the question were asked, *"Where shall the Most High be found?"* The Scriptures give many answers to the question. First, the Bible teaches that the Lord dwells in the heavens. *"Thus saith the High and Lofty One that inhabiteth eternity, whose name is holy; I dwell in the high and holy place"* (Isaiah 57:15). God fills the infinity of time and space. He fills heaven and earth; Heaven is His throne and the earth His footstool. None can flee and hide themselves from Him.

As grand as this concept is, it does not satisfy our hearts; He who is everywhere, may still be nowhere near to us. Souls need God to be more definite and near; and He is, for the Bible teaches that God dwells *"with him that is of a contrite and humble spirit"* (Isaiah 57:15). In the heart of the man, or woman, or young person who loves and fears God, and who trembles at His Word, there is a manifestation of God's presence. *"If a man love me,"* said Christ, *"my Father will love him, and we will come unto him, and make Our abode with him"* (John 14:23).

Once the Tabernacle was God's dwelling place: *"Let them make me a sanctuary; that I may dwell among them"* (Exodus 25:8). Eden had been the first place to know a manifestation of God, for the Son of God, *"the image of the invisible God"* (Colossians 1:15) had walked and talked with Adam and Eve. But they sinned, and the Lord withdrew His presence while banishing our first parents from the Garden. In shame, they fled from the face of God until they were invited to return. Blood atonement was made, and fellowship was restored.

Time passed. Again the Lord wanted to draw near to man in a more visible way, so the Tabernacle was built. Individuals found forgiveness, and pardon, in the substitutionary death of another after sacrificial blood was sprinkled on the mercy seat in the Holy of Holies. Men also found a continual symbol of the Messiah who was to come. And He did come. John the Baptist called Him, *"The Word"*, and wrote, *"The Word was made flesh, and tabernacled among us"* (John 1:14).

Where does the Most High dwell? He dwells in Christ (Colossians 2:9). *"In Him dwelleth all the fullness of the Godhead bodily."* And yet, though *"God was in Christ"* (2 Corinthians 5:19), the question of His abode is not at an end, for the Scriptures declare that the Church is *"builded together for an inhabitant of God through the Spirit"* (Ephesians 2:22), and so is God's dwelling place now on earth?

By His Spirit, through Christ, *"God is in us of a truth"* (1 Corinthians 14:25). In spiritual terms, the Church is an extension of the Incarnation; as God was in Christ, the Head, so is He now in the Church, the body. *"Know ye not that ye are the Temple of God, and that the*

Spirit of God dwelleth in you? The Temple of God is holy, which Temple ye are" (1 Corinthians 3:16, 17). *"Ye are the Temple of the Living God; as God hath said, I will dwell in them and walk in them"* (2 Corinthians 6:16).

Here then are five different senses of the concept of God's dwelling place. God dwells in the heavens; dwelt in the Tabernacle and in the Temple; dwells in the Person of Christ; dwells in individual Christians; He dwells in the Church. The challenge that arises is to know the reality, and the power of being a fit dwelling place for the God who made us, loves us, and redeemed us for Himself!

Is Jesus God? Romans 1:3

As the Apostle Paul continues his salutation to the Church of Rome, he declares that the gospel he was separated unto, was preached in the Old Testament, as it focused upon the person and work of Jesus Christ, who is called *"the Son of God"* (Romans 1:4). Here is the heart of the Christian faith. Either Jesus Christ is the Son of God and very God of very God, or He is not. Either Jesus is who He claimed to be, or He is a lunatic; or worse yet, He is a liar.

Because of Jesus' claim it is of paramount importance to examine the question, *"Is Jesus God?"* The historic Orthodox Church has always affirmed that Jesus is God. Many declarations in the Scriptures affirm the deity of Christ.

1. The deity of Christ is declared in the gospels in the power that He displayed. Jesus is declared to be all-powerful. *"And Jesus came and spake unto them, saying, All power is given unto me in heaven and in earth"* (Matthew 28:18).

    - The power of the Lord is manifested over affliction: *"And he stood over her, and rebuked the fever; and it left her: and immediately she arose and ministered unto them"* (Luke 4:39).

    - The power of the Lord is manifested over the demons of darkness: *"And Jesus rebuked him, saying, Hold thy peace, and come out of him. And when the devil had thrown him in the midst, he came out of him, and hurt him not"* (Luke 4:35).

- The power of the Lord is manifested over the matters of men: *"And as Jesus passed forth from thence, he saw a man, named Matthew, sitting at the receipt of custom: and he saith unto him, Follow me. And he arose, and followed him"* (Matthew 9:9).

- The power of the Lord is manifested over the forces of the universe: *"And he saith unto them, Why are ye fearful, O ye of little faith? Then he arose, and rebuked the winds and the sea; and there was a great calm"* (Matthew 8:26).

- The power of the Lord is manifested in His ability to forgive sin: *"And he entered into a ship, and passed over, and came into his own city. 2 And, behold, they brought to him a man sick of the palsy, lying on a bed: and Jesus seeing their faith said unto the sick of the palsy; Son, be of good cheer; thy sins be forgiven thee"* (Matthew 9:12).

- The power of the Lord is manifested over the tradition of the times: *"And it came to pass, as Jesus sat at meat in the house, behold, many publicans and sinners came and sat down with him and his disciples. 11 And when the Pharisees saw it, they said unto his disciples, Why eateth your Master with publicans and sinners?"* (Matthew 9:10, 11).

- The power of the Lord is manifested over the dread of death: *"And he came and touched the bier: and they that bare him stood still. And he said, Young man, I say unto thee, Arise. 15 And he that was dead sat up, and began to speak. And he delivered him to his mother"* (Luke 7:14, 15).

2. The deity of Christ is revealed not only in His power, but also in His wisdom.

    - Jesus knew all about the personal activities of Nathanael: *"Nathanael saith unto him, Whence knowest thou me? Jesus answered and said unto him, Before that Philip called thee, when thou wast under the fig tree, I saw thee"* (John 1:48).

- Jesus knew about the plot of Judas to betray Him: *"Jesus answered them, Have not I chosen you twelve, and one of you is a devil?"* (John 6:70).

- Jesus knew the self-righteousness in the hearts of the Pharisees: *"And Jesus knew their thoughts, and said unto them, Every kingdom divided against itself is brought to desolation; and every city or house divided against itself shall not stand"* (Matthew 12:25).

- Jesus knew the secret thoughts of the scribes: *"And, behold, certain of the scribes said within themselves, This man blasphemeth. 4 And Jesus knowing their thoughts said, Wherefore think ye evil in your hearts?"* (Matthew 9:34).

- Jesus discerned the sincerity of one single scribe: *"And when Jesus saw that he answered discreetly, he said unto him, Thou art not far from the kingdom of God. And no man after that durst ask him any question"* (Mark 12:34).

- Jesus was familiar with the sordid past of the Samaritan woman: *"Come, see a man, which told me all things that ever I did: is not this the Christ?"* (John 4:29).

- Jesus was aware of the burning ambition of His disciples: *"Then there arose a reasoning among them, which of them should be greatest. 47 And Jesus, perceiving the thought of their heart, took a child, and set him by him"* (Luke 9:46, 47).

3. The deity of Christ was also displayed by His universal presence. John 3:13 explains. Jesus said, *"And no man hath ascended up to heaven, but he that came down from heaven, even the Son of man which is in heaven."*

4. The deity of Christ was revealed by the worship He received.

- The angelic host of heaven worshipped Jesus: *"And again, when he bringeth in the first begotten into the world, he saith, And let all the angels of God worship him"* (Hebrews 1:6).

- The faithful shepherds worshipped Jesus: *"And it came to pass, as the angels were gone away from them into heaven, the shepherds said one to another, Let us now go even unto Bethlehem, and see this thing which is come to pass, which the Lord hath made known unto us"* (Luke 2:15).

- Jesus was worshipped by the wise men from the east: *"Saying, Where is he that is born King of the Jews? For we have seen his star in the east, and are come to worship him"* (Matthew 2:2).

- A loathsome leper worshipped Jesus: *"And, behold, there came a leper and worshipped him, saying, Lord, if thou wilt, thou canst make me clean"* (Matthew 8:2).

- A ruler of the synagogue worshipped Jesus: *"While he spake these things unto them, behold, there came a certain ruler, and worshipped him, saying, My daughter is even now dead: but come and lay thy hand upon her, and she shall live"* (Matthew 9:18).

- A Syro-Phoenician woman worshipped Jesus: *"Then came she and worshipped him, saying, Lord, help me"* (Matthew 15:25).

- A worried mother worshipped Jesus: *"Then came to him the mother of Zebedee's children with her sons, worshipping him, and desiring a certain thing of him"* (Matthew 20:20).

- A madman worshipped Jesus: *"But when he saw Jesus afar off, he ran and worshipped him"* (Mark 5:6).

- A man born physically blind worshipped Jesus: *"And he said, Lord, I believe. And he worshipped him"* (John 9:38).

- His doubting disciple, named Thomas, worshipped Jesus: *"And Thomas answered and said unto him, My Lord and my God"* (John 20:28).

- The Gentiles worshipped Jesus: *"And there were certain Greeks among them that came up to worship at the feast: 21 The same came therefore to Philip, which was of Bethsaida of Galilee, and desired him, saying, Sir, we would see Jesus"* (John 12:20, 21).

- The disciples, following His resurrection, worshipped Jesus: *"And as they went to tell his disciples, behold, Jesus met them, saying, All hail. And they came and held him by the feet, and worshipped him"* (Matthew 28:9).

5. Because He is very God of very God, Jesus has the right to render just judgments: *"For the Father judgeth no man, but hath committed all judgment unto the Son."* Jesus also has the power to save souls from their sins. John 10:28, *"And I give unto them eternal life; and they shall never perish, neither shall any man pluck them out of my hand"* (John 5:22).

6. As the deity of Christ is declared in the gospels, so it is set forth in the rest of the Scriptures. There is the testimony of Stephen, in the book of Acts. With his dying breath, Stephen prayed to Christ. *"And they stoned Stephen, calling upon God, and saying, Lord Jesus, receive my spirit"* (Acts 7:59). Then there is the worship that the eunuch gave to the Lord. *"And Philip said, If thou believest with all thine heart, thou mayest. And he answered and said, I believe that Jesus Christ is the Son of God"* (Acts 8:37). The Ethiopian believed and was baptized.

7. In the epistles written by Paul, Peter, Jude, James, and John, the deity of Christ is affirmed.

- Galatians 2:20, *"I am crucified with Christ: nevertheless I live; yet not I, but Christ liveth in me: and the life which I now live in the flesh I live by the faith of the Son of God, who loved me, and gave himself for me."*

- Colossians 2:9, *"For in him dwelleth all the fullness of the Godhead bodily."*

- 1 Peter 3:22, *"Who is gone into heaven, and is on the right hand of God; angels and authorities and powers being made subject unto him."*

- 2 Peter 1:17, *"For he received from God the Father honor and glory, when there came such a voice to him from the excellent glory, This is my beloved Son, in whom I am well pleased."*

- Jude 1:25, *"To the only wise God our Savior, be glory and majesty, dominion and power, both now and forever. Amen."*

- James 2:1, *"My brethren, have not the faith of our Lord Jesus Christ, the Lord of glory, with respect of persons."*

- 1 John 5:20, *"And we know that the Son of God is come, and hath given us an understanding, that we may know him that is true, and we are in him that is true, even in his Son Jesus Christ. This is the true God, and eternal life."*

- Revelations 1:18, *"I am he that liveth, and was dead; and, behold, I am alive forever more, Amen; and have the keys of hell and of death."*

8. Perhaps the greatest proof of the deity of Christ is displayed by His sinlessness. The Bible declares that He knew no sin.

    - 2 Corinthians 5:21, *"For he hath made him to be sin for us, who knew no sin; that we might be made the righteousness of God in him."*

    - 1 Peter 2:22, *"Who did no sin, neither was guile found in his mouth."*

    - Hebrews 4:15, *"For we have not an high priest which cannot be touched with the feeling of our infirmities; but was in all points tempted like as we are, yet without sin."*

    - 1 John 3:5, *"And ye know that he was manifested to take away our sins; and in him is no sin."*

    - John 14:30, *"Hereafter I will not talk much with you: for the prince of this world cometh, and hath nothing in me."*

9. Honest individuals, and even His enemies, acknowledged the sinlessness of Christ.

- Pilate, the governor of Jerusalem, said that Jesus was innocent: *"Pilate therefore went forth again, and saith unto them, Behold, I bring him forth to you, that ye may know that I find no fault in him"* (John 19:4).

- The wife of Pilate said Jesus was an innocent man: *"When he was set down on the judgment seat, his wife sent unto him, saying, Have thou nothing to do with that just man: for I have suffered many things this day in a dream because of him"* (Matthew 27:19).

- Judas Iscariot realized too late that Jesus was perfect: *"Saying, I have sinned in that I have betrayed the innocent blood. And they said, What is that to us? See thou to that"* (Matthew 27:4).

- The dying thief on the cross perceived the righteousness of Christ: *"but this man hath done nothing amiss"* (Luke 23:41).

- The Roman centurion sensed that Jesus was holy: *"Now when the centurion saw what was done, he glorified God, saying, Certainly this was a righteous man"* (Luke 23:47).

10. The Church has historically taught that Christ could sin and also that the Lord could *not* have sinned.

    "The point of view that Christ could sin is designated by the idea of peccability, and the fact that He could not sin is expressed by the term impeccability. To suggest the capability or possibility of sinning would disqualify Christ as Savior, for a peccable Christ would mean a peccable God. Holiness is far more than the absence of sin; it is positive virtue. The advocates of peccability say, 'Christ could have sinned, but He did not.' To say that He could have sinned is to deny positive holiness.

    To deny positive holiness, therefore, is to deny the holy character of God. Holiness is positive virtue that has neither room for nor interest in sin.

    The Lord Jesus could not sin because the days of His flesh meant only addition of experience, not variation of character. Holy humanity was united to Deity in one indivisible person, the impeccable Christ. Jesus Christ cannot have more holiness because He is perfectly holy; He cannot have less holiness because He is unchangeably holy" (Studies in the Person and Work of Jesus Christ, W.E. Best).

The Impeccability of Christ

In discussing the doctrine of the impeccability of Christ, a person must remember several foundational truths.

First, Jesus is the fulfillment of all the Old Testament prophecies that are grounded in the eternal decrees of God. The divine decree foreordained that the Messiah would be without sin and therefore a worthy Savior. To say that Jesus could not have sinned, is to say that the decrees of God could not fail, as they were manifested in fulfilled prophecies.

Second, there is moral certitude. There are parents who would die before they harmed their child in a horrible manner. The soul of Jesus Christ was so holy and so pure that the suggestion of any sin was abhorrent. Jesus could not sin.

Third, it must never be forgotten that Jesus was not two persons in one body. He was one Person, with two natures. While He was truly human, He was altogether God, and as the God-man, He could not sin.

Fourth, the capacity to sin is not what makes man. If there were no capacity to sin, man would still be man; for there was no sin in Adam when he was first created, yet he is called man (Genesis 2:7). In our resurrected bodies, we will still be human, but without the sin nature. Whatever constitutes man as man does not necessitate sin or a sin nature. Therefore, it was not necessary that Jesus have the moral capacity to sin in order to be true humanity.

Finally, to embrace a concept that there was the possibility of Jesus' sinning but that He simply chose not to, might make one feel psychologically good; it might make Jesus seem to be more like "me." But Jesus is not like "me." No one who is born of a virgin is just like "me." No one who is truly God is just like "me." Jesus did not come into the world to be just like other men. He came to rescue fallen men from the depths of sin into which they had fallen.

To believe that Jesus could have sinned if He so chose is an unworthy thought of Him, for it presupposes that there is still something in His nature susceptible to sin. Logically, this means that Christ was not, and is not quite perfect. Christ was not perfect because He consistently chose not to sin. He was perfect, and therefore He was without sin. Jesus was perfect in Mary's womb. He was perfect in the hour of His birth. He was perfect as a child. He was perfect as a man in His ministry. He was perfect in His death. And He is perfect today in His glorified, resurrection body. To say that Christ could have sinned, is to say that Christ could still sin yet, He just chooses not to. The peccability of Christ is unacceptable to a high view of Christology. Jesus Christ is the same today, yesterday, and forever. He did not and He could not sin. Early Church councils were called to give form to, and defend this truth.

Main Points Proving the Impeccability of Christ

1. In the year AD 451, the Council of Chalcedon met and formulated the faith of the Church respecting the person of Christ, and declared Him *"to be acknowledged in two natures, inconfusedly, unchangeably, indivisibly, inseparably; the distinction of the natures being in no wise taken away by the union, but rather the property of each nature being preserved, and concurring in one Person and one Subsistence, not parted or divided into two persons."*

2. The great truth enunciated is that the eternal Son of God, took upon Himself our humanity, which includes making choices, and not that the man Jesus acquired divinity.

3. Vehement argument has raged around the question, *"Did the Lord's deity render sin impossible, and consequently make His temptations unreal?"* The following proposition is place for consideration: *"If, to Christ, sin was impossible, then His temptation by Satan was a meaningless display, and His victory a mere delusion, and His coronation* (Philippians 2:6) *a shadow."*

4. One answer to this problem is to argue for both positions. *"We may say it was impossible Jesus would sin. We dare not say it was impossible He could not sin."*

5. While this response would please many, for others, it does not do justice to either the Scriptures, or to the person of Christ. It is a matter of records, that once the concept is conceded that Jesus could sin, the temptation comes to teach, and believe, that He did sin, or that He was less than very God of very God.

6. From the very beginning, the Church has argued that Jesus was free, both from hereditary depravity, and from actual sin.

   - Jesus never offered a sacrifice for sin.

   - Jesus never prayed for forgiveness. Jesus frequently went up to the Temple, but He never offered sacrifice. He prayed, *"Father, forgive them"* (Luke 23:34), but He never prayed: *"Father, forgive me."*

   - Jesus taught that others needed the new birth. He said: *"Ye must be born anew"* (John 3:7); but the words indicated that He had no such need. Jesus not only yielded to God's will when made known to him, but also sought it: *"I seek not mine own will, but the will of Him that sent me"* (John 5:30). It was not personal experience of sin, but perfect resistance to it that made Jesus fit to deliver us from it. The choices that Jesus made to behave and honor the will of the Father were consistent with His essence, where there was nothing which sin could touch.

   - Jesus challenged others to convict Him of a single sin. And the angel answered and said unto her, The Holy Ghost shall come upon thee, and the power of the Highest shall overshadow thee: *"therefore also that holy thing which shall be born of thee shall be called the Son of God"* (Luke 1:35). *"Which of you convinceth me of sin? And if I say the truth, why do ye not believe me?"* (John 8:46). *"Hereafter I will not talk much with you: for the prince of this world cometh, and hath nothing in me"* (John 14:30). There was not the slightest evil inclination upon which temptation could lay hold of Christ.

7. Another question arises, *"If in Christ there was no sin, or tendency to sin, how could He be tempted?"*

8. The answer is that Jesus was tempted in the same way that Adam was tempted, which is susceptibility to all the forms of innocent desire. To these desires, temptations may appeal. Sin consists, not in these desires, but in the gratification of them, out of God's order, and contrary to God's will. So Satan appealed to our Lord's desire for food, for applause, and for power (Matthew 4:11). Because most temptations are addressed either to desire, or fear, it can be said that Christ *"was in all points tempted like as we are"* (Hebrews 4:15). The first temptation, in the wilderness, was addressed to His desire; the second, in the garden, was addressed to His fears. Satan, after the first temptation, *"departed from him for a season"* (Luke 4:13), but returned when Jesus was in the Garden of Gethsemane. Still, the Lord was able to say that *"the prince of the world cometh: and he hath nothing in me"* (John 14:30). Satan was trying to deter Jesus from His work at Calvary, by rousing within Him, vast and agonizing fear, with which His holy soul was moved. But it did not work, *"He was without sin"* (Hebrews 4:15).

9. To press the point of the Impeccability of Christ more closely, we ascribe to Christ not only natural, but also moral, integrity or moral perfection that is sinlessness. This means not merely that Christ could avoid sinning, and did actually avoid it, but also that it was impossible for Him to sin, because of the essential bond between the human and the divine natures.

10. The sinlessness of Christ is clearly testified to in the following passages:

- Luke 1:35, *"And the angel answered and said unto her, The Holy Ghost shall come upon thee, and the power of the Highest shall overshadow thee: therefore also that holy thing which shall be born of thee shall be called the Son of God."*

- John 8:46, *"Which of you convinceth me of sin? And if I say the truth, why do ye not believe me?"*

- John 14:30, *"Hereafter I will not talk much with you: for the prince of this world cometh, and hath nothing in me."*

- 2 Corinthians 5:21, *"For he hath made him to be sin for us, who knew no sin; that we might be made the righteousness of God in him."*

- Hebrews 4:15, *"For we have not an high priest which cannot be touched with the feeling of our infirmities; but was in all points tempted like as we are, yet without sin."*

- Hebrews 9:14, *"How much more shall the blood of Christ, who through the eternal Spirit offered himself without spot to God, purge your conscience from dead works to serve the living God?"*

- 1 Peter 2:22, *"Who did no sin, neither was guile found in his mouth."*

- 1 John 3:5, *"And ye know that he was manifested to take away our sins; and in him is no sin."*

11. While Christ was made to be sin judicially, yet ethically, He was free from both hereditary depravity, and actual sin.

12. Part of the problem for those who do *not* embrace the impeccability of Christ, is the tendency to believe that Jesus is but a man. Yet, there is at the same time, a longing to ascribe to Him the essence of God. There is also the desire to affirm divinity for Christ, in virtue of the immanence of God in Him, and the powerful presence of the indwelling Holy Spirit. The tension does not do justice to the truth of the two natures in Christ: He is both Divine and Human, in one Person, forever (*Studies in the Person and Work of Jesus Christ*, W.E. Best).

The Humanity of Jesus Christ: Romans 1:3

1. The doctrine of the person of Christ, properly called Christology, is one of the most important doctrines of the Bible. The

Scriptures present Christ as very God and yet true man. Because of this doctrine, Christ is perfect Mediator between God and mankind because He partakes fully of the nature of both.

2. The title *Son of Man* was the Lord's preferred way of referring to Himself (Luke 7:33-34; 9:58; Mark 8:31; 9:12; 14:21; 14:49).

3. Only once in the Gospels was Jesus referred to as the Son of Man by anyone other than Himself. Stephen, condemned by the Jewish Sanhedrian, saw *"the Son of Man standing at the right hand of God"* (Acts 7:56).

4. The humanity of Christ is revealed in many passages.

   - Jesus had a human genealogy. *"And, behold, thou shalt conceive in thy womb, and bring forth a son, and shalt call his name, Jesus"* (Luke 1:31). *"But when the fullness of the time was come, God sent forth his Son, made of a woman, made under the Law"* (Galatians 4:4).

   - He had a human body, soul, and spirit.

     - Body. Matthew 26:12, *"For in that she hath poured this ointment on my body, she did it for my burial."*

     - Soul. John 12:27, *"Now is my soul troubled; and what shall I say? Father, save me from this hour: but for this cause came I unto this hour. Matthew 26:38 Then saith he unto them, My soul is exceeding sorrowful, even unto death: tarry ye here, and watch with me."*

     - Spirit. Mark 2:8, *"And immediately when Jesus perceived in his spirit that they so reasoned within themselves, he said unto them, Why reason ye these things in your hearts?"* Luke 23:46 *"And when Jesus had cried with a loud voice, he said, Father, into thy hands I commend my spirit: and having said thus, he gave up the ghost."*

   - Jesus appeared to others as a man, because He was truly human.

- To a Samaritan woman, Jesus looked like a Jew: *"Then saith the woman of Samaria unto him, How is it that thou, being a Jew, askest drink of me, which am a woman of Samaria? For the Jews have no dealings with the Samaritans"* (John 4:9).

- To the Jews Jesus looked to be of normal age: *"Then said the Jews unto him, Thou art not yet fifty years old, and hast thou seen Abraham?"* (John 8:57).

- To Mary, the body of Jesus was real for she wanted to bury His body: *"Jesus saith unto her, Woman, why weepest thou? Whom seekest thou? She, supposing him to be the gardener, saith unto him, Sir, if thou have borne him hence, tell me where thou hast laid him, and I will take him away"* (John 20:15).

5. Jesus was true flesh and blood: *"Forasmuch then as the children are partakers of flesh and blood, he also himself likewise took part of the same; that through death he might destroy him that had the power of death, that is, the devil"* (Hebrews 2:14).

6. Jesus grew from infancy to adulthood like any normal person: *"And the child grew, and waxed strong in spirit, filled with wisdom: and the grace of God was upon him"* (Luke 2:40).

7. Jesus learned, by asking thoughtful questions: *"And it came to pass, that after three days they found him in the temple, sitting in the midst of the doctors, both hearing them, and asking them questions"* (Luke 2:46).

8. Jesus acquired wisdom: *"And Jesus increased in wisdom and stature, and in favor with God and man"* (Luke 2:52).

9. In certain areas, Jesus was limited in immediate knowledge. This limitation was self-imposed. According to Philippians 2:58, certain divine attributes, while here on earth were voluntarily abstained from being used, that He might totally depend upon the power and wisdom of the Holy Spirit. This truth helps to explain certain passages.

- Mark 5:30, *"And Jesus, immediately knowing in himself that virtue had gone out of him, turned him about in the press, and said, Who touched my clothes?"*

- John 11:34, *"And said, Where have ye laid him? They said unto him, Lord, come and see."*

- Mark 11:13, *"And seeing a fig tree afar off having leaves, he came, if haply he might find any thing thereon: and when he came to it, he found nothing but leaves; for the time of figs was not yet."*

- Mark 13:32, *"But of that day and that hour knoweth no man, no, not the angels which are in heaven, neither the Son, but the Father."*

10. Jesus prayed, often, and alone: *"And in the morning, rising up a great while before day, he went out, and departed into a solitary place, and there prayed"* (Mark 1:35). *"And it came to pass, that, as he was praying in a certain place, when he ceased, one of his disciples said unto him, Lord, teach us to pray, as John also taught his disciples"* (Luke 11:1).

11. Jesus was tested in all points, like others: *"Then was Jesus led up of the Spirit into the wilderness to be tempted of the devil"* (Matthew 4:1). *"For in that he himself hath suffered being tempted, he is able to succor them that are tempted"* (Hebrews 2:18). *"For we have not an high priest which cannot be touched with the feeling of our infirmities; but was in all points tempted like as we are, yet without sin"* (Hebrews 4:15).

12. Jesus went to the school of divine obedience: *"Though he were a Son, yet learned he obedience by the things which he suffered"* (Hebrews 5:8).

    - Jesus knew the pains of hunger: *"And when he had fasted forty days and forty nights, he was afterward an hungered"* (Matthew 4:2). *"Now in the morning as he returned into the city, he hungered"* (Matthew 21:18).

    - Jesus knew the violent thirst for water: *"There cometh a woman of Samaria to draw water: Jesus saith unto her, Give me to drink"* (John 4:7).

- Jesus was subject to fatigue: *"Now Jacob's well was there. Jesus therefore, being wearied with his journey sat thus on the well: and it was about the sixth hour"* (John 4:6).

13. Jesus grew weary, and went to sleep: *"And, behold, there arose a great tempest in the sea, insomuch that the ship was covered with the waves: but he was asleep"* (Matthew 8:24).

14. Jesus knew how to love others: *"Then Jesus beholding him loved him, and said unto him, One thing thou lackest: go thy way, sell whatsoever thou hast, and give to the poor, and thou shalt have treasure in heaven: and come, take up the cross, and follow me"* (Mark 10:21).

15. Jesus had a heart that was very tender: *"But when he saw the multitudes, he was moved with compassion on them, because they fainted, and were scattered abroad, as sheep having no shepherd"* (Matthew 9:36).

16. Jesus knew how to become angry: *"And when he had looked round about on them with anger, being grieved for the hardness of their hearts, he saith unto the man, Stretch forth thine hand. And he stretched it out: and his hand was restored whole as the other"* (Mark 3:5).

17. Jesus knew how to cry: *"Jesus wept"* (John 11:35).

18. Jesus knows the lovely feeling of joy: *"Looking unto Jesus the author and finisher of our faith; who for the joy that was set before him endured the cross, despising the shame, and is set down at the right hand of the throne of God"* (Hebrews 12:2).

19. Jesus manifested great concern for others: *"When Jesus therefore saw her weeping, and the Jews also weeping which came with her, he groaned in the spirit, and was troubled"* (John 11:33).

20. Jesus bled: *"And being in an agony he prayed more earnestly: and his sweat was as it were great drops of blood falling down to the ground"* (Luke 22:44).

21. Jesus suffered: *"Forasmuch then as Christ hath suffered for us in the flesh, arm yourselves likewise with the same mind: for he that hath suffered in the flesh hath ceased from sin"* (1 Peter 4:1).

22. Jesus died, as other men have died: *"Jesus, when he had cried again with a loud voice, yielded up the ghost"* (Matthew 27:50).

26. Jesus was buried, as those who die are buried: *"And when Joseph had taken the body, he wrapped it in a clean linen cloth, And laid it in his own new tomb, which he had hewn out in the rock: and he rolled a great stone to the door of the sepulcher, and departed"* (Matthew 27:59, 60).

Doctrine of Kenosis

Closely related to the doctrine of the humanity of Christ, is the doctrine of *"kenosis."* The word *"kenosis"* comes from Philippians 2:7, where Paul writes that Christ *"emptied Himself."* The word *"kenosis"* has become a technical term for the humiliation of the Son in the incarnation. But what does it mean when it says that Christ *emptied* Himself?

1. The rendering, *emptied*, is a somewhat misleading translation. In the NT, *"kenoo"* is commonly used in the metaphorical, rather than the literal meaning as per Romans 4:14; 1 Corinthians 1:17; 9:15; and 2 Corinthians 9:3. In all of these passages, the word is used figuratively and means, *"to make void;" "of no effect; of no account;" "of no reputation."*

2. Specific statements of the New Testament indicate that Jesus retained His divine nature, and attributes (Matthew 1:23; 11:27; Mark 1:1; John 3:13; 14:9; Romans 1:4).

3. The doctrine of the incarnation requires the continuing divinity of Jesus.

4. The immutability of God makes an *emptying* inconceivable.

5. Christ made of Himself of no account, and of no reputation. He did not assert His divine prerogative, but took the form of a

servant. But what does His becoming a servant involve? Becoming a servant involves a state of subjection, in which one is called upon to render obedience. The opposite of this is a state of sovereignty, in which one has the right to command.

6. The Scriptures bear witness that Christ never emptied Himself of His divinity in order to become true humanity. Moreover, the immutability of God is plainly taught in such passages as Malachi 3:6 and James. 1:17. A mutable God is not the God of the Bible.

7. What Christ did do, in becoming man, was to give up the independent exercise of the divine attributes. Although subsisting in the form of God, Christ did not regard His equality with God as a thing to be forcibly retained, but emptied Himself, by taking the form of a servant, that is, by being made in the likeness of men.

9. And being found in outward condition as a man, He, the incarnate Son of God, yet further humbled Himself by becoming obedient unto death, even the death of the cross.

10. It is important to notice that what Christ divested Himself of, in becoming man, is not the substance of His Godhead, but the *form of God* in which this substance was manifested.

11. This *form of God* can be only that independent exercise of the powers and prerogatives of Deity that constitutes His *equality with God*. This Jesus surrendered, in the act of *taking the form of a servant*, or becoming subordinate, as man.

12. The Lord Jesus, as God and man united, submitted Himself, consciously and voluntarily, to the humiliation of a shameful death, in order to save sinner.

A Resurrection from the Dead: Romans 1:4

The reality of the resurrection of Christ is the foundation upon which the Christian faith is built. If Christ be not raised from the dead, then He is not the Son of God with power, and there is no Spirit of holiness. Faith collapses, and the world is plunged into spiritual darkness, if Christ is not the true Light of the world, ascended into heaven, and seated at the right hand of God the Father. Because of the centrality of the resurrection, we consider this doctrine once more, by turning to 1 Corinthians 15.

Doctrine of the Resurrection

1. The prominence of the resurrection of Christ is set forth in Scripture. *"And if Christ be not risen, then is our preaching in vain, and your faith is also vain"* (1 Corinthians 15:14).

2. The fact of the resurrection is declared in simple eloquence, as the essence of the true gospel. *"Moreover brethren, I declare unto the gospel which I preached unto you, which also ye have received and wherein ye stand"* (1 Corinthians 15:1).

3. The time of the resurrection of Christ is said to be on the third day: *"For I delivered unto you first of all that which I also received, how that Christ died for our sins according to the scriptures; And that he was buried, and that he rose again the third day according to the scriptures"* (1 Corinthians 15:34).

4. A possible date, and time of the crucifixion, was AD 30, the 15th of Nisan, which fell on Friday (April 7), between 9 AM, and 3 PM. During those six hours, the world was changed.

5. That the day was Friday is indicated in various passages.

    - Mark 15:42 *"the day before the Sabbath"* (Saturday)

    - Matthew 27:62 *"the day of preparation"*

    - Luke 23:54 *"that day was the preparation, and the Sabbath* (Saturday) *drew on"*

    - John 19:14 *"it was the preparation of the Passover"* Friday is called preparation day, because the meals for the Sabbath were prepared on the sixth day, as no fires were allowed to be kindled on the Sabbath (Exodus 16:5).

6. Some modern theologians have suggested that the day on which Christ died was really Wednesday, and not Friday. The reason for this view is grounded in a concern for exact literalism of such passages as Matthew 12:40. The Bible says, *"For as Jonah was three days and three nights in the whale's belly; so shall the Son of Man be three days and three nights in the heart of the earth."* As interesting as the concept is, the idea that Jesus died on Wednesday is not necessary to embrace for a variety of reasons.

- All the other events of the Last Week would need to be condensed in time, and reassigned to other days.

- The Jews considered part of a day, to be a full day thereby fulfilling the prophecy of Matthew 12:40.

- The natural reading of the gospel narratives indicates a weekly Sabbath, not a special Sabbath.

- The earliest tradition of the Church honored Friday as the day Christ died. Those closest to the scene of action would surely be more familiar with the events, than others two thousand years later. New interpretations of the scripture, should always give more honors to the historical position of the Church, when that position has always been consistent.

- Conservative Christian scholars down through the centuries have recognized Good Friday as the day on which Christ died. *"The day of the week on which Christ suffered on the cross was a Friday, during the week of the Passover, in the month of Nisan, which was the first of the twelve lunar months of the Jewish year, and included the vernal equinox"* (Philip Schaff, *History of the Christian Church*, Vol. I., p. 133). Alfred Edersheim who wrote *The Life and Times of Jesus the Messiah* concurs.

7. The reason for the resurrection (1 Corinthians 15:3). Christ was not a martyr dying for His faith, but a Savior dying for our sins.

He did not say, *"I am finished,* but *it is finished!"* All three Persons of the God head were involved in the Lord's death and resurrection: The Father (John 3:16; Acts 2:24); The Son (John 10:11, 18); The Holy Spirit (Hebrews 9:14; Romans 1:4).

8. The results of the resurrection include the salvation of souls (1 Corinthians 15:2). *"By which also ye are saved, if ye keep in memory what I preached unto you, unless ye have believed in vain."*

9. Christ made at least seventeen, personal, post resurrection appearances.

• Mary Magdalene	John 20:11-18
• The other woman	Matthew 28:9-10
• The two disciples	Luke 24:13-22
• Simon Peter	Luke 24:33-35
• Ten Apostles	Luke 24:36-44
• Eleven apostles	John 20:26-31
• Seven apostles	John 21:1-14
• Five hundred disciples	1 Corinthians 15:6
• James, the Lord's brother	1 Corinthians 15:7
• The eleven apostles on Mt. Olivet	Luke 24:44-49
• Stephen	Acts 7:160
• Paul (five times)	
At Damascus	Acts 9:19
In Corinth	Acts 18:9
While at Jerusalem	Acts 23:11
On board a ship	Acts 27:23
At Lystra	2 Corinthians 12:14
• John, Isle of Patmos	Revelation 1:12

10. Because the resurrection of Christ is essential to the gospel (1 Corinthians 15:12, 19), it has been challenged. Several alternative theories have emerged, to explain what might have happened.

    - **The Fraud Theory** suggests that the early disciples simply lied. But then the question emerges, *"Would the disciples die, for a known lie?"* All but John died a martyr's death.

- **The Swoon Theory** maintains that Jesus did not die at Calvary but merely swooned. Later, in the cool of the cave he revived and was able to escape. The response to this concept is that the soldiers who killed Christ knew death. They had stared it in the face. Also, the armed guards would have kept anyone from stealing the body.

- **The Vision Theory** argues that since the men and women who loved Christ wanted to see Him alive again, they had a vision and the vision became a verbal reality.

- **The Spirit Theory** sets forth the novel concept that only the Spirit of Jesus was resurrected.

- **The Heart Theory** appeals to modern Biblical liberalism, by teaching that the historical facts of the resurrection do not matter. Jesus is resurrected in our hearts.

11. All of the theories of the resurrection are unworthy of the gospel, and of Christ. It has been said, that if the resurrection of Christ is not true, then all gospel preaching has been, and is, now useless; all gospel preachers are liars, and, or, fools; all souls are still in their sins; all holy reasons for life are destroyed; the body of Christ has deteriorated, and is dry dust in a Middle Eastern graveyard; Christian ordinances, such as baptism are silly; suffering for the Savior is meaningless; and a life of hedonism (pleasure) should be embraced (1 Corinthians 15:32).

12. But, the resurrection of Christ is true. He is the First Fruits from among the dead (1 Corinthians 15:20-28; Leviticus 23).

13. And, because the resurrection is true (1 Corinthians 15:33, 34), Christians are to awake to righteousness, and sin not (1 Corinthians 15:34). Moreover, they are to withdraw their fellowship from those who deny the resurrection, and live as the hedonist (1 Corinthians 15:33).

14. The resurrection of Christ becomes a pattern for the resurrection of Christians, and a preview of things to come (1

Corinthians 15:35-38). It is still true, that the body of the saints will, like a grain of wheat, one-day die. No human power can stop this process. But, like a grain of wheat, there is change in death (John 12:24), for death does not suppress life but releases it. The body will not lose its ultimate identity (1 Corinthians 13:12), and shall one day live again.

15. What shall the resurrected body be like? The Bible offers a contrast of the resurrection body with the old. The old, natural body goes to the grave in corruption (1 Corinthians 15:42), dishonor (1 Corinthians 15:43), and weakness, liable to diseases and infirmities (1 Corinthians 15:43). It is sown a natural body governed by the Laws of nature (1 Corinthians15:44). But thanks be unto God, the new resurrection body is raised incorruptible so that it can never again perish (1 Corinthians 15:42). It is raised in glory, to enjoy existence in a new heaven and a new earth (1 Corinthians 15:43). It is raised in power so that it is not vulnerable to disease and death (1 Corinthians 15:43). It is raised a spiritual body and is not subject to the known Laws of nature (1 Corinthians 15:44).

16. Because the teaching of the resurrection sounds too good to be true, the Bible offers assurances that it will happen (1 Corinthians15: 50-53). The Bible states plainly, that all Christians shall all be changed suddenly. Corruption will put on incorruption, and mortal persons will put on immortality. And wonderful change will happen at the Second Advent. (Hebrews 9:28) Some who are living will not die (1 Thessalonians 4:16, 17; 1 Corinthians 15:51).

17. The resurrection will be majestic, and glorious (1 Corinthians 15:54) as it defeats physical death (1 Corinthians 15:26; Psalms 55:4), and spiritual death (Revelation 2:11; John. 5:24; 8:51), not to mention the world (Galatians 1:4; 1 John. 2:15), the flesh (Romans 7:18; Galatians 5:17), and the devil (Matthew 13:39; Ephesians 6:11).

Grace and Apostleship: Romans 1:5

Having exalted the Lord Jesus Christ, as the living Son of God with power, Paul continues, by stating that he had personally received grace (Romans 1:5). Grace is one of the great words of the Christian vocabulary. It has been defined as *"**G**od's **R**iches **A**t **C**hrist's **E**xpense."* Grace is God's unmerited favor, extended toward sinners. Grace indicates not only the power to bestow undeserved favor upon another but also a willingness to do the same. That God is a God of great grace is manifested in many ways. In grace, God gives life to a creation that does not know Him, or even care to have fellowship with Him. God makes the sun to shine on the just, and the unjust alike. He gives health and wealth, fame and fortune in continuous acts of common grace. Paul knew how long-suffering the grace of God could be for he was the recipient of common grace.

He was also the recipient of saving grace. Paul never forgot the day he traveled the Damascus road and met the Master. Whenever the opportunity arose, a personal word of testimony was given how saving grace was provided to the chief of all sinners.

In addition to common grace and saving grace, are spiritual gifts of grace. At the moment of salvation, the Holy Spirit sovereignly bestows spiritual gifts upon individuals. Some are given gifts of giving. Others have the gift of helps. Martha had the gift of serving. Some are given the ability to teach. Others can preach. Church leadership is also a spiritual gift. Historically, the Church has recognized three main offices of spiritual leadership: Apostle, Elder, and Deacon. Paul considered himself an apostle.

The Called of Jesus Christ: Romans 1:6-7

The purpose for which Paul received the position of being an apostle was that he might be obedient to the faith among all nations. In particular, Paul was commissioned to go forth and preach the gospel among the nations of the world, and Paul was obedient to the faith. In the name of Jesus and for the name of Christ, Paul journeyed from city to city with the good news of redeeming grace. As Paul went, he called men to repentance and belief of the gospel. Among those called upon to believe in Christ were the citizens of Rome. Many individuals who came into contact with the gospel responded in a positive way and were converted. They heard not only the external call of the gospel in the mouth of the minister but also the internal call of the Holy Spirit. Being objects of distinguishing grace, beloved of God, the souls in Rome were now called saints. It is important to realize there is an external call of the gospel, but an internal call as well. The Scriptural evidence is compelling.

1. While the external call, the gospel is preached to all people indiscriminately. Anyone can hear it, but not all will respond to the spiritual truths communicated (Matthew 22:1-14).

2. In the external call of the gospel, the good news is sown. Gospel truth falls upon rocky soil and good soil alike.

3. In the external call, the gospel is easily dismissed. The internal call is not.

4. The internal call of the gospel is the voice of the Holy Spirit effectively applying the gospel message to the hearts of individuals with sovereign power to repentance, faith, salvation, and service.

- Mark 2:17, *"When Jesus heard it, he saith unto them, they that are whole have no need of the physician, but they that are sick: I came not to call the righteous, but sinners to repentance."*

- Luke 5:32, *"I came not to call the righteous, but sinners to repentance."*

- Acts 2:39, *"For the promise is unto you, and to your children, and to all that are afar off, even as many as the Lord our God shall call."*

- Mark 1:20, *"And straightway he called them: and they left their father Zebedee in the ship with the hired servants, and went after him."*

5. The external call gives spiritual power for the dead soul to live in order to believe the gospel.

6. The internal call cannot be denied nor does the renewed heart want to reject the gospel. There is the effective evocation of faith by the Holy Spirit.

- Romans 8:30, *"Moreover, whom he did predestine, them he also called: and whom he called them he also justified: and whom he justified them he also glorified."*

- 1 Corinthians 1:9, *"God is faithful, by whom ye were called unto the fellowship of his Son Jesus Christ our Lord."*

- Galatians 1:15, *"But when it pleased God, who separated me from my mother's womb, and called me by his grace."*

- 2 Timothy 1:9, *"Who hath saved us, and called us with holy calling, not according to our works, but according to his own purpose and grace, which was given us in Christ Jesus before the world began."*

- Hebrews 9:15, *"And for this cause he is the mediator of the new testament, that by means of death, for the redemption of the transgressions that were under the first testament, they which are called might receive the promise of eternal inheritance."*

- 1 Peter 2:9, *"But ye are a chosen generation, a royal priesthood, an holy nation, a peculiar people; that ye should shew forth the praises of him who hath called you out of darkness into his marvelous light."*

- 2 Peter 1:3, *"According as his divine power hath given unto us all things that pertain unto life and godliness, through the knowledge of him that hath called us to glory and virtue."*

7. The reason why so many can turn away from the Lord, and reject Christianity is that they have yet to hear the internal call of the gospel.

8. Once the internal call is heard, there are ethical implications. A worthy walk is demanded (Ephesians 4:1) to be characterized by holiness, patience, and peace (1 Thessalonians 4:7; 1 Peter 1:15; 1 Peter 2:21; 1 Corinthians 7:15; Colossians 3:15).

It would not be wrong to talk honestly to people, and ask them if they have heard the internal call of Christ, which converts the soul and causes the heart to love Jesus. The curse of the modern Church is that people sit in pews, accepting the outward signs of salvation, while secretly being unsure whether Jesus is the Son of God, and the Savior of the world, who was crucified, was buried, and rose again the third day. The question should be asked of every person, as to whether there is assurance, of having asked the Lord to grant the gospel grace of being able to hear the internal call to salvation.

A person can know that they have been called of God when the gospel is believed without reservation. He will experience a new spiritual hunger for the Bible; a desire for righteousness, and a holy life; a love for the Church; and gospel obedience manifested in such acts as baptism.

What Paul Was Thankful For: Romans 1:8

To have a grateful heart, is to have a good heart. The heart of man, by nature, tends to be greedy and unthankful, so that the more a person has, the more a person wants. But the renewed heart is able to appreciate the grace, and good deeds it receives. Paul had a grateful heart to God. He was grateful for his personal salvation. Once a religious zealot without understanding, Paul persecuted the Church of Christ. Then came that glorious moment, when the scales of spiritual darkness fell from his eyes, and he was able to see clearly the glorious resurrected Christ.

As Paul was grateful for his own faith, so he could rejoice that the faith of others was spoken of throughout the whole world. All over the Roman Empire, people were discussing the faith of the Church at Rome. Their faith was powerful, prevailing; and it became popular. People were impressed, and the question arises as to, *"Why? Why was the faith of the Church of Rome spoken of throughout the whole world? Was Paul exaggerating? Was he using literary license or was something really happening?"* The answer is this: Paul was not exaggerating. The Church of Rome had faith. But what did that mean?

Primarily, the Church had a core of doctrines that were nonnegotiable, unshakable, and rooted in Scriptures. Among the foundation doctrines, were the substitutionary death of Jesus Christ,

His burial according to the Scriptures, and His resurrection. These cardinal truths do not just make an interesting story they form the bedrock of belief. No person will ever get to heaven, who does not believe, with all the heart that Jesus Christ is the Son of the Living God, and the Savior of the world. No one will ever be saved who does not, from the heart, confess oneself a sinner, and call upon the name of Christ for salvation.

Of course, pretending is easy to pretend to have faith—but God knows the heart, and God will not be deceived or mocked. The Bible warns that all liars shall have their place in the Lake of Fire. Revelation 22:14-15 says, *"Blessed are they that do his commandments, which they may have right to the tree of life, and may enter in through the gates into the city. For without are dogs, and sorcerers, and whoremongers, and murderers, and idolaters, and whosoever loveth and maketh a lie."* Judas Iscariot once pretended to have faith. He could not disbelieve that Jesus was the Messiah. He could not disbelieve the Lord's miraculous power. He could not disbelieve the truths he had heard taught. They were too powerful to protest.

But the absence of unbelief does not constitute saving faith. Biblical faith, saving faith is more than mental assent to sound doctrine. If that were all to saving faith, the Devil and every demon would be saved as well as all the Pharisees, for they knew that Jesus arose from the dead. They had to believe in the physical resurrection of Christ. The evidence was super-abounding. Saving faith is something more positive than the suspension of judgment. Saving faith is the casting of one's entire heart and life on the person of Jesus Christ. Saving faith is a rushing to Christ, a closing with Christ, and an embracing of Christ with every fiber of the heart. Saving faith is Thomas' crying out, *"My Lord and my God!"* Saving faith is Saul's asking, *"Lord, what wilt Thou have me to do?"*

Saving faith is Peter's weeping because he has wounded Christ. Saving faith is John on the isle of Patmos seeing spiritual truths. Saving faith is the Philippian jailer's screaming out at midnight, *"What must I do to be saved?"* The people in the Church of Rome had such saving faith.

In addition to doctrinal truth, the Church of Rome had sustaining faith. Sustaining faith is the faith that sustains the soul during the struggles of life. Sustaining faith is that faith which sees the silver lining in the storm clouds of life. Sustaining faith is that which believes in the Lord and loves Him, despite death, diseases, economic disaster, dislocation of a job, or the destruction of the toys of time. George Frederick Handel, the great musician, lost his health; his right side was paralyzed; his money was gone; and his creditors seized his property and threatened to imprison him. Handel was so disheartened by his tragic experiences that he almost despaired, for a brief time.

But his faith prevailed, and he composed his greatest work, *"The Hallelujah Chorus,"* which is part of his majestic *Messiah*. The Apostle John wrote, *"This is the victory that overcometh the world, even our faith."* Sustaining faith is that which lays hold of Jesus and will never let Him go. *"Though he slay me,"* cries faith, *"I will never let Him go."*

The Church at Rome had such faith, for individuals knew what it was to suffer the demented behavior of the Emperor Nero; Nero, who grew foolish as reason was overcome by madness; Nero, who thought it was clever to burn Christians in his garden parties; Nero, who sang a song while Rome burned; Nero, who thought himself a great actor. Nero, the Beast of the Revelation, whose number was 666, was no match for the Christian community that he tried to destroy.

The Church at Rome had a faith that sustained them through social unrest, and their faith encouraged the hearts of others throughout the world. As there is saving faith and sustaining faith, so there is sanctifying faith. The Bible says that without holiness no man shall see God. One of the signs of salvation is a desire to bring every thought into captivity for Christ and to do those things that are pleasing in His sight. All the strongholds of sin must be assaulted. Private addictions and personal obsessions no longer bring pleasure. Spiritual freedom is sought. A life of holiness and humility is believed to be beautiful.

Passing the Test of Time

The sustained testimony of the Church of Rome reminds us that our faith cannot be false for long. We may go through certain externals, but genuine faith cannot be hidden, nor can it be duplicated. In just a little while, the truth is revealed, for out of the heart all people will speak. It took time for the faith of the saints to be revealed to others. Word did spread of their faith, but not all at once. Faith must pass the test of time. Only he who endures to the end shall be saved. It was not just the faith of a person or two that was spoken of but the faith of the Church, as a whole. How wonderful it is when a Church is known for faith. What an honor that reputation must be. It is a goal for all God's people so that when others reflect upon the assembly, the heart must spontaneously say, *"First, I thank my God through Jesus Christ for you all, that your faith is spoken of throughout the whole world."*

The Sanctified Ego of Saint Paul: Romans 1:9-16

One cannot read this section of Romans without becoming aware of the number of personal pronoun references. This practice is really unusual for Paul. Rarely does he inject himself into the narrative as often as he does here. As we examine his usage of the personal pronoun, it is obvious that the Apostle is not promoting himself or boasting, for he has a sanctified ego reflected in the fact that he gives thanks to God for the faith of others (Romans 1:8).

Second, Paul testified that he was a servant of God from his heart (Romans 1:9). Paul served the Lord with his spirit in a positive way. He was not just fulfilling an obligation. It is for such spirits that the Lord is looking. Jesus said we must worship the Father *"in spirit and in truth."* External religion reduces the heart to something that is cold and callous. External religion breeds resentment. External religion makes a person feel trapped; but religion that is from the heart and in the spirit is free, joyous, spontaneous, and lasting.

Then third, Paul testifies that he was a man of prayer (Romans 1:9). At all times the Church of Rome was upon his heart. Paul had much to be happy about with the Roman congregation. *"No one had come to Paul to report disorders and divisions at Rome such as moved him to write to the*

Corinthians (1 Corinthians 1:11), and he had not received a letter of inquiry from Rome (1 Corinthians 7:1). The Romans were neither divided nor disorderly. Their faith was worldwide in its reputation (Romans 1:8), and they were full of goodness (Romans15: 14). The Romans were in no danger from Judaizing teachers as were the Galatians, so that Paul, in sore apprehension, had to write them not to abandon the liberty in Christ (Galatians 5:1) for the bondage of the Law" (James M. Stifler, *The Epistle to the Romans*).

So Paul prayed for the Church, and his prayer life was very specific. In particular he asked God if he might be allowed to visit with the saints (Romans 1:10). As the apostle to the Gentiles, Rome would be a natural place for Paul to preach. Rome was the center of the wheel of the Roman Empire. If he could convert souls to Christ at Rome, like the moving spokes on a wheel, individuals would spread out, taking the gospel with them so that in just a little while the gospel would reach the whole world. It was for strategic as well as personal reasons that Paul wanted desperately to get to Rome. But Paul's intention had to be according to the will of God. In this effort, the sanctified ego of Paul is manifested.

In summary, a sanctified ego recognizes the faith of others (Romans 1:8), serves the Lord from the heart in the gospel (Romans 1:9), prays without ceasing (Romans 1:9), seeks only the will of God, longs to impart one's spiritual gift (Romans 1:11) in order to build up the body of Christ (Romans 1:11), is comforted by the shared common faith (Romans 1:12), longs for spiritual fruit (Romans 1:13), is ready to proclaim the gospel (Romans 1:15), and is not ashamed of Christ (Romans 1:16) or His gospel. No new gospel has to be created to replace the old, old story of Jesus and His love.

A Gift of Apostolic Grace

If Paul did get to Rome, he wanted to convey unto the saints a spiritual gift in order to establish them more in the faith. What was this spiritual gift that Paul wanted to share that would make the believers stronger in their faith? Perhaps it was his gift of teaching. By imparting to the Church of Rome his spiritual gift of teaching, Paul knows that he will be personally blessed and comforted because of the mutual faith that existed between the saints of Rome and himself (Romans 1:12).

The content of his teaching would be the gospel. It is the gospel that Paul wanted to proclaim. It was the gospel that he was ready to preach. It was the gospel that is the power of God unto salvation (Romans 1:16). It is the gospel of which he was not ashamed.

I Am Not Ashamed Anymore: Romans 1:16

Paul was not ashamed of Jesus Christ, for he saw in the Lord Someone most excellent. First, Jesus is most excellent in that He is the Son of God, which means that He is very God of very God. Here is a great mystery, but it is one that we are asked to believe with all of our hearts. The Bible declares that *"In the beginning was the Word, and the Word was with God, and the Word was God"* (John 1:1). Jesus often declared that He was the Son of God, thereby making Himself equal to God. The Jews understood what Christ was saying and took up stones to kill Him for blasphemy. However, as the Son of God, Jesus proved Himself the same by healing the sick, raising the dead, and teaching as no one else has ever taught.

Second, Jesus is most excellent in that He is sinless. Sin is the curse of this fallen world. Sin has caused agonizing diseases and placed the dew of death upon the brow of our loved ones. Sin is the culprit that has captured the hearts of millions, and made them addicted to harmful substances. Sin is the Evil Tyrant that promises life, and delivers damnation. Sin stalks all that is decent to overthrow it and turns laughter into sorrow, freedom into bondage, love into lust, and joy into despair. Every child of Adam knows the self-destructive and other destructive nature of sin. Sin casts forth its black whip and drives the tongue to speak abominations.

Sin compels the heart to grow callous and cruel when the inclination is to cry out for forgiveness. Sin demands its own self-will, at the expense of all other things. Sin destroys, and annihilates what truth and beauty create. The children of Adam are enslaved to sin by birth, and by choice. Sin becomes the secret delight of the depraved heart. Like a powerful magnet, sin draws souls back into its sphere of influence. However, what the natural heart loves, Jesus hates. His righteous soul was undefiled by sin. Even when Christ was on the Cross He was just and pure. No one could ever find fault with Christ, though many tried. He was separate from sinners, for sin never touched His Holy heart.

Then third, Jesus is most excellent, in that He is the Sovereign Savior of the world. Glorious men throughout human history have helped others; for example, some have become champions for the oppressed. In ancient Rome, Spartacus led a slave revolt. He tried to free other slaves like himself by organizing an army. Ultimately, Spartacus was defeated on the field of battle, and was crucified. Abraham Lincoln became the Great Emancipator for the African Americans in 1863, when he issued the Emancipation Proclamation. In the end he was assassinated. Lincoln literally gave his life for others. But on a far grander scale, Jesus Christ stands alone, more excellent than all men, for He is the Savior of the *"world"* (1 John 2:2). From every walk of life, men and women, boys and girls, rich and poor, educated and uneducated, can know eternal salvation through the substitutionary work of Christ at Calvary. Here is a gospel that is so great, so full of good news, that one would be amazed that someone else would be ashamed of it. What is there to be ashamed of? The gospel is the good news of redeeming love.

The gospel is the good news of salvation. The gospel is the good news of how fallen men can be forgiven. What is there about the gospel that would cause anyone to hesitate sharing it with others? Should we be ashamed that the gospel is so bloody? Some people do not like to talk about bloodshed; yet the Bible says that without the shedding of blood, there is no remission of sins. God has always required a blood sacrifice since the Garden of Eden.

Foolishly did Cain try to offer God a bloodless sacrifice, only to be rejected. Abel offered the first of his flock to the Lord and was well received. It is the blood that God has required as atonement for sin. It is the blood of Jesus Christ, God's Son that keeps on cleansing us from all of our sins. The blood of Christ is precious, and priceless. It is the basis of the gospel.

Should Christians be ashamed that the gospel calls men *"sinners"*? Not at all, for it is sin that obscures the truth, with words that lead gentle souls to temporal and eternal destruction. The power of words to destroy is well documented. During World War II, the Nazis wanted to move people from populated areas, to death camps, with little protest. They discovered that if they talked about *"transporting"* communities, they met with vigorous resistance. However, when the Nazi government began to talk about *"transplanting"* communities, there was less opposition.

The word *"transplanting"* conveyed the idea of a quiet relocation that was peaceful and permanent so with cunning words, the Nazis lured people into their chambers of horror. The Christian gospel does not use smooth words to lead people to temporal or eternal destruction. It boldly speaks the truth to warn individuals to flee from the wrath to come. Christians should be proud of a message that speaks the truth in grace, for the gospel teaches that God loves sinners. *"While we where sinners Christ died for us."*

Should Christians be ashamed of the gospel because of possible rejection? Some people are. But we know that the preaching of the Cross is foolishness to men, and that most will reject it. Jesus said this rejection would happen. The Lord said that salvation is rare, and difficult. A broad path leads to destruction while the path to eternal life is narrow, and few there are that walk on it. Men walk on the broad path to destruction because they still believe that they can still earn or deserve salvation. The Bible teaches that the works of the flesh shall justify no man. It is only when we humble ourselves and accepts God's way of salvation, that the Lord of Glory, in grace, lifts us higher than we have ever been before. Because of these things, all Christian should say with Paul, *"I am not ashamed of the gospel of Christ. I am not ashamed of the blood offering required. I am not ashamed of Jesus. I am not ashamed of the truth that the gospel teaches. I am not ashamed of the ridicule the gospel receives from foolish people. I am not ashamed of the gospel of Christ."*

Once, Paul was ashamed of the gospel. He was embarrassed that another Jew was claiming to be the Messiah and the Savior of the world. He was embarrassed that the gospel was becoming so popular that it was undermining Judaism. He was ashamed of a free gospel of free grace. Then Saul met Jesus personally and was forever changed. He became Paul, and then he who once ruthlessly persecuted the Church, began to preach what he formerly protested, to the point of death. Paul discovered the power of God unto salvation to everyone that believeth. Oh, to be able to believe!

That is the greatest of all privileges: To be able to believe that Jesus is the Christ the Son of God; To be able to believe that all of our sins are forgiven; To be able to believe in a glorified resurrected Savior; To believe that Jesus is the Only Wise God and Ruler of the Universe. The gospel staggers the mind. It strains the intellect as it invites belief. Still, let the word go forth and let people know that we are not ashamed anymore!

A Life of Faith: Romans 1:17

There can be four responses to the Law. (1) We can attempt to keep the Law as the Pharisees tried to observe all of the many demands the Law made. (2) Life can be lived in a religious response to the Law but with no real effort arriving at its essential righteousness. (3) The Law can be willfully abandoned for a life of hedonism. (4) In the person of Christ the Law can be kept.

Retaining Respect for the Law while Rejecting Regeneration

It was the testimony of Paul that he was ready to preach the gospel to those in Rome. He was ready emotionally because of His great love for Jesus. Once Paul hated Jesus until the resurrected Lord met him and changed his heart. It would have been easy for Christ to kill Saul that day on the road to Damascus when first He appeared. It would have been within the boundaries of Divine justice for Christ to blast Saul of Tarsus into eternity with the brightness of His glory. But where sin abounded, grace did much more abound and Saul was spared. His heart was changed, and he saw Jesus as the Savior for sinners.

Saul was a great sinner. He was guilty of pride and prejudice. He could be charged with covetousness, and cruelty, for he had consented to the death of Stephen. But again, instead of punishment,

Saul found grace, and mercy, in the eyes of the Lord. As a result, he wanted to spend the rest of his life apologizing and preaching the gospel of redeeming grace. As Paul was prepared emotionally he was prepared psychologically. He knew that much danger awaited him in Rome. A trial awaited, and he might lose his life. Still, Paul was not going to change his message. He was totally committed. Many years ago, a young African pastor wrote the following words, and tacked them on the wall of his house.

My Commitment As A Christian

I'm part of the fellowship of the unashamed. I have Holy Spirit power. The die has been cast I have stepped over the line. The decision has been made. I'm a disciple of His. I won't look back, let up, slow down, back away, or be still.

My past is redeemed, my present makes sense, and my future is secure. I'm finished and done with low living, sight walking, small planning, smooth knees, colorless dreams, tamed visions, mundane talking, cheap living, and dwarfed goals.

I no longer need preeminence, prosperity, position, promotions, plaudits, or popularity. I don't have to be right, first, tops, recognized, praised, regarded, or rewarded. I now live by faith, lean on His presence, walk by patience, lift by prayer, and labor by power.

My face is set, my gait is fast, my goal is heaven, my road is narrow, my way rough, my companions few, my Guide reliable, my mission clear. I cannot be bought, compromised, detoured, lured away, turned back, deluded or delayed. I will not flinch in the face of sacrifice, hesitate in the presence of the adversary, negotiate at the table of the enemy, ponder at the pool of popularity, or meander in the maze of mediocrity.
I won't give up, shut up, let up, until I have stayed up, stored up, prayed up, paid up, and preached up for the cause of Christ. I am a disciple of Jesus. I must go till He comes, give till I drop, preach till all know, and work till

> *He stops me. And when He comes for His own, He will have no problems recognizing me, my banner will be clear!*

In addition to emotional and mental preparation for preaching the gospel, Paul was prepared theologically. Illuminated by Divine revelation under the guidance of the Holy Spirit, Paul had thought through the implications of the gospel. His irrevocable position was that the gospel was nothing to be ashamed of, because it was the power of God unto salvation, to everyone that believeth. Furthermore, in the gospel the righteousness of God is revealed. Prior to Christ, Paul, like all orthodox Jews, looked to the Law, for the righteousness of God was revealed therein. It was to the Law that men looked, for the way of salvation. People were taught that righteousness consisted in keeping the Law, for the Law was holy, just, and good.

However, the problem was that no one could keep the Law. Many tried. Sacrifices were offered. The Scriptures were studied. Special days were observed. The Law of the Lord was loved. But was this righteousness? Was this ceremonial activity the righteousness of God? These were the haunting questions for thinking men and women. And the honest answer was, *No!* The attempts to keep the Law seemed inadequate, for no one could keep it perfectly. The Law was too demanding. It was precise, exacting, and far above what men could produce. The Law condemned individuals with a sensitive conscience.

The Law condemned the best efforts of men as individuals realized that the righteousness of God was not just a matter of degrees whereby one man kept 20 percent of the Law and another person kept 80 percent and God kept it all. No. The righteousness of God was part of His essence. God's righteousness is not a matter of submission to external commandments. God's righteousness is His attribute. Fallen man does not have the innate righteousness of God. The best he can now do is to seek after it. But in the seeking, the discovery is made that the soul will always fall short of the high and holy standard.

Once Israel realized that the Law could not be kept perfectly, several groups were formed. Into one group were those who were still determined that they would at least keep as much of the Law as possible. Such were the Scribes and the Pharisees. They hoped that somehow, someday their good lives would be accepted after all.

In another group were those who decided to enjoy life by being religious if not righteous. Life would be lived without any real concern with the demands of the Law. Still another group just decided to forget the Law and embrace a lifestyle of hedonism. This group of people is described in Romans 1:21-32.

Different from all of these groups was one more. It was much smaller than the rest. It could be called the elect for it was a remnant according to grace. Into this group of people came the glorious light of gospel truth that the just shall live by faith. How did the gospel come to this group? Very simply, one person told another so that from the faith of one soul the faith of the other was strengthened. In the process of sharing messages several truths were communicated, the most important being that it is the gospel that displays the righteousness of God.

The gospel tells us that God is distinct from mankind. The gospel reveals that God is absolute holiness, righteousness, and goodness. His holiness is not something to fear, but to honor and respect. While God's righteousness condemns sinners, it causes some souls to want to be holy in His sight. But how is that possible? By keeping the Law? No. By faith! The gospel message declares that, *"not all the blood of beasts on Jewish altars slain, Could give the guilty conscience peace, or wash away the stain."*

But Christ the heavenly Lamb takes all our sins away; A sacrifice of nobler Name and richer blood than they. By faith the righteous shall live. The righteous shall live in time. It is a new life, not of works but of faith. It is life not of striving but serving. It is a life, not of trying but of trusting. Oh what freedom there is in a life of faith. There is freedom from fear, freedom from failure, and freedom from future condemnation. Christ clothes Christians with garments of His own righteousness so that we can step forth into the company of the saved. We step out of the sphere of death and into life and sing,

> *Jesus, Thy blood and righteousness,*
> *My beauty are, my glorious dress;*
> *Mid flaming worlds in these arrayed*
> *With joy shall I lift up my heart.*

To every heart the gospel comes asking, *"Are you living a life of faith? Are you trusting in Jesus?"* To trust in Christ means to cast oneself upon Him for salvation. This concept is not always easy to communicate.

Stretch Thyself Out

In the early days of the gospel in the South Pacific isles, many missionaries were killed by the natives who were in a state of savage cannibalism. Finally, John G. Paton arrived at his destination in the New Hebrides and by one of the acts of Providence, which unbelieving men call chance, he came to the island at the moment when there was a terrible epidemic that had decimated the population.

He entered into the huts of the sick and began to care for them. He buried the dead and tended to the sick. When the epidemic had passed, he was received by all and began to take up his life with them. His first thought was to learn their language, and he began to listen to their speech and write down in his note book all the words and phrases which he learned.

The natives became accustomed to having him stop them in the middle of a sentence, repeating words, and waiting while he wrote them down. Then came a time when John decided that he would begin to translate some of the gospel stories into their language. But to his dismay, when he began the task he discovered that there was no word in his book for faith, confidence, trust, and belief. You will not get very far in translating the Bible without such words, and he turned his full attention to finding something that would convey the missing idea. Nothing availed.

He imagined stories that would bring up possible conversations that would contain such a word. The natives knew that he was seeking something, but they could not imagine what it was. After some time of frustration he went on a hunting trip with one of his helpers. They shot a deer-like animal and several smaller game and started to carry their kill back to the house of the missionary. The equatorial weather was oppressive; the hill in which they hunted was trackless; and they arrived at the house almost exhausted. They dropped their heavy burden, and then cast themselves down on the grass to rest. The native said, after a moment, *"Oh, it is good to stretch yourself out here in the shade."*

John Paton revived on the instant. Excitedly he had his companion repeat the sentence again and again. He put every bit of it down in his book; and, when the Gospels were ultimately translated, this was the word that was used to convey the idea of faith and belief. *"For God so loved the world that He gave His only begotten Son that whosoever stretcheth Himself out on Him, shall not perish, but have everlasting life. And stretch yourself out on the Lord Jesus Christ and thou shalt be saved."* And again, *"If thou shalt confess with thy mouth the Lord Jesus, and in thine heart stretch thyself out on the fact that God hath raised Him from the dead, thou shalt be saved; for with the heart one stretcheth himself out unto righteousness, and with the mouth confession is made unto salvation."*

This Is the Life of Faith

Sometimes discovering this simple truth takes a long time. That was the case with Martin Luther. For many years Luther tried to know the righteousness of God by keeping the Law. Then the hour came when God revealed to Him the true meaning of salvation in Romans 1:17. Of this whole experience Boreham of Australia wrote the following. *"It goes without saying that the text that Martin Luther made history with a vengeance. When, through its mystical but mighty ministry, Martin Luther entered the newness of life, the face of the world was changed. It was as though all the windows of Europe had been suddenly thrown open, and the sunshine came streaming in everywhere. The destiny of empires was turned that day into a new channel."*

Thomas Carlyle (1795-1881) has written in a stirring manner to show that every nation under heaven stood or fell according to the attitude that it assumed toward Martin Luther. *"I call this Luther a truly great man. He is great in intellect, great in courage, great in affection and integrity one of our most lovable and gracious men. He is great, not as a hewn monolith is great, but as an Alpine mountain is great; so simple, honest, spontaneous; not setting himself up to be great, but there for quite another purpose than the purpose of being great!"*

"A mighty man," he says again, *"What were all emperors, popes and potentates in comparison? His life to flame as a beacon over long centuries and epochs of the world; the whole world and its history was waiting for this man!"* And elsewhere he declares that the moment in which Luther defied the wrath of the Diet of Worms was the greatest moment in the history of men. Here, then, was the man; what was the text that made him?

"Let us visit a very interesting European library. Here, in the Covenant Library at Erfurt, we are shown an exceedingly famous and beautiful picture. It represents Luther as a young monk of four and twenty, poring in the early morning over a copy of the Scriptures to which a bit of broken chain is hanging. The dawn is stealing through the open lattice, illumining both the open Bible and the eager face of its reader. And on the page that the young monk so intently studies is to be seen the words: 'the just shall live by faith.'

These are the words that made the world all over again. If we want to live a life of faith, then let us resolve to be like the saints of old and say, 'I will, like Paul, forget those things that are behind and press forward. Abraham trusted implicitly in my God. I will, like Moses, choose rather to suffer than to enjoy the pleasures of sin for a season. I will, like Daniel, commune with my God at all times. I will, like Caleb and Joshua, refuse to be discouraged because of superior numbers. With Joseph, I will turn my back to all seductive advances. Gideon, advance even though my friends be few. With Isaiah, I will consecrate myself to do God's work. Like Andrew, I will strive to lead my brother into a closer walk with Christ.

As John leaned upon the bosom of the Master and imbibed of His Spirit, so will I. As Stephen manifested a forgiving spirit toward all who hurt him, so will I. After the manner Timothy, I will study the Word of God. With the heavenly hosts, I will proclaim the message of peace on earth and good will to all men. I will, by faith, rely upon Christ for I can do all things through Christ which strengtheneth me.'"

This is the life of faith.

The Wrath of God: Romans 1:18

The concept of a God angry at sin and hostile to sinners in His holiness is not well received among men. Many would rather think of God as docile, distant, and disinterested in daily living. In many ways men have tried to remove the idea of an all-powerful God holding His creation to a high level of accountability. Because of ungodliness, because of unrighteousness men suppress the truth. It is not that the truth is sought but cannot be found, but rather that, confronted with the truth—which is clearly seen Romans 1:20, fallen humanity seeks to block and deny its influence. It is this suppression of the truth in unrighteousness that produces the wrath of God. The Creator is being ignored by His creation, and that rejection is unacceptable. Consider briefly some of the philosophical concepts that have been advocated in unrighteousness.

- **Atheism.** Atheism says that there is no God. One of the most infamous atheists who advocated this position to his generation was Robert Green Ingersoll (1833-1899). This son of a Calvinistic conservative Protestant minister was born in Dresden, New York. An exceptionally bright man, at the age of twenty-one Robert was admitted to the bar at Mount Vernon, Illinois.

  He started to practice Law with his brother Ebon Clark Ingersoll in Shawneeville, Illinois, and then moved to Peoria in 1857. After fighting in the Civil War, in which he was taken prisoner, Ingersoll served as attorney general of Illinois (1867-1869).

  In 1879 he moved to Washington, DC, to engage in the practice of federal Law; in 1885 he settled in New York City, where he continued to be a successful trial Lawyer. Ingersoll rebelled against what he considered an unduly harsh religious childhood. When Charles Darwin's *Origin of the Species* was published in 1859,

Ingersoll became an ardent exponent of the doctrine of evolution.

He began attacking orthodox Christian beliefs while defending atheism in public lectures. One of his lectures was on what he called *Some Mistakes of Moses*. Known for his oratorical gifts, exemplary private life, and noble character, he was an effective champion of atheism.

- **Agnosticism.** Most people are not as bold as Robert Ingersoll. Most people would not just come out and say there is no God though not a few would admit to being an agnostic. An agnostic is a polite atheist. Such a person is willing to share his skepticism and leave the door open for discussion lest he be accused of being closed-minded. In essence the practicing agnostic who lives life without God is no better than the professing atheist who says there is no God.

- **Evolution.** If there is no God, if there is no Creator, if there is no Supreme Being, how then did the universe came into existence? The modern scientific answer is that man evolved from a common ancestor with the animals! But even that answer does not solve the problem for the universe is still complex. Is life all a cosmic chance? Does it not take enormous faith to believe that the great mystery of life just happened? No wonder God is angry at such foolish reasoning. He has endowed men with more sense than that. Why would men suppress the truth? Do men hate the Lord that much? And if so, Why? What has God done that deserves so much hostility?

- **Self-esteem.** In more recent years, men have gone from arrogantly dismissing God to entertaining the notion that man is God. Catchy slogans are coined. What the mind of man can conceive, the ability of man can achieve. This arrogance comes in part because of creative successes. Does man dream of flying with the birds? It is done! Does man wish to build a superstructure that towers hundreds of feet above the earth? It is done! Does man conceive of going to the moon? His ability can achieve it! Does man wish to dam up the mighty rivers of the world and control them as easily as turning on the faucet on the home? It is done! What modern man forgets is that all of these things and more are the gifts of God who long ago gave man permission to subdue the Creation. But man has never been given permission to think that he is the Creator! That thinking is going too far, and it is suppressing the truth. In the end man is proved to be just another created entity among the beasts of the field as he goes to the dust from which he came. He is not God. And the wrath of God will be revealed against him.

Now even though this message of the wrath of God may not be popular, it is the duty of the faithful minister to teach the truth. That is what Paul meant when he said in his last address to the Church at Ephesus, *"For I have not shunned to declare unto you all the council of God"* (Acts 20:27). In Romans 1:18 mankind is being indicted. The argument of the prosecution in the case against man is that man, the creature of God, has a rich history of sin and is presently in a hopeless condition. This is the charge.

If the charge is true, the concept of a God of wrath should not surprise anyone. A God without wrath would be a crippled God. He would in fact be a monster, for He would never right any wrong. But the attributes of God are balanced. As He is perfect love, so He is also perfect justice. He is of purer eyes than to behold evil (Habakkuk 1:13). In Hebrews 1:9 we read, *"Thou hast loved righteousness and hated lawlessness; Therefore God, Your God, has anointed You with the oil of gladness more than your companions."*

God hates lawlessness! Therefore, the love of God must not be presented to the exclusion of His wrath. There are two different words in Greek for wrath. One of them means a hot, vehement, surge of anger, while the other refers to a slowly rising indignation. *"Thumos"* is a wrath that signifies a panting rage. That is not the word used here. But the word *"orga"* is used. This word signifies an indignation that has risen gradually and became more settled. Thayer, a Greek scholar defines this term as *"that in God which stands opposed to man's disobedience, obduracy, especially in resisting the gospel, and sin, and manifests itself in punishing the same."* The revelation of just how much

God hates sin and is willing to punish it is displayed at the Cross. At Calvary the wrath of God is fully displayed.

Prior to Calvary, God occasionally burst forth to protest the offenses of sin. But at Calvary the full fury of Divine anger was poured out upon Christ. Prior to the Cross, it could be said that there were times of ignorance which God winked at (Acts 17:30), but not any longer. Prior to Calvary, people thought that they could sin with impunity. Some dared to provoke God to judge them and were almost amazed when He did not destroy them. Perhaps a simply illustration can tell why.

The story is told that the godly farmers in a western community were greatly shocked one summer Sunday morning, when they drove up to the little Church in the country, to see that the man who owned the forty acres across from the Church was in the midst of plowing, and that he had evidently been turning the furrows since dawn. The people went on into the Church and could hear the rise and fall of the noise of the tractor as it approached and then went on to the other side of the field. The farmer who was doing this worked other fields all week and came back on the following Sunday to complete the job. And so on through the spring, summer and fall, he plowed, disked, harrowed, dragged, fertilized, drilled and cultivated the field, and finally cut, stacked and husked the corn and carried it to the crib. Then he wrote a letter to the editor of the local weekly, pointing out that he had done all this on Sunday and yet had the highest yield per acre of any farm in the country; and he asked the editor how the Christians could explain this. The editor, with great common sense, printed the letter, but followed it with the simple statement, *"God does not settle His accounts in the month of October."*

But God does settle His accounts, which truth is why the gospel warning comes in Acts 17:30, 31 saying that God *"now commands all men everywhere to repent, because He has appointed a day on which He will judge the world in righteousness by the Man whom He has ordained."*

There is a need for a Day of Judgment for Man's inhumanity to man makes countless thousands mourn. In the Day of Judgment, in the day of wrath, righteousness will triumph. This may be hard to believe, for it does not seem that justice will ever be vindicated. Only the revelation of the wrath of God at the Cross of Jesus Christ can tell us that the Lord will finish what He has started.

If He who spared not His own Son judged sin in Him, how shall the rest not be judged who neglect so great a salvation? Now notice that the source of the revelation of God is said to be from heaven. We have known of the wrath of man being revealed on Earth. It is an awesome and terrible thing. But this coming Divine wrath will be revealed from heaven. We see a foretaste of it at Calvary; for on that day, the Earth shook and the sky turned black. Terror gripped the hearts of people. Some cried out in fear. The wrath of God was being revealed. Oh, how glad the Church is that the wrath of God fell upon Christ. No wonder the Church sings songs of gratitude.

"Beneath the Cross of Jesus
I fain would take my stand,
The shadow of a mighty Rock,
Within a weary land.

A home within the wilderness,
A rest upon the way,
From the burning of the noontime heat,
And the burden of the day.

Oh, safe and happy shelter!
Oh, refuge tried and sweet!
Oh, trusting place where Heaven's love
And Heaven's justices meet.

As to the holy patriarch
That wondrous dream was given,
So seems my Savior's cross to me
A ladder up to Heaven.

There lies beneath its shadow,
But on the farther side,
The darkness of an awful grave
That gapes both deep and wide;

> *And there between us stands the Cross,*
> *Two arms outstretched to save,*
> *Like a watchman set to guard the way*
> *From that eternal grave."*

But what happens when the Church stops singing and stops remembering? What happens when men forget that the wrath of God will still be revealed against sin? One commentator, William Newell, knows for he writes, *"It will not only fail to help us, but will seriously harm us, to study the awful arraignment of God against human sin, unless we apply it to ourselves, thereby discovering our own state by nature... Christendom is rapidly losing sin consciousness, which means losing God consciousness; which means eternal doom: As it was in the days of Noah...and it came to pass in the days of Lot...they knew not. Because iniquity abounds, the love of many professing Christians is waxing cold."*

Despite the clear teaching of the Bible about the wrath of God, there are still those who deny it. Some of the cults such as the Jehovah Witnesses were started because they do not believe in hell. They do not believe in the wrath of God. But they should.

The Things Which God Hath Shown: Romans 1:19-20

As the gospel reveals the righteousness of God and the wrath of God against sin, so nature reveals the fact of God 1:19. Unfortunately, not all men can see God, or so they say. But there is a reason for this. Men suppress or hold down the truth that God exists. *"Man's apostasy from God is not the act of an ignorant mind but the act of a determined will"* (*Romans*, Donald Grey Barnhouse). Man wants to shut God out of His own universe. He does this by pretending that God cannot be known. It can be conceded that much about God is veiled but this is by design. God has not chosen to reveal everything about Himself which can be appreciated, for we as humans practice self-concealment and self-disclosure.

Very few people know all there is to know about someone else. Even individuals who have been married for a long time are surprised at what they learn or discover about their mates. We veil ourselves, and we disclose ourselves. That is our privilege. It is God's privilege as well. And God has veiled much about Himself. He has wrapped Himself in mystery and majesty and is accountable to no one. But God has also revealed some things, for we read, *"That which may be known of God."* This is a very important statement in the Bible because it crosses the frontier between natural religion and revealed religion. In natural religion man looks at nature and he discerns two things: man has a conscience, and there is a Designer to the Universe.

- **Man has a conscience**. But where did he get this conscience? Where did man get his sense of right and wrong? Many years ago an editorial was written by a former superintendent of the public schools in California. The writer said that he might be inclined to accept evolution except for the fact that the theory cannot explain how man came to be a creature with a conscience and a moral sense of right and wrong. No lion has every apologized for killing a zebra. No cobra has ever felt remorse for eating a rabbit. No crocodile has every shed a tear for robbing the nest of another animal for food. Man is unique among the living creatures, for he shows sorrow in the injury of others.

- **As man discerns that he has a conscience and so is different from the animal kingdom, he looks at nature and discerns that this great universe must have a Designer.** The universe is glorious and grand. Man discovers that he is in the middle of material creation. There is something beyond him, and there is something below him as well. The telescope is created, and it is discovered that there is more to the universe than is visible to the eye. We are surprised to learn that we are but a speck of dust in the midst of universes upon universes. The microscope is invented and we are excited to find the universe of the atoms with their whirling protons, electrons, neutrons, deuterons, and mesons. There are subatomic particles. And while our eyes have not seen this invisible world, it exists. Scientists are able to discern the effects of their movements and to formulate laws that govern these movements. The proof that the scientific talk is more than theory has been demonstrated by the ruins of Hiroshima and the meltdown at Chernobyl. In the early eighteenth century, Joseph Addison understood that God has manifested Himself in all of nature, and he wrote,

"The spacious firmament on high,
With all the blue ethereal sky,
And spangled heav'ns, a shining frame,
Their great Original proclaim,
Th' unwearied sun from day to day,
Does his Creator's pow'r display,
And publishes to every land,
The work of an Almighty hand.

Soon as the evening shades prevail,
The moon takes up the wondrous tale,
And nightly to the listening earth
Repeats the story of her birth;

Whilst all the stars that round her burn,
And all the planets in their turn,
Confirm the tidings as they roll,
And spread the truth from pole to pole.

What tho' in silence all
Move 'round this dark terrestrial ball;
What tho' no real voice nor sound

Admist their radiant orbs be found;
In reason's ear they all rejoice,
And utter forth a glorious voice;
Forever singing as they shine,
The Hand that made us is Divine!"

As wonderful as natural theology can be, in revealed religion God speaks more plainly. The Christian faith teaches that God has spoken more plainly and revealed Himself in the pages of Scripture and in the Person of Jesus Christ so *"That which may be known of God is manifest."* One of the things, which are manifest, is that God loves us, for there is a place called Calvary. If there had been no Calvary, we could never really know that God loves us. Creation itself is no confirmation of this Divine attribute, for Satan and sin have taken creation captive. Daily provisions of food and water and shelter would be no confirmation of the love of God, for all these things are subject to change. Food can perish on the vine. Water can become polluted. Shelter can be blown away.

Something else must be seen to know the love of God. And so we read that Jesus was lifted from the earth so that all men might look and see that *"God so loved the world, He gave His only begotten Son."* Now if God has manifested Himself in nature through conscience and a marvelous creation; if God has manifested Himself through the special revelation of the Scriptures and His own Son, surely men are without excuse. No one has a reason for anyone to reject Jesus Christ as Lord and Savior. There is no reason for anyone to resist being a disciple of Christ.

There is no reason for anyone to repeat harmful behavior unchallenged. It is one thing to struggle with sin; it is another thing to justify the same. The Bible teaches that all men are without excuse, but no man is without hope; for the blood of Jesus Christ, God's Son, cleanses from all sin. It is the privilege of every student of the Bible to agree with God's Word, acknowledge that a Savior is needed, and long for the cleansing power of the Holy Spirit.

When Bad Behavior is Excused

1. When the Lord confronted Adam with the sin of disobedience, Adam excused his behavior by shifting blame to God Himself.

    - Genesis 3:12-13, *"And the man said, The woman whom thou gavest to be with me, she gave me of the tree, and I did eat. And the LORD God said unto the woman, What is this that thou hast done? And the woman said, The serpent beguiled me, and I did eat."*

2. When Moses did not want to go back to Egypt as a leader, he told God that the people would not listen to him.

    - Exodus 4:1, *"And Moses answered and said, But, behold, they will not believe me, nor hearken unto my voice: for they will say, The LORD hath not appeared unto thee."*

3. Then Moses tried to suggest that he was not a good speaker (Acts 7:22).

   - Exodus 4:10, *"And Moses said unto the LORD, O my Lord, I am not eloquent, neither heretofore, nor since thou hast spoken unto thy servant: but I am slow of speech, and of a slow tongue. 11 And the LORD said unto him, Who hath made man's mouth? Or who maketh the dumb, or deaf, or the seeing, or the blind? Have not I the LORD? 12 Now therefore go, and I will be with thy mouth, and teach thee what thou shalt say. 13 And he said, O my Lord, send, I pray thee, by the hand of him whom thou wilt send. 14 And the anger of the LORD was kindled against Moses, and he said, Is not Aaron the Levite thy brother? I know that he can speak well. And also, behold he cometh forth to meet thee: and when he seeth thee, he will be glad in his heart."*

4. Aaron tried to blame the persistence of the multitude as an excuse for his allowing a golden calf to be made.

   - Exodus 32:22, *"And Aaron said, Let not the anger of my lord wax hot: thou knowest the people, which they are set on mischief. 23 For they said unto me, Make us gods, which shall go before us: for as for this Moses, the man that brought us up out of the land of Egypt, we wot not what is become of him. 24 And I said unto them, Whosoever hath any gold, let them break it off. So they gave it me: then I cast it into the fire, and there came out this calf."*

5. The Israelites tried to excuse themselves from knowing the Word of the Lord by pretending that it was too far away to know.

   - Deuteronomy 30:11, *"For this commandment which I command thee this day, it is not hidden from thee, neither is it far off. 12 It is not in heaven, that thou shouldest say, Who shall go up for us to heaven, and bring it unto us, that we may hear it, and do it? 13 Neither is it beyond the sea, that thou shouldest say, Who shall go over the sea for us, and bring it unto us, that we may hear it, and do it? 14 But the word is very nigh unto thee, in thy mouth, and in thy heart, that thou mayest do it."*

6. Gideon tried to suggest that he was too poor and humble to obey the known will of God.

- Judges 6:12, *"And the angel of the LORD appeared unto him, and said unto him, The LORD is with thee, thou mighty man of valor. 13 And Gideon said unto him, Oh my Lord, if the LORD be with us, why then is all this befallen us? And where be all his miracles which our fathers told us of, saying, Did not the LORD bring us up from Egypt? But now the LORD hath forsaken us, and delivered us into the hands of the Midianites. 14 And the LORD looked upon him, and said, Go in this thy might, and thou shalt save Israel from the hand of the Midianites: have not I sent thee? 15 And he said unto him, Oh my Lord, wherewith shall I save Israel? Behold, my family is poor in Manasseh, and I am the least in my father's house. 16 And the LORD said unto him, Surely I will be with thee, and thou shalt smite the Midianites as one man. 17 And he said unto him, If now I have found grace in thy sight, then shew me a sign that thou talkest with me."*

7. Elisha almost missed being part of a spiritual ministry because of family ties (Matthew 8:21, 22; Luke 9:61, 62).

    - 1 Kings 19:19, *"So he departed thence, and found Elisha the son of Shaphat, who was plowing with twelve yoke of oxen before him, and he with the twelfth: and Elijah passed by him, and cast his mantle upon him. 20 And he left the oxen, and ran after Elijah, and said, Let me, I pray thee, kiss my father and my mother, and then I will follow thee. And he said unto him, Go back again: for what have I done to thee? 21 And he returned back from him, and took a yoke of oxen, and slew them, and boiled their flesh with the instruments of the oxen, and gave unto the people, and they did eat. Then he arose, and went after Elijah, and ministered unto him."*

8. The King of Syria almost excused himself from being healed because he thought the river Jordan was too dirty to bathe in.

    - 2 Kings 5:10, *"And Elisha sent a messenger unto him, saying, Go and wash in Jordan seven times, and thy flesh shall come again to thee, and thou shalt be clean. 11 But Naaman was wroth, and went away, and said, Behold, I thought, He will surely come out to me, and stand, and call on the name of the LORD his God, and strike his hand over the place, and recover the leper. 12 Are not Abana and Pharpar, rivers of Damascus, better than all the waters of Israel? May I not wash in them, and be clean? So he turned and went away in a rage. 13 And his servants came near, and spake unto him, and said, My father, if the prophet had bid thee do some great thing, wouldest thou not have done it? How much rather then, when he saith to thee, Wash, and be clean? 14 Then went he down, and dipped himself seven times in Jordan, according to the saying of the man of God: and his flesh came again like unto the flesh of a little child, and he was clean."*

9. Jeremiah tried to excuse himself from a prophetic ministry because he was afraid of the people.

   - Jeremiah 1:1, *"The words of Jeremiah the son of Hilkiah, of the priests that were in Anathoth in the land of Benjamin: Jer 1:4 4 Then the word of the LORD came unto me, saying, 5 Before I formed thee in the belly I knew thee; and before thou camest forth out of the womb I sanctified thee, and I ordained thee a prophet unto the nations. 6 Then said I, Ah, Lord GOD! Behold, I cannot speak: for I am a child. 7 But the LORD said unto me, Say not, I am a child: for thou shalt go to all that I shall send thee, and whatsoever I command thee thou shalt speak. 8 Be not afraid of their faces: for I am with thee to deliver thee, saith the LORD. 9 Then the LORD put forth his hand, and touched my mouth. And the LORD said unto me, Behold, I have put my words in thy mouth. 10 See, I have this day set thee over the nations and over the kingdoms, to root out, and to pull down, and to destroy, and to throw down, to build, and to plant."*

10. Some will use the family as an excuse not to follow Jesus.

    - Matthew 8:21, *"And another of his disciples said unto him, Lord, suffer me first to go and bury my father. 12. People reject the gospel using very foolish excuses."*

    - Luke 14:18-20, *"And they all with one consent began to make excuse. The first said unto him, I have bought a piece of ground, and I must needs go and see it: I pray thee have me excused. And another said, I have bought five yoke of oxen, and I go to prove them: I pray thee have me excused. And another said, I have married a wife, and therefore I cannot come."*

11. Felix said he would not come to Christ because it was not convenient.

   Acts 24:25, *"And as he reasoned of righteousness, temperance, and judgment to come, Felix trembled, and answered, Go thy way for this time; when I have a convenient season, I will call for thee."*

12. The pseudo intellectual refuses to have faith because he cannot see God in a tangible manner.

   Romans 1:20, *"For the invisible things of him from the creation of the world are clearly seen, being understood by the things that are made, even his eternal power and Godhead; so that they are without excuse:"*

In all these cases people are without excuse for their condemnation of others according to Romans 2:1. *"Therefore thou art inexcusable, O man, whosoever thou art that judgest: for wherein thou judgest another, thou condemnest thyself; for thou that judgest doest the same things."* Sometimes, it is far better not to be too demanding of others, but to be silent before the Lord in humility.

When man moved against God, God moved against man. The Bible says that in judgment:

God gave the heart up to uncleanness, so that intense desires consumed the soul.

He allowed men to dishonor their bodies, by using the body parts in a way that is contrary to nature.

He allowed truth to be exchanged for a lie.

He allowed the creation to be worshipped, rather than the Creator, and silly questions to be asked. "Cosmic universe, do you hear?" "Astrological chart, do you care?" "Signs of the Zodiac, will you help me today?"

In His wrath, God allowed women to prefer women to men, and he allowed men to prefer men to women. Despite the modern day rhetoric, homosexuality, and lesbianism are not natural. They are signs of the wrath of God being poured out upon a nation.

In His wrath, God allows a multitude of sin to saturate the soul.

When people allow sin to bring a disdain for true value, and risk abandonment by God, when people allow a spirit of licentiousness to prevail (Romans 1:29-31), God will give people exactly what they want. But there is no need for suppression of the truth in unrighteousness, for God has always revealed Himself. His attributes of omnipotence, omniscience, omnipresence, justice, immutability, veracity, holiness, and absolute righteousness, are clearly seen in nature (Romans 1:20). Men are without excuse.

Why then, do men insist on committing Deicide? The answer is rather simple: men hate God. Men know God, but they do not glorify Him as God. Neither are men thankful. Allowing themselves futile thought, allowing their hearts to be darkened, men professed themselves to be wise, and changed the glory of God into a corruptible being through an act of the will. Is there any hope for such desperate souls?

The answer, surprising enough is, yes! But the Divine remedy is not easy. It is free, but not cheap. Man must stop suppressing the truth, and admit to being enslaved to sin. Man must confess sin as sin. Man must ask forgiveness. Man must forsake sin. How? By faith! A life of righteousness must be cultivated. God must be pursued as much as sin was. Not one of these steps can be eliminated. To whatever degree individuals engage in, they will know the wrath of God, or the greatness of His glory and grace.

Professing Wisdom While Practicing Foolishness: Romans 1:21

It is a matter of record, that men in all societies are religious by nature. No matter how primitive the social gathering may be in a given culture, there is an element of religion. When Charles Darwin took his famous journey in the Beagle, he returned to England, and reported on a tribe of savages on the island of *Tierra del Fuego*, who appeared to have no religion whatsoever. The Christians in England formed a missionary society to send someone to minister the gospel to these people. Their language and customs were soon learned, and then it was discovered that the people did have well-developed concepts, and ideas, and practices of religion, even though they were not obvious to the eyes of Darwin.

The truth of the matter is that all men, everywhere, have always had an idea of God. Originally, it was a high idea, reflected by Adam and Eve in the Garden of Eden. They knew God as their Creator. They knew God as a personal Friend. They knew God as the Object of worship. They knew God as an intimate Confidant, to whom they could tell the longings of their heart, as Adam did when he realized that each of the animals had a mate, and that he did not. Man did not evolve or develop a high view of God with the passing of time, as modern sociology teaches.

Many modern experts, in human behavior, declare that man started out with a low sight of God, and then came up with a nobler picture of Him. In this way, Biblical history is retold. People are taught that Noah's mean-spirited God destroyed the earth with a flood. Abraham's God was bloodthirsty, demanding a bloody sacrifice. The God of Moses frightened everyone from Mt. Sinai amidst smoke and thunder and lightening. David's God was a little more ethical, but still responded to the terrible imprecatory prayers of the people.

By the time of the prophets, God was beginning to change, at least in the minds of men. He was concerned with ethical considerations, and hated social injustices. In the teachings of Jesus the idea of God was marvelous, for God was viewed as a Father, and the brotherhood of mankind was made manifest. Today, the idea of God is most mature, for He is a God of infinite love who will not send anyone to hell. No wonder Frederick W. Nietzsche asked, *"Is man only a blunder of God? Or is God a blunder of man?"*

The answer is, *"Neither."* God did not make a mistake when he made man, and man certainly did not create God. God revealed Himself as

Creator to mankind and man worshipped Him and Him alone until his thinking degenerated from monotheism to polytheism. How did this happen? It happened in two stages. The first phase involved deception. Satan deceived Eve into believing that she too could be a god (1 Timothy 2:14). Eve sincerely believed that if she ate of the forbidden fruit, she would be like God. So she ate and offered her husband fruit, which led to the second phase, whereby sin entered into the world. In the eating of the forbidden fruit, Eve was farther from being like God than ever before, for God has never, and will never, experience sin.

Adam was not deceived by Eve. Rather, he consciously and deliberately ate of the forbidden fruit, thereby placing his will against the will of God. And, in that moment, all of creation was transformed. Creation began to groan as if suddenly afflicted with a deadly poison. The nature of animals changed. Some of the herbivores turned immediately into carnivores. A new nature was given to the beasts of the fields so that they would become territorial, and defensive. Soon creation was red in tooth and claw.

The nature of man also changed in an instant. His mind was darkened. Fear gripped his soul. Innocence was lost. The covering of holiness vanished, and man knew he was unclothed in the sight of God. And yet, for all of this, after the Fall, man still had knowledge of the one true God, for we read that, *"By faith Abel offered unto God a more excellent sacrifice than Cain, by which he obtained witness that he was righteous, God testifying of his gifts: and by it he being dead yet speaketh"* (Hebrews 11:4). *"And Enoch also, the seventh from Adam, prophesied of these, saying, Behold, the Lord cometh with ten thousands of His saints, To execute judgment upon all, and to convince all that are ungodly among them of all their ungodly deeds which they have ungodly committed, and of all their hard speeches which ungodly sinners have spoken against him"* (Jude 1:14, 15).

Then there was Moses, who, *"Esteeming the reproach of Christ greater riches than the treasures in Egypt: for he had respect unto the recompense of the reward"* (Hebrews 11:26). Man knew God, even after the Fall, through nature. Man knew that there was one Supreme Being. Man knew God through his conscience that was sensitive to wrong attitudes and wrong actions. Man knew God through Scriptures. And man knew

God through the prophets, for the Lord has always had a witness unto Himself in every generation. But, knowing God as God, the Bible teaches that mankind did several things.

First, man failed to worship Him as a personal God. *"They glorified [praised] Him not as God."* Why? Because man wanted to be left alone. He did not, and does not want to be held accountable for his attitude and actions. *"Leave me alone!"* is the violent cry of the sinner who is unrepentant. It was the cry of Adam and Eve. When God came calling for them, they were silent. They did not want to praise Him. They wanted to be left alone.

Second, because man wants to be left alone with his sin, he is not thankful that God comes looking for him. This was true of Adam and Eve. After their transgression, they were not thankful for the regular hour of fellowship with the Lord in the cool of the evening. They did not want anything to do with God. The Garden of Eden had become a place of painful memories. William Shakespeare wrote, *"I hate ingratitude more in a man than lying, vainess, babbling, drunkenness or any taint of vice."* The reason for ingratitude is sin. Through the prophet Isaiah, the Lord lamented saying, *"The ox knoweth his owner and the ass his master's crib: but Israel doth not know, my people doth not consider"* (Isaiah 1:3).

There is something else. Sin has caused man to become conceited in his imagination, making his foolish heart to be darkened. It has been said that those who leave God in religion, and manners, will soon leave him in their mind. Still, *"The Lord knoweth the thoughts of man, that they are vanity"* (Psalms 94:11). God knows that, *"the preaching of the cross is to them that perish foolishness; but unto us which are saved it is the power of God"* (1 Corinthians 1:18).

In the darkness of his mind, man remains hostile to God. *"Because the carnal mind is enmity against God: for it is not subject to the Law of God, neither indeed can be"* (Romans 8:7). Even in the Person of Jesus Christ, man is hostile to God, for the Lord is the Light of the World. *"And the light shineth in darkness; and the darkness comprehended it not"* (John 1:5). *"He was in the world, and the world was made by Him, and the world knew Him not"* (John 1:10).

In Scriptural language, the world's imagination has been captured by sin so that it cannot even consider Christ rationally. Because the origin of sin in the soul rests in the imagination, it is important to protect this facet of the heart. The imagination is a powerful influence on what is said and done, for both good and evil, so the imagination must be guarded at all times. In contrast to a person using the imagination for evil, selfish self-help, or for false religious purposes, the exhortation of Scripture is to use the imagination in a wholesome way, to think about God, to consider the Cross of Calvary, and to engage the mind on things which are holy.

Doctrine of Imagination

1. Prior to the Flood, every imagination of the thoughts of men was only evil (Genesis 6:5).

2. After the Flood, the Lord knew that man's imaginations would continue to be evil (Genesis 9:21).

3. The Lord has promised to judge the person, who is determined to follow sinful behavior produced by a wicked imagination (Deuteronomy 29:19, 20).

4. God knows every thought, and every imagination in the heart of man (Deuteronomy 31:21).

5. David prayed that the Lord would allow the people of Israel to have holy imaginations (1 Chronicles 29:18).

6. It was the promise to Jeremiah that the day would come when the people of God would no longer walk after the imaginations of their evil hearts (Jeremiah 3:17).

7. Despite divine pleas, men continually give their hearts to evil imaginations (Jeremiah 7:23, 24).

8. When men break fellowship with the Lord, He will use the covenant relationship as a basis for divine discipline (Jeremiah 11:8).

9. Man insists on his own imaginations (Jeremiah 13:10) in part because he loses faith in God (Jeremiah 18:12).

10. False prophets provide false peace to people who walk in the evil imaginations of their own hearts (Jeremiah 23:17).

11. God is still sovereign over the wrong usage of the imagination (Luke 1:51).

12. One of the seven deadly sins of Proverbs 6:18, is a heart that deviseth wicked imaginations.

13. Paul speaks of a vain, or empty imagination (Romans 1:21).

14. The Christian is commanded to cast down imaginations that are not pleasing to the Lord (2 Corinthians 10:5).

The Greatness of God's Glory: Romans 1:22-25

When mankind rebelled against God, the Bible says that he became a fool, all the while professing wisdom. Here is the great irony of life. What appears to be wisdom in man is in the sight of God, foolishness. The word for *"fool"*, in the original, means to *"make or act as a simpleton."* The *"foolish"* person is the *"simple"* person. Thinking himself to be intellectually deep, the natural man is really shallow. Numbers of illustrations document this Biblical truth.

- **Communism.** No one has to guess about the beliefs, the aims, or the purposes of Communism. No one has to be fooled by high ideals. The truth is in writing for anyone to read. The basic doctrine and beliefs of Communism are set out clearly in *"The Communist Manifesto"* written in 1848 by Karl Marx, and by Frederic Engels, a German, living at the time in England, as was Marx. Fundamentally, as the *"Manifesto"* states, *"The Communists *everywhere support revolutionary movement against the existing social and political order of things."*

Again, *"The Communists...openly declare that their ends can be attained only by the forcible overthrow of all existing social conditions. Let the ruling classes tremble at a Communist revolution."* Still again, *"the theory of the Communist may be summed up in the simple sentence: abolition of private property."* And finally, *"Communism abolishes eternal truths, it abolishes all religion and all morality, instead of constituting them on a new basis; it therefore acts in contradiction to all historical experience."*

The Communists believe that men are the victims of their material environment only, which may be manipulated by changing that environment. In order to do this, there must be a dictatorship of the proletariat, to command, and achieve the ultimate perfect state. The dictatorship established in the Soviet Union is not the dictatorship demanded by Marx, and planned by Lenin—a dictatorship of the working people. It is a dictatorship exercised by the few men who control the Communist Party. Joseph Stalin made this shift. The fate of 200 million people was to be ruled by only 3% or 4% of their number who had been accepted into the Communist Party. It has taken a large portion of the world many years, and untold misery to realize that Communism is an evil empire. But long ago the Bible called it foolish, for we read, *"The fool has said that there is no God."*

- **Humanism.** Humanism is the study of man. This is not wrong, per se, except that Humanism as a philosophy believes that all there is to man is what scientific behavior, and social analysis can reveal. Because humanism does not recognize any Divine commentary, people are left with whatever prepositional thinking other humans can be persuaded to embrace. One of the basic beliefs of Humanism is that man is basically good but that he is ruined by society.

Man in his pristine state is in harmony with nature. When this worldly wisdom was first being developed in Europe in the 18th century, the American Indian was considered a prime example of the Noble Savage. Indian cultures could be savage, and they could also be noble as well, just like any European society. In other words, the Indians of America, and the individuals in Europe, were no different by nature.

- **Self-Deification.** Another example of worldly wisdom is the New Age Movement, which goes beyond saying that man is good, to declaring that man is God. Just how man became *God* differs according to cultural interpretation. In the Western world, which emphasizes individuality, man becomes his own god. In the Eastern part of the world, which emphasizes the collective society, man becomes absorbed in the stream of life, for all is *God*, and *God* is all.

It is foolish for man to believe that he is a god, but that mindset does not stop the articulation of the wisdom of this world. For man to believe himself to be god is just as irrational for a sophisticated computer to suddenly print out a message saying, *"I am man!"* These illustrations help us to realize that there is so much foolishness in the world, despite the academic, intellectual, philosophical, thought-provoking packaging it all comes in. Ultimately, all that the foolish thinking does is to change people in such a way that their behavior reflects their beliefs.

Here is a spiritual principle. Behavior is the product of belief. Does the Communist believe that private property is bad? Then extraordinary means must be used to make the world better just as no one would hesitate to kill a mad dog whose bite would destroy the family. Does humanism believe that man is the captain of his soul and the master of his fate? Then right and wrong are only what man says they are on any given day. Truth is relative. There does seem to be a common element to all the worldly wisdom of man and that is an assault upon God.

Communism says there is no God. Humanism teaches that man cannot know God. The New Age Movement says that man is *God*. Paganism causes the glory of God to appear in the form of a creature. This ungodly effort to transform God into something less than He is comes because people do not like to feel inferior. We see this tendency in human relationships by the need at times to find fault with someone who appears to be more successful.

We do not mind finding something wrong with the person. So it is that man wants to have something against God. Fallen man wants Him to be *corruptible,* but the Bible says He is *incorruptible* or *undecaying.* God has never decayed or changed in His essence or continuance. His creation is constantly changing as it goes from order to disorder; but God is the same yesterday, today, and forever. In His holiness, God is still righteous. In His presence, God is still everywhere. In His wisdom, God is still without equal. In His power, God is still sovereign.

In His grace, God is still matchless. In His love, God is still constant. When men insist upon changing the glory of God, God may react by giving individuals over to *akatharsia* or *impunity.* The means God uses is the intense desires of the heart. Jesus has told us what the heart of man is like by nature and what will come out of the heart. No one has to look around to discern what uncleanness is like. Any person can simply look inward and be honest about what is seen. Generally speaking, men will dishonor their bodies (Romans 1:24), and they will change the truth of God into a lie.

They will worship and serve the creature more than the Creator. Paul believed this to be true for he says, *"Amen. I believe that man's nature is depraved and I believe that God is blessed [eulogestos; well spoken of] forever."* The glory of God remains intact.

Doctrine of Glory

1. One of the most common Hebrew words for glory is *kabowd,* which refers to something that has weight. In a figurative sense it means *"splendor"* or *"honor."*

2. Jacob was accused, by the sons of Laban, of stealing all the family's possessions in order to have glory, or weight, in the eyes of men (Genesis 31:1).

3. After Joseph revealed himself to his brothers, he wanted them to go back to Israel and tell Jacob of all his glory as a ruler of Egypt (Genesis 45:13).

4. The children of Israel were allowed to see the glory of the Lord, revealed in a cloud of Divine provision (Exodus 24:16; Leviticus 9:6; 9:23).

5. The glory of the Lord rested upon Mount Sinai (Exodus 24:1617; Deuteronomy 5:24).

6. The garments that the high priest wore were designed for glory and for beauty, to reflect God (Exodus 28:2; 28:40).

7. The glory of God sanctifies or sets apart a place (Exodus 29:43).

8. Moses pleaded with God to show him His glory (Exodus 33:18).

9. The glory of the Lord filled the Tabernacle in the wilderness (Exodus 40:34; Numbers 14:10).

10. A Divine promise has been made, that the Earth, shall one day, be filled with the glory of the Lord (Numbers 14:21).

11. Hearts and lives will not be changed because men see the glory of the Lord (Numbers 14:22; 16:19; 16:42).

12. There is a transient glory associated with men (Deuteronomy 33:17).

13. Part of confessing sin is to give glory to God by acknowledging His holiness (Joshua 7:19).

14. God will allow glory to come to men (1 Samuel 2:8).

15. Sometimes the glory of the Lord will depart from a place (1 Samuel 4:21, 22).

16. Those who worship idols are commanded to repent, and give glory to God (1 Samuel 6:5).

17. Sometimes the glory of God's presence is so overwhelming, that men cannot stand before it, and live (1 Kings 8:11; 2 Chronicles 5:14; 7:2).

18. Christians are not to glory in the flesh, but in the Lord (1 Chronicles 16:10).

19. The glory of God is to be proclaimed among all nations (1 Chronicles 16:24; 16:28-29; Psalms 96:3).

20. Where God is, there is His glory (1 Chronicles 16:27).

21. Divine deliverance is to be prayed for, so that the saints can glory in praise of God (1 Chronicles 16:35).

22. A prayer of praise was offered by David at the end of his life (1 Chronicles 29:11).

23. At the dedication of Solomon's Temple, fire fell from heaven consuming the offering, and manifesting God's glory (2 Chronicles 7:1).

24. A glimpse of God's glory will elicit worship (2 Chronicles 7:3; Psalms 97:6).

25. Sometimes God will test men, by removing from them their reflective glory (Job 29:20; Job 19:9).

26. Compared to God, man has only faded glories (Job 40:10).

27. The glory of God is a source of spiritual protection for believers (Psalms 3:3; 84:11).

28. It is within the nature of sinful man to try to turn the glory of God into shame (Psalms 4:2).

29. The glory of God is set above the heavens (Psalms 8:1; 113:4).

30. At his original creation, man was given inherent glory so that he is more than an animal (Psalms 8:5).

31. The heavens declare the glory, or majesty, of God (Psalms 19:1).

32. The glory of God is great in salvation (Psalms 21:5).

33. If the Church will wait and watch, the King of Glory will come (Psalms 24:79).

34. Thinking men, will speak in awe, of the glory of God (Psalms 29:9).

35. One reason why God gives healing is to turn man's glory into praise (Psalms 30:11ff).

36. Human glory is transitory (Psalms 49:16-17).

37. The heart of the saint is jealous of God's glory (Psalms 57:5, 11; 57:78; 72:19).

38. The Christian has no glory, apart from God (Psalms 62:7; 63:11).

39. Christians long to see God's glory (Psalms 63:12; 90:16; 106:5; 108:5; 115:1).

40. Holiness in the heart brings glory to the righteous (Psalms 64:10).

41. Heaven is a place of glory (Psalms 73:24).

42. When God's people sin, He will allow His glory to be dishonored, as a form of Divine discipline (Psalms 78:61).

43. The glory of God is a basis of prayer for spiritual help (Psalms 79:9).

44. When people fear God, His glory will dwell in the land (Psalms 85:9).

45. God is the ultimate glory of the spiritual strength of the saints (Psalms 89:17).

46. The glory of the ungodly will fall before the greatness of God (Psalms 89:44).

47. One day, all the kings of the Earth shall fear the name, and the glory of God (Psalms 102:15-16; 145:11; 148:13).

48. The glory of the Lord [alone] shall endure forever (Psalms 104:31).

49. Sinful men constantly seek to diminish the glory of God (Psalms 106:20).

50. The glory of God is the basis of true security (Psalms 138:5; 149:5).

51. The wise shall inherit glory (Proverbs 3:35).

52. Old age, and glory, are associated together (Proverbs 16:31).

53. The glory of children is their fathers (Proverbs 17:6).

54. The glory of young men is their strength (Proverbs 20:29).

55. One reason many of our transgressions are not revealed is that the goodness and kindness of God can be manifested, and in this, He is glorified (Proverbs 25:2).

56. There is glory in the majesty of God (Isaiah 2:10, 19, 21).

57. Nature is a reflection of the glory of God (Isaiah 6:3).
58. When God reigns in righteousness, there is glory (Isaiah 28:5).

59. Even those who live in desert places can know of the glory of the Lord (Isaiah 35:2; 40:5).

60. When the Church lives close to the Lord, and receives from Him divine strength, they then want to glory in His greatness (Isaiah 41:16).

61. God will never share His essential glory with anyone (Isaiah 42:8; 48:11). This truth disallows idolatry, and the concept of men, or angels, ever becoming God.

62. Those who are chosen by God for salvation were selected to manifest His glory (Isaiah 43:7; 45:25; 60:1, 2; Romans 9:23; Ephesians 1:12).

63. The earth is to be filled with the glory of the Lord (Isaiah 59:19; 66:18).

63. Men are not to glory in their wisdom, riches or strength, but in the Lord (Jeremiah 9:23, 24; 1 Corinthians 1:31; 2 Corinthians 10:17).

64. The glory of the Lord came to the Second Temple (Hag. 2:9).

65. The Son, Jesus Christ, shares the glory of His Father (John 17:5; 17:22; 1 Peter 5:10) and we as Christian will share the Son's glory.

66. At the Second Coming much glory will be revealed (Matthew 16:27; 19:28; 24:30; 25:31).

67. Sinful men try to bring dishonor to the glory of God (Romans 1:23).

68. All men have come short of the glory of God (Romans 3:23).

69. There is glory in being saved from the power, pollution, and presence of sin (Romans 2:10; 8:18; 9:4).

70. There is a crown of glory that *fadeth not away* (1 Peter 5:4), which is the soul winner's crown.

71. Men are to fear God and to give Him the glory (Revelation 14:7).

The Depths of Human Depravity: Romans 1:26-32

The path of human degradation descends by an easy slope at first. Then the descent toward self-destruction and eternal damnation accelerates. The soul that finds itself in the strong grip of sin may or may not want to continue the journey, but sin has its own strength that no mortal can control. Like a child on board a runaway locomotive on a steep hill, no human power to reverse, slow down, or stop the process.

The only hope is for a sovereign work of Divine grace to do something. If God does not show grace, He will manifest His justice by giving individuals to the natural process of perverted passions. God will give people up into their own burning desires. Women will exchange the natural use of the bodies into that which is against nature (Romans 1:26), and men will leave women in a fatal attraction for another man (Romans 1:27). Why does this perversion happen? Because men do not like to retain God in their knowledge, so they challenge God in attitudes and actions just like Cain of old. Jude 1:11 speaks of *"the Way of Cain,"* which is the way of self-will and superficial substitution of spiritual sacrifices. God had appointed a place of worship. God had appointed a plan of worship.

Cain went to the place where God was to be met with his own plan. Instead of bringing the required blood offering, Cain brought a sacrifice of his own hand, only to be rejected. But instead of repenting, and returning with an appropriate sacrifice, Cain went from the presence of God to kill his brother, Abel. If he could not come to God, and be accepted on his own terms, he would make sure Abel did not come either. So Cain killed Abel, and thus established the true pattern of brotherhood. It is one of jealousy and violence. Cain and Abel could have worked together before God, but Cain's spirit of jealousy gripped his heart, and led him to murder.

The Way of Cain is the way of men and women today; and when it is followed, God may allow people to pursue it with a vengeance. God will more often than not, give people over to this worthless, reprobate mindset of Cain, to do those things that are not convenient or fitting. This truth is important to understand, because it is contrary to one popular concept of the Lord; that is, that He sits in heaven, and stops people from sinning. The idea is that man wants to have a little fun; he wants to have his own way, but God will not let him.

But the truth of the matter is that God will let man have his own way. God will withdraw the Holy Spirit. God will take away His Word. God will send away gospel ministers. God will allow people to do those things that are not proper. When certain people of Israel rejected the ministry of the Lord Jesus Christ because of unbelief, the Bible says that He went away without doing any mighty works (Matthew 13:58). The Light of the world left men in darkness. Love turned back without helping. The springs of Living Water dried up, and souls remained thirsty.

Grace and mercy moved on, and men were given over to do those things that are not right. God does allow men to commit evil. God does not always stop, control, or contain the filth of the flesh. Rather, He opens the floodgates of moral depravity so that raw sewage can stream forth, over self and society. The Apostle Paul identifies this abomination of the flesh that fills to overflowing individual lives. Twenty-one sins are spoken of; Dr. Donald Grey Barnhouse guides us in the understanding of them (*Romans*).

- **Unrighteousness** (*adikia*). This is a term that is used in the Scriptures for injustice in a judge, for unrighteousness of heart and life, unrighteousness by which others are deceived. It is the word used by our Lord in speaking of deceitful riches, and the word used for the reward of iniquity—the thirty pieces of silver that Judas received, for betraying our Savior.

  Lord Palmerston, in a letter to Lord Clarendon, wrote, *"There is a passion in the human heart stronger than the desire to be free from justice and wrong, and that is the desire to inflict injustice and wrong upon others, and men resent more keenly an attempt to prevent them from oppressing other people than they do the oppression from which they themselves suffer."*

- **Fornication.** This word in the Authorized Version is not found in the original manuscripts.

- **Wickedness** (*poneria; sexual impropriety*). The word is used for *depravity, iniquity, evil purposes* and *desires, wicked ways*. It is the word used in Ephesians 6:12 for the followers of Satan in the spiritual realm, the *hosts of wickedness,* and a kindred word is used for the Devil whenever he is called *the wicked one.* When David had the opportunity of killing King Saul in the cave, he refused to do it; and, in crying out to Saul afterwards, he reminded him that there was a proverb of the ancients, *"Wickedness proceedeth from the wicked"* (1 Samuel 24:13). Once more, it is the human heart that is seen to be the fountain of evil waters.

- **Covetousness** (*pleonexia; avarice,* i.e., by implication, *fraudulence, extortion*). This word is used for people who are grasping, who are itching for more, and who are extortioners, wishing to make gain from the losses of others. This is the characteristic described in this word. It is much more prevalent than thought. Liddell and Scott include in its definition, *"To take advantage of another's simpleness, to overreach, defraud."* The Holy Spirit defines covetousness as idolatry (Colossians 3:5), and idolatry, of course, is the worship of another object rather than God.

- **Maliciousness** (*kakia; badness,* i.e., [subjectively] *depravity,* or [actively] *malignity,* or [passively] *trouble*). The word denotes *ill will, malice, malignity,* and *a desire to inju*re. It is wickedness that is not ashamed to break the Laws. It is a word that means *a vicious disposition.* Thomas Jefferson wrote to Madison, *"Malice will always find bad motives for good actions."*

- **Full of envy** (*phthonos; ill will* [as detraction] i.e., *jealousy or spite*). The Oxford English Dictionary defines the word, *"To feel displeasure and ill will at the superiority of another in happiness, success, reputation, or the possession of anything desirable; to regard with discontent another's possession of some superior advantage which one would like to have for oneself."* We remember that Scripture tells us, in connection with the crucifixion of our Lord, that, *"Pilate knew that for envy they had delivered him"* (Matthew 27:18). It was when the Lord healed the man on the Sabbath day that the leaders of the Pharisees held a council against Him, how they might destroy Him (Matthew 12:14). They should have been more holy and were not. They knew that He was holy and powerful, and they envied Him, and therefore hated Him.

- **Murder** (*honos*; *to slay, to murder*). is the taking of another's life because he has something that one wants, or because he has offended the ego of the murderer, who arrogates to himself the place of God to take the life of his enemy. Murder follows envy not only in our list but also in life.

- **Debate** (*eris*; *a quarrel*, i.e., [by implication] *wrangling*). The concept here is that of strife, contention and wrangling.

- **Deceit** (*dolos*; a trick [bait], i.e., [figuratively] wile). This word in the Greek means *fish bait*, and by extension came to mean to lure, to ensnare, to beguile, and to deceive. The prophet Habakkuk describes men as fishing for other men, and snaring them in their nets. They succeed so well that *"they sacrifice unto their net, and burn incense unto their drag; because by them their portion is fat, and their meat plenteous"* (Habakkuk 1:16).

- **Malignity** (*kakoetheia*; bad character, i.e., [specially] mischievousness). The word refers to bad character, depravity of heart and life, malignant subtlety, malicious craftiness, and taking all things in the evil part (Aristotle, Rhetoric).

- **Whispers** (*psithuristes*; *a secret calumniator*). The word means *"secret slander"* or *"to speak in one's ear."* In Ecclesiastes, Solomon says, *"The serpent will bite without enchantment; and a babbler is no better* (10:11)." God Almighty has stamped gossip with the nature of a snakebite. Chrysostom said, *"slander is worse than cannibalism."* Jeremy Taylor, in one of his sermons said, *"Slander rends in pieces the very heart and vital parts of charity: it makes an evil man part and witness, and judge, and executioner of the innocent."*

- **Backbiters** (*katalalos*; *talkative against*, i.e., *a slanderer*). This refers to open slander. There are some who are not content to whisper into the ear of the listener, but who will publicly flaunt false charges against their fellow man. But whether it is the secret gossip, or the public slanderer, we may be sure that all forms of the vice of false witness are rooted in the heart of man.

- **Haters of God** (*theostuges; hateful to God,* i.e., *impious*). The word here means hateful to God. There are some men who are so odious, so detestable, that God must hate them.

- **Despiteful** (*hubristes; an insulter,* i.e., *maltreater*). Insolent people are so uplifted with pride, that they either heap insulting language upon others, or do them some shameful act of wrong.

- **Proud** (*huperephanos; appearing above others (conspicuous),* i.e., [figuratively] *haughty*). The word means to be haughty. It is that arrogant showing of oneself above others, with an overwhelming sense of one's means of merits; despising others, or treating them with contempt.

- **Boaster** (*alazon; braggart*). The empty pretender who prates of that which he does not possess. It is the empty wagon that rattles.

- **Inventors of evil things** (*epheuretes a discoverer,* i.e., *contriver*). In the Psalms, we read that men provoked God to anger with their inventions (Psalms 106:29), and *"that they went a whoring with their own inventions"* (Psalms 106:39). Man turns to evil, even with the inventions that are full of potential good.

- **Disobedient to parents** (*apeithes; unpersuadable,* i.e., and *contumacy*). Children will not be compliant to the wishes of parents.

- **Without understanding** (*asunetos; unintelligent;* [by implication] *wicked*). The human race is by nature without spiritual or moral understanding. *"The natural man receiveth not the things of the Spirit"* (1 Corinthians 2:14). A wicked man has no mind for the things that make for salvation. Even the greatest minds of earth, are born into this world as spiritual morons.

- **Covenant breakers** (*asunthetos*; *i.e., treacherous to compacts*). Literally, *without good faith*. A German emperor precipitated World War I when he called a solemn treaty *a scrap of paper*. Individuals break confidences without consideration of the horror of their sin.

- **Without natural affection** (*astorgos*; *hardhearted towards kindred*). It is possible for a society to become so sinful that men and women put off a husband or a wife as easily as they put off a coat. It is possible for a nation to allow its children to be murdered legally. It is possible for a people to kill the sick and elderly at will.

- **Implacable** (*aspondos*; [literally] *without libation* [which usually accompanied a treaty], i.e., [by implication] *truceless*).

- **Unmerciful** (*aneleemon*; *merciless*). Positive cruelty has been the mark of sinful men. The Tartars and the Huns and the Vandals and the Nazis have left their names behind them for their deeds. One philosophical writer named Schopenhauer has written, *"Man is little inferior to the tiger and hyena in cruelty and savagery."*

It is bad enough that men commit such sins, but the depravity of the human heart goes deeper still, for in Romans 1:32 we read that those who commit evil deeds have pleasure in others that do them as well. Eve was glad when Adam took of the forbidden fruit. Herodias was delighted when Herod agreed to marry her even though it meant leaving his brother Philip as wife (Matthew 14:13). And she was furious at John for protesting what heaven condemned. The men of Sodom and Gomorrah did not care that Lot was disturbed with their homosexuality. They were just glad that he did not condemn them. Absalom was delighted that he could steal the hearts of his countrymen away from his father to the point that they would join him in his unholy rebellion. All of this perverse delight in sin comes because the conscience can be defiled.

The Bible warns of evil. Nevertheless, when the warnings are not heeded and when the conscience is confirmed in evil, man is still blameworthy (Romans 1:32) because he knows that God is just to judge him. That point is important to understand. Man knows the judgment of God. Even when men teach their lies about universal salvation, soul sleeping, annihilation, conditional immortality, the final restoration of all beings, God being some All in all, and hell's not being eternal, he knows the truth. Man knows the judgment of God. He knows that the wrath of God is just and that all men deserve death at the hands of the Creator whom they have outraged by their continual rebellion and rewriting of the truth. But what is one more sin, that of telling lies like Satan, the Father of Lies, when the conscience is hardened and the soul is saturated in self? Such is the heart given up by God and given over to a reprobate mind.

Is there no hope when the heart is hardened, when the conscience is seared? Is there no hope if the heart realizes that its pleasure in sin is itself a perversion and a sign of divine wrath? The answer is, *Yes!* There is hope for where sin abounds, grace does much more abound. There is a Savior and His name is Jesus. And He invites all to look to Him for deliverance from the power and pollution of sin.

But be careful. Before that can happen, the honest heart must get a clearer sight of self, and confess all known sin. Only then will the blood of Jesus Christ, God's Son, cleanse from sin. When sin is washed away, God will give a new mind, a new heart, and a new will to serve Him with. It is for such a mind and for such a heart, that we must now plead.

Doctrine of the Conscience

1. The word for conscience is *suneidesis, which* literally means *a knowing with (sun, with, oida, to know). Suneidesis* is *knowledge with oneself.*

2. With the conscience we come to know what is right and what is wrong based upon a sense of innate justice.

3. Every person has a conscience that is developed according to personality, society, and religious instruction.

4. When the Law of God, summarized in the Ten Commandments, is violated, there is a sense of guiltiness before God (Hebrews

10:2). The guilt is healthy because individuals are kept sensitive to sin. Confession of guilt is elicited, and righteousness is sought.

5. The Law of God can be violated apart from any personal knowledge of Holy Scripture, as per Romans 2:15, as the conscience distinguishes between what is morally good and bad. While societies differ according to custom and Law, certain acts are universally recognized as wrong such as murder, stealing, lying, and adultery.

6. In the conscience the peace of God can be discerned and find confirmation with the Holy Spirit (Romans 9:1).

7. When a Christian lives with integrity, there is an awareness of that fact in the conscience (2 Corinthians 1:12).

8. The way to live with integrity is to do what is right because conscience requires it (Romans 13:5).

9. Christians are not to question or violate the integrity of the conscience of others in doubtful matters (1 Corinthians 10:28, 29).

10. The Christian is to live so as to commend himself to every man's conscience (2 Corinthians 4:2; 5:11).

11. It is possible to have a conscience that is not strong enough to discern between what is lawful and what is unlawful (1 Corinthians 8:7, 10, 12).

12. The presence of God prevails the life of the believer through the conscience. (1 Peter 2:19)

13. The sacrifices of old could never cleanse or perfect the conscience (Hebrews 9:9).

14. The conscience is described in different ways.

    - A good conscience   Acts 23:1; 1 Timothy 1:5,19;

	Hebrews 13:18; 1 Peter 3:16, 21
• A clear conscience	Acts 24:16
• A weak conscience	1 Corinthians 8:8; Titus 1:15
• A pure conscience	1 Timothy 3:9; 2 Timothy 1:3
• A seared conscience	1 Timothy 4:2
• A purged conscience	Hebrews 9:14
• A guilty conscience	Hebrews 10:22

2

Romans 2

Without Excuse: Romans 2:1

The word *"therefore"* in verse 1, serves as a transitional link between the contents of chapter one and the contents of chapter two. Some one has well said that when you see the word *"therefore"* in the Bible, you should pause and ask, *"What is it there for?"* The word *"therefore"* is written to remind the reader that the fact of the tremendous wickedness of the Gentiles has been established, and recognized by heaven and earth. The age in which Paul lived and worked, was an age of shame. Many customs were out of control. Virgil wrote: *"Right and wrong were confounded; so many wars the world over, so many forms of wrong; no worthy honor is left to the plough; the husbandmen are marched away and the fields grow dirty; the hook has its curve straightened into the sword blade."*

It was a world of violence. When Tacitus wrote of this period he said, *"I am entering upon the history of a period, rich in disasters, gloomy with wars, rent with seditions, savage in its very hours of peace...All was one delirium of hate and terror; slaves were bribed to betray their masters, freedmen their patrons. He who had no foe was destroyed by his friend."* Suetonius, writing of the reign of Tiberius, said: *"No day passed but someone was executed."* Despite the terror, it was an age of luxury. In the public baths of Rome the hot and cold water ran from silver taps. Caligula sprinkled the floor of the arena of the forum with gold dust instead of sawdust. Juvenal said, *"A luxury more ruthless than war broods over Rome...No guilt or deed of lust is wanting since Roman poverty disappeared."* Seneca spoke of money as *"the ruin of the true honor of things."*

The extravagance of the Roman Empire allowed open immorality. Not a single case of divorce was recorded in the first 520 years of the history of the Roman Empire. But during the days of Paul, *"women were married to be divorced and divorced to be married"* according to Seneca. Juvenal even sites the shameful case of Agrippina, the empress herself, the wife of Claudius, who at night used to leave the royal palace to go down to serve in a brothel for the sheer joy of sensuality. From the highest strata to the lowest, society was saturated with sin. Fourteen of the first fifteen Roman Emperors were homosexuals.

No wonder we read in Romans 1 that God abandoned men and women to their own selves as His wrath was poured out upon them. Yet, Paul was still eager to come to Rome to preach the gospel of Jesus Christ. He knew that it was the power of God unto salvation to all that believed (2 Corinthians 10:45). Paul wanted the Gentiles to believe, and he wanted other Jews to believe as well. But there was a problem. The Jews thought that they were morally superior to the Gentiles. While the Gentiles might need a message of redeeming grace, many Jews felt no need. They believed themselves to be morally superior with a right to sit in judgment upon those who had not the Law of God.

When the Jews considered the situation of the Gentiles as presented in Romans 1, they immediately agreed with the apostolic assessment. There was shame in society. Society abounded in excessive violence and open immorality. The Jews looked at the Gentiles and expressed disgust. Now Paul must show the Jews their own guilt.

Paul must teach the Jews that in judging the Gentiles the Jews have begun the process of condemning themselves, for they too, are guilty of great sin in the sight of God. It is this point which the apostle will press home in chapter two as he teaches that whenever a person stands in judgment upon another, he stands in judgment upon himself. The person who has accused another person about lying has not been guiltless of shading the truth. When David became angry upon hearing about a wealthy man who took the one little lamb of another, he was condemning himself, as the prophet Nathan soon reminded him. David had taken the wife of one of his subjects, Uriah the Hittite.

When Peter declared that the people before him in the temple area in Jerusalem, on the Day of Pentecost, had taken the Lord of Glory and denied Him, Peter was also condemning himself. He too had denied the Lord Jesus Christ. Every parent who tells a child not to whine, not to talk back, not to show disrespect, not to waste money, or to be hateful, has been guilty of those very things and more.

In light of this truth, the point becomes clear: When judgment is passed upon another, self is usually condemned because the same acts have been done. Does this practice make everyone hypocritical? Should individuals never judge someone else? Is that what Paul is saying? The immediate answer is, *No!* People are not hypocritical because they offer criticism of another, nor should moral evaluations in life stop. People are critical of each other, in part, because every person has a God given conscience. Man is made in His image, and it is the nature of God to evaluate and judge what is right, and what is wrong. Therefore, it is part of man's nature as well.

Of course, the world, the flesh, and the devil would like mankind to stop being critical. The popular wisdom of society is that no one should be judgmental of others. The argument is set forth that there should be no moral condemnation rendered by anyone on anyone else including those who engage in sodomy, lesbianism, adultery, pimping, prostitution, stealing, lying, robbing, murdering, or extortion. None of this is logical. If the philosophy of being nonjudgmental were truly and universally implemented, then there would be no need for judges on the bench or lawyers in the courtroom.

There would be no rationale for policemen, security systems, or locks on doors, for no one would ever say or do anything that is evil. But here is the reality: right or wrong exist. Nature declares it as well as one's own conscience. The imperfections of others are seen and criticism is offered because there is recognition of a proper code of conduct. In Romans 2, Paul reminds his audience that any judgments rendered are uttered by those who themselves are guilty of the same acts to one degree or another. By realizing this, the heart of the Christian at least might want to sing the old Negro spiritual which reminds us that it's *"Not my brother, nor my sister, but it's me, O Lord, standin' in the need of prayer."* By singing such songs, believers can take their place in the seat of the accused and the condemned. Because Christians are in need of prayer and God's grace, they will want to be careful in their judgment of others in specific areas.

Doctrine of Wrath

1. There are two basic words translated *"wrath"* in the Authorized Version. One word is *"orge."* Another word-translated *"wrath"* is *"thumos"* which refers to, *"hot anger, passion." "Thumos"* is translated *wrath* in Luke 4:28; Acts 19:28; Romans 2:8; *"wraths"* in 2 Corinthians 12:20; and *"fierceness"* in Revelation 16:19; 19:15.

2. Many passages speak of wrath.

   - Matthew 3:7, *"But when he saw many of the Pharisees and Sadducees come to his baptism, he said unto them, O generation of vipers, who hath warned you to flee from the wrath to come?"*

   - Luke 3:7, *"Then said he to the multitude that came forth to be baptized of him, O generation of vipers, who hath warned you to flee from the wrath to come?"*

   - Luke 4:28, *"And all they in the synagogue, when they heard these things, were filled with wrath (thumos)."*

   - Luke 21:23, *"But woe unto them that are with child, and to them that give suck, in those days! For there shall be great distress in the land, and wrath upon this people."*

   - John 3:36, *"He that believeth on the Son hath everlasting life: and he that believeth not the Son shall not see life; but the wrath of God abideth on him."*

   - Acts 19:28, *"And when they heard these sayings, they were full of wrath, and cried out, saying, Great is Diana of the Ephesians."*

- Romans 1:18, *"For the wrath of God is revealed from heaven against all ungodliness and unrighteousness of men, who hold the truth in unrighteousness."*

- Romans 2:5, *"But after thy hardness and impenitent heart treasurest up unto thyself wrath against the day of wrath and revelation of the righteous judgment of God."*

- Romans 2:8, *"But unto them that are contentious, and do not obey the truth, but obey unrighteousness, indignation and wrath."*

- Romans 4:15, *"Because the Law worketh wrath: for where no Law is, there is no transgression."*

- Romans 5:9, *"Much more then, being now justified by his blood, we shall be saved from wrath through him."*

- Romans 9:22, *"What if God, willing to shew his wrath, and to make his power known, endured with much long-suffering the vessels of wrath fitted to destruction."*

- Romans 12:19, *"Dearly beloved, avenge not yourselves, but rather give place unto wrath: for it is written, Vengeance is mine; I will repay, saith the Lord."*

- Romans 13:4, *"For he is the minister of God to thee for good. But if thou do that which is evil, be afraid; for he beareth not the sword in vain: for he is the minister of God, a revenger to execute wrath upon him that doeth evil."*

- Romans 13:5, *"Wherefore ye must needs be subject, not only for wrath, but also for conscience' sake."*

- Galatians 5:20, *"Idolatry, witchcraft, hatred, variance, emulation, wrath, strife, seditions, heresies."*

- Ephesians 2:3, *"Among whom also we all had our conversation in times past in the lusts of our flesh, fulfilling the desires of the flesh and of the mind; and were by nature the children of wrath, even as others."*

- Ephesians 4:26, *"Be ye angry, and sin not: let not the sun go down upon your wrath."*

- Ephesians 4:31, *"Let all bitterness, and wrath, and anger, and clamor, and evil speaking, be put away from you, with all malice."*

- Ephesians 5:6, *"Let no man deceive you with vain words: for because of these things cometh the wrath of God upon the children of disobedience."*

- Ephesians 6:4, *"And, ye fathers, provoke not your children to wrath: but bring them up in the nurture and admonition of the Lord."*

- Colossians 3:6, *"For which things' sake the wrath of God cometh on the children of disobedience."*

- Colossians 3:8, *"But now ye also put off all these; anger, wrath, malice, blasphemy, filthy communication out of your mouth."*

- 1 Thessalonians 1:10, *"And to wait for his Son from heaven, whom he raised from the dead, even Jesus, which delivered us from the wrath to come."*

- 1 Thessalonians 2:16, *"Forbidding us to speak to the Gentiles that they might be saved, to fill up their sins alway: for the wrath is come upon them to the uttermost."*

- 1 Thessalonians 5:9, *"For God hath not appointed us to wrath, but to obtain salvation by our Lord Jesus Christ"* (Study 1 Timothy 2:8; Hebrews 3:11; Hebrews 4:3; Hebrews 11:27; James 1:19; James 1:20; Revelation 6:16, 17; 11:18; 12:12; 14:8; 14:10; 14:19; 15:1; 15:7; 16:1; 16:19; 18:3; 19:15).

3. Paul speaks of the wrath of God three times: Romans 1:18. Ephesians 5:6, and Colossians 3:6.

4. In Romans 5:9 Paul speaks about being saved from the wrath.

5. In Romans 12:19 he advises men not to take vengeance, but to leave evildoers to the wrath.

6. In Romans 13:5 he speaks about the wrath as being a powerful motive to keep men obedient.

7. In Romans 4:15 he says that the Law produces wrath.

8. And in 1 Thessalonians 1:10 he says that Jesus delivered us from The Wrath to come.

9. Paul speaks about the wrath, and yet from that very wrath Jesus saves men. What is meant?

10. To understand the wrath of God is to return to the Hebrew prophets. Their message was simple: *"If you do not obey God, the wrath of God will involve you in ruin and disaster."* Ezekiel stated it plainly when he said, *"The soul that sins shall die"* (Ezekiel 18:4).

11. The universe consists of a moral order, and the person who transgresses it shall suffer. J. A. Froude, the great historian, said *"One lesson, and one lesson only, history may be said to repeat without distinctness, that the world is built somehow on moral foundations, that, in the long run, it is well with the good, and, in the long run, it will be ill with the wicked."*

12. The conclusion is clear: The moral order is the wrath of God at work. God made this world in such a way that if we break His Laws, it is to our ruin.

13. Those who break God's Laws consistently shall risk being abandoned by God (Romans 1:24).

The Goodness of God: Romans 2:2-5

In Romans 1 the Apostle Paul has set forth the sad state of the Gentiles. He has argued that they were without God, for sin had captured their imaginations, their passions, and their reasoning, so that all of their activities were only evil continually. What Paul said was true. The depravity of the Gentiles was openly displayed, so that in a spirit of self-righteousness the Jews looked at the Gentiles, and held them in contempt. This moral arrogance made it necessary for the Apostle to confront his kinsmen with being censorious of others, and conceited, even though they themselves were not without fault (Romans 2:1). In strong language Paul says, *"Thou art inexcusable, O man, whosoever thou art that judgest.* He goes on to ask, *Thou who teachest another teachest thou not thyself?"*

While the Jews loved to teach the Law of the Lord to others, they did not like to make personal application of the rules they taught. So the Jews looked with disgust and disdain upon the Gentiles, while excusing themselves from similar forms of bad behavior. Because the Jews were guilty of breaking the Law of God Paul is able to establish the fact that they had made themselves worthy of Divine condemnation.

The argument is further made by the apostle that the Jews are guiltier than the Gentiles, for whereas they have the Light of the Law, the Gentiles only had the light of nature. To press his point, and to elicit a strong sense of conviction of guilt, the apostle sets forth the righteousness and justice of God, which Paul declares, is *"according to truth."* By this declaration, Paul means that eternal rules of justice and equity exist based upon an objective truth. Sometimes we listen to a person to find the truth about a certain situation, but we do not know whether we are hearing it. Truth can be very elusive.

Though men have trouble discerning what is true and what is false, God does not, for He looks at the heart (1 Samuel 16:7). When God looks at the human heart, He looks as One who is no respecter of persons. He does not play favorites. God does not excuse one person while condemning another. The Lord does not justify the Jews while condemning the Gentiles though the Jews would have very much liked to think that God favored them. No, God sees the truth in all and about all.

Man listens for it, but God sees it, which, in reality, is one reason why the Lord is never impressed with those who merely speak out against sin. God knows how easy it is to be verbally indignant about something, only to go and plunge headfirst into the same cesspool of sin. Matthew Henry reminds us all that denouncing transgressions harshly will never atone for the guilt of practicing them. The Jews were guilty of practicing what they denounced and Paul wanted them to understand that God would not tolerate that. On this point, the Jews are invited to consider the situation, as Paul writes, *"Thinkest thou this, O man?"*

For Paul, the case is so plain, that anyone can comprehend the principle of Divine justice involved. *"Does any person really think that they can escape the judgment of God when they commit what they condemn?"* Logic forbids such a conclusion. One reason that the Jews may have thought that they could get away with doing wrong, was the passage of time. When Israel sinned as a nation, she was not always immediately disciplined. There is something about not being instantly caught in sin that leads to a feeling of false security. We need to be reminded that *"The most plausible politic [astute of] sinners, who acquit themselves before men with the greatest confidence, cannot escape the judgment of God; [they] cannot avoid being judged and condemned"* (Matthew Henry).

People never stop trying to get away with doing wrong, for *"the heart is deceitful above all things and desperately wicked."* Consider the case of the covetous man. Some people give every fiber of their soul, every beat of their heart and every waking moment of their life to making money by fair means or foul. What will God do with such a covetous soul? What will God do with the passionate heart, which will have its way through the force of temper tantrums? What will God do to the person with the tongue of a serpent that causes discord needlessly? What will God do with the careless who confess love for His Church and for the Bible all the while neglecting both? Do such people really think that they can escape the judgment of God? They cannot! God will judge all men, and He will do so according to truth. And the truth will reveal that those who practice and those who speak out against sin while practicing the same are guilty of two things. They are guilty of slighting the goodness of God (Romans 2:4), and they are guilty of provoking His wrath (Romans 2:5).

First, there are those who are guilty of slighting the goodness of God, which means that they trade on His mercy. They take advantage of His kindness. The Jews of the first century were certainly slighting God's mercy. They had received so many expressions of Divine favor over the years a belief was embraced that they were a privileged nation above all others. They had as their fathers Abraham, Isaac, and Jacob. They had the prophets. They had Moses and the Law. They had the miracles of the Exodus Generation. They had so much, and yet they appreciated so little. And so the Jews sinned against all of the privileges that they had received. They sinned against Light, and they sinned against Love. They held the goodness of God in contempt, as they persisted in living in arrogance, willfulness, pride, rebellion, and greed.

As a nation, Israel became known to be a people without much mercy and without much compassion. As a nation, they grew legalistic, and formal in their worship. The Jewish men would find a woman and cast her at the feet of Jesus wanting Him to give the word to stone her, while their own hearts burned with unholy passions. The Jews would curse the Lord of Glory for curing a sick man on the Sabbath; but if an ox fell into a ditch on the Sabbath, they would not hesitate to help it out. The Jewish rulers would eagerly collect the temple money, but refuse to help the poor.

Jewish men and women would condemn a murderer, while harboring hatred in their heart toward the Samaritans. The Jewish nation would pray for the Messiah and then kill Him when He came. And because God did not destroy Israel at once, individuals grew bolder and bolder in their sins, for such is the nature of the human heart. I have read the history of some of the Americans who have spied upon our country for money. They each have a similar initial story to tell, in that they were all surprised at how easy it was to perform acts of espionage without getting caught. The very ease they enjoyed encouraged their hearts to continue. Rather than stop, the spies grew bolder and more reckless in their activities. What happens in the secular world, happens in the spiritual. Some in the Church have learned how easy it is to exploit others and take the money of Christians. Promises are made to the saints of health and wealth and power. People are made to think that they can know the future under the guise of prophecy. It has been so easy for shameless charlatans to make money off of God's people, that they are emboldened to more acts of spiritual depravity.

But God will not always conceal sin. His goodness is now being manifested, but only so that there will be time for repentance. The patience of God has never been designed to lead His people to continue a life of presumptuous sinning despite what some people think, such as Heinrich Heine. Heine was a German poet, and critic, who lived from 1797-1856. He made an infamous, cynical statement when he declared that he was not concerned with the world to come because he was confident that God would forgive him for all of his sins. When asked why he was so sure of that, Heine replied, *"It is His trade."* It is a terrible thing to go on sinning against God's grace and love. Still, that is what many do. This is what the Jews were doing in Paul's day. They were abusing God's great grace and patience.

While grace is being offended, the call of the gospel to repentance, and a new life, is still being offered. God now commands all men to repent. But God will not drive men to repentance, for the most part. He would rather draw individuals to Himself with cords of love, while appealing to reason (Hosea 2:4; 11:4). *"Come now and let us reason together, saith the Lord: though your sins be as scarlet, they shall be as white as snow; though they be red like crimson, they shall be as wool"* (Isaiah 1:18).

Those who will not come to the Lord and listen to reason, and love, will discover something in the spiritual world described as a *hard and impenitent heart* (Romans 2:5). The heart of a person becomes hard when it walks in a way that is known to be contrary to the will of God. As bad as a person having a hard heart is, it is worse to have an impenitent heart. The hardhearted may yet be converted, while the impenitent-hearted never will be. Rahab was a harlot. She had a hard heart for no one can live the way Rahab lived unless the heart had been made callused. But Rahab did not have an impenitent heart, for her name is listed in faith's hall of fame. Jesus said that He came to call sinners to repentance.

Sinners have hard hearts but they can yet have good hearts by redeeming grace. In 1855 C.H. Spurgeon spoke of a sailor who was sixty years old. He had sailed the seas and lived without God. Then sovereign love took hold of him and he was converted. The old sailor came to Church and said, *"Pastor, sixty years have I been sailing under the colors of the devil; it is time I should have a new owner; I want to scuttle the old ship and sink her altogether; then I shall have a new one, and I shall sail under the colors of Prince Emmanuelle."*

The man became a praying man. He walked before God in all sincerity. He had a hard heart, but it was melted by the sunshine of God's love. The distinction between a hard heart, and an impenitent heart is important to recognize, for the latter will know the certainty of divine judgment. This judgment is called the treasure of wrath (Romans 2:5). Normally, we think of a treasure as being something valuable. But in the divine economy is a treasure of wrath, concerning which three things can be said: the treasure of wrath is in abundance; the treasure of wrath is something secret; and the treasure of wrath is stored up for the future.

First, the treasure of wrath is abundant to the point that eternity itself will not exhaust its supply. People do not like to hear of an eternal damnation, but the Bible plainly teaches it, and the faithful Christian will proclaim what God reveals. The grace of God is abundant, but so is His divine wrath.

Second, the treasure of wrath that the unthinking and the impenitent store up is connected with secrecy. Because most sins are committed in secret, God will allow judgment to be secretly stored up.

Finally, the spiritual treasure of wrath is being stored up for a future occasion that the Bible calls the Day of Judgment. One day God will break open the spiritual treasures of wrath. In that day there will be no clever arguments, no boldness of sin, no self-justification, no explanation of evil.

There will be weeping and wailing and gnashing of teeth, as God's anger towards the impenitent is made manifest. When will this day come? No one knows. It may be very soon; it may be centuries in the future. Many people believe that history is rapidly approaching Armageddon, but no one knows for sure. What is known, is that God is angry at the wicked every day. What is known, is spiritual wrath is being stored up in the hearts of the impenitent. What is known, is that it is not reasonable to sin against love and the light of the Law of God. What is known, is that now is the day of salvation. What is known, is that we must examine ourselves to see if we have a hard heart. And more alarming still, do we have an impenitent heart? Do we have a heart that will not give up that which we know is displeasing to the Lord? God is not asking if we will speak against evil. He is watching to see if we will cease to practice the evil that we do. The Lord's goodness is present, and so is His grace. What will we do with each?

Four Principles of a Just Judgment: Romans 2:2-16

One of the great themes of Romans 2 is the judgment of God. The concept of judgment may be positive and negative. For a person who is blameless, there is nothing to fear; however, a person who is willful and wicked should be terrified. The terror of the wicked will increase when they understand that the judgment of God will take place according to four great principles. The first principle of just judgment is stated in Romans 2:2a and amplified in Romans 2:2b-5. The second principle is set forth in Romans 2:6 and discussed in Romans 2:7-10.

In Romans 2:11, the third principle of divine judgment is recorded and then treated in Romans 2:11-15. Finally, Romans 2:16 declares the fourth principle of divine judgment.

The First Principle of a Just Judgment in Romans 2: 2 is that God will base His findings upon truth; therefore, He will be absolutely impartial in the judicial proceedings. *"But we are sure that the judgment of God is according to truth against them that commit such things."* The specific acts which God will judge have been listed in Romans 1:29-32. These are vile things indeed and are worthy of just condemnation, followed by a severe penalty. Neither Jew nor Gentile will escape the Divine evaluation of sinful activity in life. In this way, the judgment of God is far different from human justice. In any manmade judicial system, the person who violates human Laws has at least four chances of escape.

- It is possible that a person who violates the Law shall never be known. Each year countless murders, rapes, and robberies go unsolved, because the legal authorities do not know the offender.

- It is possible that a person who breaks the Law can successfully flee, and escape beyond the boundary of jurisdiction.

- It is possible that a failure in the legal process, after arrest, will set a person free who has broken the Law.

- It is possible that a person may escape from prison, and hide from the arm of the Law. But not one of these maneuvers will prevail with any person in regard to divine justice. God has no lack of knowledge or power, or will, to execute righteousness.

The Second Principle of a Just Judgment, as stated in Romans 2:6, is that God will deal with every person upon the basis of absolute equity, whether it be to render punishment or reward (Proverbs 24:12). *Who* [God] *will render to every man according to his deeds.* While judgment will be passed upon every man, the punishment, or reward, will be distributed to two classes of men, and only two, for there is no third class. Righteousness knows no middle ground, no gray areas. Men are either on one side of the Law of God, or on the other. There is no neutrality. This fact means that in every family, in every community, in every state, in every nation in the world, either men and women and young people can, and will, be characterized as being *"patient in well doing and seeking for glory and honor and immortality,"* or they will be characterized as being *"contentious [headstrong], and do not obey the truth, but obey unrighteousness."*

Every person alive falls into one of these two classes. Every person you know comes under one of these categories. Every person who shall yet live will find his or her way into one of these two groups. Because this statement is true, the reward will be far different for each group. One group will be rewarded with eternal life, as per Romans 2:7 while the other will find the result of their life has brought them *"wrath and indignation"* (Romans 2:9).

There will be no exceptions. The Jews will receive either eternal life, or sorrow and misery. The Gentiles will receive either eternal life, or sorrow and misery. The only preference that the Jews might have over all others is that they will be judged first. In the day of ultimate judgment, it may be that the Jews will go before others to receive eternal life, or tribulation and anguish.

After the Jews are judged, God will evaluate the Gentiles. Some will be given eternal life; most will suffer sorrow and misery. Those who are part of the damned, will suffer what the Bible calls, The Second Death (Revelation 20). It is instructive to note that nowhere in the Scriptures is the future of the wicked ever called by the term, life. While they exist forever in the burning fires of eternal wrath, such a state of existence could hardly be called life. It is really an eternal death.

The Third Principle of a Just Judgment can be found in Romans 2:11, which declares God is no respecter of persons. Some people have taken these words to mean that God treats all people equally. But that is not true. Some individuals are born with great intelligence, while others are mentally challenged. Some people are born with physical health, while others suffer from birth, with defects. Some people are born into poverty while others are *"born with a silver spoon in their mouth"* to use an old expression. Some people are born to condemnation, such as Judas, while others will know the love of God (Romans 9). However, there is one place where all men are treated equally by God, and that is before the bar of divine justice.

When it comes to Justice, God will be no respecter of persons. Even Moses declared this great truth (Deuteronomy 10:17): *"For the Lord your God is God of gods, and Lord of lords, a great God, a mighty, and a terrible, which regardeth not persons, nor taketh reward:"* (Acts 10:34; Ephesians 6:9; Colossians 3:25; James 2:9; 1 Peter 1:17). God has never been a respecter of persons, and He never will be. God provides justice for all, and this justice will be administered according to the standard that they have. Not all men have within their possession the same moral standard in the same form. For example, the Jews had the written Law of Moses, while the Gentile world did not. Since the Jews had the Mosaic Law, that Law shall judge them.

Those who kept the Law shall be honored, and those who broke the Law will be judged by it. That is Paul's teaching. Meanwhile, God will also deal with the Gentiles, who had not the Mosaic Law.

The Gentiles must come for judgment, because God is no respecter of persons. The Gentiles must come for judgment because they too have been given a moral Law to live by. This concept is proved in three ways: (1) the matter of their conduct (Romans 2:14); (2) the matter of their conscience (Romans 2:15); or (3) the matter of their thoughts (Romans 2:15).

Paul argues, that in the heart of the Gentiles is ethical activity taking place that implies the recognition of a moral Law that can be called The Law of Nature. The Law of Nature teaches that men should not kill, steal, covet, or lie. Because every society prohibits these transgressions, all men are without excuse, and are fit candidates for divine judgment.

In the Day of Judgment, the Jews will be judged according to the Law of Moses, while the Gentiles will be judged according to the Law of Nature. In all of this discussion a principle is established that God is no respecter of persons. Despite the logic of this truth, Paul realizes that the Jews might object and try to declare that God is not just because He will be holding the Jews to a higher standard to live by than the one for the Gentiles. The Jews might complain that the Gentiles could get away with evil! Anticipating this line of reasoning, Paul reminds the Jews of the fact that Gentiles are not held to a lower form of accountability. Though it is true that they did not have the written Law of God on paper, they did have the Law of God written in their hearts (Romans 2:15).

Confirmation can be found in the fact that the Gentiles have always been very busy bringing forth accusations against one another, and putting forth defenses of bad behavior. The Roman courts were well used by the citizens of the Empire, so the Jews have no basis for objecting to God's judging them according to the Law. The Gentiles will not get away with evil. They will not be held to a lower level of accountability than the Jews.

Now, if the Gentiles try to say that they should not be punished, since they did not have the Law of God, the same reasoning will prevail. The absence of the written Word does not excuse them from just condemnation since they know what is right and what is wrong by nature. *"For when the Gentiles, which have not the Law, do by nature the things contained in the Law, these, having not the Law, are a Law unto themselves:"* (Romans 2:14). Therefore, *"For as many as have sinned without Law shall also perish without Law"* (Romans 2:12).

To understand these things, is to understand why God can justly condemn the heathen that exist in every generation, who have never heard the gospel. They are not guiltless. They too have sinned against God's moral Law. In the sight of God, they are worthy of death. If the Lord in His mercy brings many of them under the sound of the gospel and saves them, that move is according to sovereign grace. However, with or without the gospel, they are all without excuse.

The Fourth Principle of a Just Judgment, as stated in Romans 2:16, is that all men will be judged according to the gospel. A day is coming when the Jew will have one final opportunity to declare that Jesus is the Christ, the Son of the living God, or to deny that Christ is the Messiah. In like manner, a day is coming when every Gentile will have one final opportunity to declare that Jesus is King, or deny the sovereignty of the Savior.

One would think that in this coming day of ultimate judgment, all people present at the Great White Throne would immediately acknowledge the truth and the reality that confronts them, and declare that Jesus is Lord, to the glory of God. It may even be that some will try, but that they shall not be successful in their lies, for God is able to judge the secrets of the heart. God knows that those who did not love His Son in time will not love Him in eternity. God knows that those who did not adore the gospel in time will not respect it in eternity. So the secrets of the heart will be revealed, and in tremendous wrath the voice of judgment will thunder forth: *"Let him that is filthy, be filthy still!"*

The Day of Judgment will not bring forth any new acts of godly repentance. There will be only the confirmation of sin, or confirmation of righteousness. Where sin is, the revelation will come that the hearts of the wicked still harbor dark secrets. On the fateful day of the final judgment, the truth will come out that men still hate Christ despise His gospel, and long to be away from His presence. Those who rejected the gospel in time will reject it in eternity. The wicked will never love the Lord or worship Him.

Seeing the Lord in all of His majesty will not produce saving faith! It is a terrible scene that Paul sets before us. The hearts of men are so desperately wicked that God has to reveal their secrets, by Jesus Christ, according to the gospel. We could wish that men would repent. We could wish that on the final Day of Judgment men might yet fall down and receive the gospel, believe in Christ and love Him. But last moment repentance will not happen. On that day men will be confirmed in their sin. Concerning this matter of being confirmed in sin, consider several examples.

Consider the life of Saul. Saul was judged for his disobedience. Rather than respect the justice of the divine sentence and repent, Saul grew willful. He took counsel against the Lord and against His anointed, David. Saul tried to kill David. Saul was not about to submit to man or God. Rather than repent, Saul died the death of the wicked. He died confirmed in his sin.

Consider the non-elect Angels, those who were allowed to revolt with Lucifer against divine authority. The non-elect angels of God are wiser and more powerful than men in their present condition. They also know that some angels have already been placed in chains of darkness and that one-day they will join them. Why then do the fallen angels not reverse themselves? Why do they not repent? Why do the fallen angels continue to be demons? They are confirmed in evil.

Consider the larger portion of unredeemed mankind. How many times do individuals have to see the expressions of divine wrath against men and nations before they will repent? The point is established. A large portion of mankind will never repent. The spiritual affairs of this life do not matter to them. Sometimes openly, sometimes secretly, men resist the Lord. So the day will come when the secrets of men will be revealed, for there are no secrets from God. Men may pretend to be religious. Men may pretend to love God. Men may pretend to like the Church. Men may pretend to appreciate faithful pastors.

But one day, all of the pretensions of men will be openly revealed as the Lord judges justly, according to the gospel. Because all these things are true, there is but one thing for a person to do, and that is to kiss the Son. Love Christ. Plead for a good heart. Ask the Lord for a new heart that will be full of gospel truth, and not secret sins. On such souls God will have mercy. No mercy will be extended for those who are judged according to the Law of Moses. No mercy will be extended for those who are judged according to the Law of Nature. Mercy will be extended only for those who are in Christ, for He was judged at Calvary. *"There is therefore now no condemnation to those who are in Christ Jesus."* Come to Christ and love Him with all your heart.

Who is a Christian? Romans 2:17-29

The single greatest question that a person will ever consider is this: *"Am I a Christian?"* Eternity itself waits for the answer. If the answer is, *"Yes, I am a Christian,"* positive consequences will result: a belief in, and a love for Jesus Christ, as both Lord and Savior; the pursuit of holiness (Romans 2:7); a Divine evaluation of heart and life on the final Day of Judgment (Romans 2:6); the granting of eternal life (Romans 2:7).

If the answer to the great question of one's divine relationship is, *"No, I am not a Christian,"* then four consequences will follow: life will continue to be lived in rebellion to the Lord; each day sins will be added to a treasury of wrath (Romans 2:5); a day of divine evaluation will come (Romans 2:6); and tribulation and anguish will be rewarded to the unrighteous, for sinners will be confirmed in a state of wickedness (Romans 2:16).

A terrible future waits all who are outside the sphere of grace, and the mercy of God. It is also unnecessary, for the gospel invites all men to salvation and service. But the gospel also warns individuals to count the cost of spiritual commitment. Only those who endure unto the end shall be saved. Only those who follow Christ to the Cross will receive eternal life. A person who decides to commit himself to Christ will be asked another question, which is this: *"What is the evidence of salvation?"*

People may think that they are saved, when they are not. People may sincerely believe that religious activity equals salvation, but it doesn't. The greatest illustration of this delusional thinking is found in the history of the Jews.

The Jews came to a place in their religious experience when they thought they could rest. They believed in life after death, and they were confident that they had eternal life, and would live forever in the presence of God. Their confidence was built upon certain presuppositional thoughts.

- **Racial superiority**. The Jews believed in this and they believed that of all the races, they were the most excellent one (Romans 2:17).

- **The Law of Moses**. The Jews were proud that to them was given the Law of God (Romans 2:17).

- **Monotheism**. The Jews did not worship idols of wood and stone, like the Gentile nations (Romans 2:17).

- **Divine Revelation**. The Jews knew the will of God (Romans 2:18).

- **A Superior Social Code**. The Jews were able to render righteous judgment in social disputes because they judged out of the Law (Romans 2:18).

- **The Ability to Teach**. The Jews were confident that they, above all others, could be, and should be, the guide to the morally blind, and a light to all that are in darkness (Romans 2: 19-20).

Given all of this background, is it any wonder that the Jews looked at themselves as being safe and secure, and in favor with God above all others? Is it any wonder that they yielded to the sins of pride and self-righteousness? If the Church recoils at the arrogance of the Jews of old, it shouldn't because the ancient sins of Israel have become, in many cases, the modern sins of the Church. The charge can be made fairly, that a large portion of the professing Church is religious, but not regenerated. The charge can be made that a large portion of the corporate Church has become smug, and self-righteous, and spiritually satisfied. A sense of security prevails inside the Western Church at the end of the twentieth century. The Church has grown to be proud of herself for several reasons.

- The Church has a more complete Bible. If the Jews had the Law of Moses and the prophets, the Church has that, and more, for the Church has the gospel, the epistles of Paul, and the Revelation of John.

- The Church knows the Messiah. While the Jews continue to look for the Messiah, the Church has found Him.

- The Church has a rich heritage. Like the Jews, the Church honors Abraham, Isaac, and Jacob.

- The Church believes that she is now a guide to the blind and a light to those who are in darkness (Romans 2:19-20).

Is it any wonder that so many within the Church have succumbed to the temptation to be self-righteous? To both the Jews of old and to the Church today comes the gospel message that religion is not righteousness. Works of the flesh do not equal works of righteousness. The root of righteousness will produce the fruit of righteousness. It is this holy fruit which was missing in the life of the Jews according to Paul, and it is this holy fruit which is missing in the life of the Church today. Specific shocking behavior can be noticed in both ancient and modern structures.

Paul implies that the Jews were guilty of stealing. While teaching others not to steal, the Jews stole from God by failing to honor Him with their gifts. Paul implies that the Jews were guilty of committing adultery. While teaching others that God hates immorality, this practice was tearing the social fabric of society apart. Paul implies that the Jews were guilty of idolatry. While teaching others not to have any God but Jehovah, the Jews were guilty of covetous which in the sight of the Lord is idolatry. The whole argument of the Apostle is that the lifestyle of the Jews proved that they had no true spiritual life that was pleasing to God.

Every Christian man must ask himself, *"Do I blaspheme the name of God by the life I live?"* Every Christian woman must ask herself, *"Do I blaspheme the name of God by the life I live?"* Every Church must ask itself, *"Do we blaspheme the name of God by the life that we are now living?"* If the honest answer is, *"Yes!"* then the lesson needs to be learned: *"Not all Christians are Christian"* just as *"not all Jews are Jews."* If that teaching sounds confusing and contradictory, it isn't really. The Bible teaches that God recognizes different kinds of Jews and different kinds of Christians.

For example, there are the racial Jew, the religious Jew, and the regenerate Jew. The racial Jew is anyone who is a direct descendent from Abraham, Isaac, and Jacob. The religious Jew refers to those who observe the Law of Moses while the regenerate Jew has reference to those who honor and unite with the faith of Abraham, Isaac, and Jacob. So it is in the Church. Racial Christians are people who sincerely believe that they were born and baptized into the Christian faith because they are Italian, or American, or some other nationality. Salvation is identified with the race itself. Then come religious Christians, who believe that living a moral life, joining a Church, or doing good works will get them into heaven. Salvation is something that was given to them in a religious ceremony as children. Salvation then is something for them to lose; it is not a Pearl of great treasure to be found. Last, there are regenerate Christians, those who have been born from above by the Spirit of the living God. Only the regenerate Christian is truly born of God and pleases Him. Only those regenerated by the Holy Spirit have a heart of flesh.

3

Romans 3

The Place of Privilege: Romans 3:1-4

Having established the sinfulness of both Gentile and Jew, having proved that God does not prefer the racial Jew in matters of salvation, the question arises whether the Jewish nation has any advantages over others. Two rhetorical statements are made: *"What advantage then hath the Jew* [over a Gentile]*?"* And *"What profit is there of receiving in one's body the sign of a covenant relationship with God through the act of circumcision?"*

To these questions Paul responds with an emphatic reaffirmation that the Jewish nation does indeed have a tremendous advantage over other nations in many ways (Psalms 147:20; Romans 9:4). Paul does not list the many ways in which the Jews had been blessed by God above all other nations on earth, but we can mention at least one. First was the matter of being acceptable. For individuals to be acceptable in the sight of God, they had to convert to Judaism. Many did, such as Ruth the Moabitess. Ruth was willing to say, *"Thy people shall be my people and thy God my God"* (Ruth 1:16).

Naaman the Syrian became a Jewish proselyte in order to pray in an acceptable manner. Following his cleansing from leprosy, Naaman placed on the backs of two mules, large sacks of earth gathered in the land of Israel. Then he went back to Syria. In his house, Naaman spread the dirt he had brought onto the floor. Then he knelt and prayed to the Lord (2 Kings 5:17). In another time and place, when the Jews instituted the Feast of Purim, after their mortal enemy, Haman was hanged, many people became Jews according to Esther 8:17. So it went down through the corridors of time. In order to be converted, a person had to embrace the faith of Abraham, Isaac, and

Jacob. They had to embrace the Law of Moses, and if a male, they had to receive in their body the sign of the covenant. So a Jew had a great advantage. But the greatest of all advantages the Jews had over other nations is found in the fact that unto them was given the oracles of God (Romans 3:2). The word *"logia"* or *"oracle"* is used four times in the New Testament.

- The word is used in the speech of Stephen just prior to his execution, and martyrdom (Acts 7:28).

- The word is used in Hebrews 5:12, where the people are being rebuked for not understanding spiritual truths.

- The word is used in 1 Peter 4:11, where teachers are exhorted to speak as the oracles of God.

- And the word is used in Romans 3:2 to set forth the place of privilege of the Jew.

Though God spoke to other nations through His prophets, Israel was the primary recipient of the oracles, and this situation produced a practical problem for the Jews. The problem was this: The oracles of God did not seem to be effective. Many lives were not changed, despite the fact that the Scriptures had graciously been given. The simple question was, *"Why not? Why did the oracles of God not have more moral impact upon the Jewish people?"* The answer can be given in one word: unbelief (Romans 2:3).

To set the context for this stinging evaluation, Paul has been condemning the religious Jews for boasting of possessing the Law, while being lawless. A life of moral lawlessness leads to licentiousness, and that causes the name of God to be blasphemed (Romans 2:24). A holy God is not the God of an unholy people. *"Without holiness, no man shall see the Lord."* Therefore, a simple possession of the Word of God is meaningless if the Scriptures are not respected, if the Scriptures are not studied, and if the Scriptures are not obeyed.

A simple possession of the Word of God is meaningless if the Scriptures are not passed on to others, or protected from internal corruption and external destruction. Goodness is not guaranteed just because a people have been given the oracles of God. The only Divine certainty is that those who have the Scriptures do have a greater privilege, and responsibility than others; they will therefore know a greater judgment, should they fail to honor God's Word.

Dr. William Hendriksen has tried to illustrate this concept. *"Consider a youth who enrolls in college. He has the following advantages over many others: he comes from a rich family, so that paying room and board, tuition, etc., is no problem. He enjoys excellent health, and is even blessed with above average intelligence. The college he attends rates very high. His teachers are the best. In spite of all these advantages he never graduates. Why not? Because he does not make the most of his opportunities. He fritters away his time, is lazy, unfaithful to his trust"* (*Commentary on Romans*, William Hendriksen).

That college student deserves greater judgment than other students who do not have such advantages. So it was with Israel. They had been honored with being given the oracles of God, but some in Israel had been unfaithful to what was entrusted to them. Therefore, the nation discovered that the God who is faithful to His promises of kindness and mercy is also faithful to His threats when disobeyed. The sad part is that divine judgment was unnecessary, yet it came because men were unfaithful to God. Men were unfaithful because of unbelief. God spoke, only to be challenged by unbelief. Unbelief still challenges God.

The Bible says that God *"created the heavens and the earth"* and all that is in them within a seven-day period of creation. *"Not true!"* cries the unbelief of evolutionary thought. The Bible says, *"the soul that sinneth, it shall die."* *"Not true!"* says the slimy serpent into the ear of Adam and Eve. The Bible says, *"The just shall live by faith."* *"Not true!"* screams the sinner, *"Look at my works."* The Bible says that Jesus is coming the Second time for all who believe (Hebrews 9:28). Modern theology smiles knowingly and says forcefully, *"No, Jesus is coming a second and a third time."*

The Bible says that man is saved by grace through faith alone (Ephesians 2:89). *"Never! Never! Never!"* Comes the shout. *"Salvation depends upon involvement from and the free exercise of the fallen will."* The Bible says that the carnal mind is enmity against God (Romans 8:7). It is hostile to God. It hates Him. The depraved mind of man needs divine grace. The Bible says that all Scripture is God breathed. Unbelief gnashes its terrible teeth and hisses that the Bible is the product of religious zealots full of all the frailties of humanity.

The Bible says that Jesus is coming for His Bride, the Church, whom He loves with a passion. Unbelief laughs and throws back the challenge, *"Where is the sign of His coming?"* The Bible says that God was in Christ Jesus who is the expression of the Godhead bodily. *"That is not true!"* says unbelief. *"Jesus is the illegitimate offspring of a Roman soldier. He died and was buried two thousand years ago, if he ever did live."*

Countless are the attacks against the oracles of God. Without number are the temptations to express unbelief. Multiple are the times of wretched faithlessness. However, *"Does the unbelief and faithlessness of men make the faithfulness of God ineffectual?"* The answer to that question is, *"No!"* Paul shudders at the very idea. *"Yea, let God be true, but every man a liar."* Human mendacity, or treachery, shall never overthrow divine veracity.

Regardless of circumstances, in spite of current events, no matter what the penetrating intelligence of the profane may imagine, despite the persuasiveness of eloquent speeches that are hostile to God, what the Lord has decreed, what the Lord has promised will come to pass. What is written in the oracles of God is certain. Neither the spade of the archaeologist, the telescope of the astronomer, the speculations of philosophers, or the faithlessness of man, can overthrow God and prove Him to be faithless or untrue.

The Jews may have been faithless, to their part of the covenant relationship. The Jews may have disobeyed the Law of God. The Jews may have trampled the Word of Truth into the ground like swines move around in mud. The Jews may even have killed the Lord of Glory, yet God will still be faithful to fulfill the covenants He has made with mankind. Specifically, in the Abrahamic covenant, God promised that in Abraham, all the families and all the nations on earth would be blessed (Genesis 22:18). This has happened, for in the fullness of time the Messiah was born. God sent forth His Son, *"made of a woman, made under the Law, to redeem them that were under the Law"* (Galatians 4:4, 5).

God has always been faithful to His word so that He might be justified in His integrity and silence all that are the objects of His judgment (Romans 3:4). David understood this concept. David had sinned grievously. He sinned against Bathsheba. He sinned against Uriah the Hittite. He sinned against the nation of Israel. He sinned against His own body. But most of all he sinned against God. David was faithless to God. David was faithless to the covenant relationship. But God was not faithless. In marvelous grace, God sent a prophet to the wayward king to bring him to repentance. In the agony of his soul David cried out saying, *"Oh God, I confess to Thee all things that thou mayest be proved right in Thy words and prevail in Thy judging"* (Psalms 51:4b).

David wanted to make his own confession of sin as open as possible in order that in his unrighteousness, the righteousness of God might be revealed. David wanted God to triumph. Here then is another perspective on confessing sins. We confess our sins, not only to feel better, we confess our sins not only to be forgiven, we confess our sins openly and honestly that the righteousness of God might be established. We want God's righteousness to triumph against the background of our unrighteousness.

We want the glory of grace to shine forth. In one of Rembrandt's paintings named *Night Watch*, are dark shadows. The shadows are rather gloomy, but they do enhance the bright spot of light that is present on the main subject. In the blackness of the night the light explodes all the more brilliantly. In like manner, there is a way in which the unrighteousness of man causes God's righteousness to be accentuated.

The conclusion of the matter covered in this section, is that the Gentiles are the objects of God's wrath because of their sinful practices. Even though they did not have the Law, they are guilty because the Law of Nature is written in their consciences. But the Jews are also under divine judgment, for they have sinned with the Law. They who have had great advantages have been faithless. Nevertheless, man's faithlessness will not negate God's faithfulness.

The life of David proved this point. Your life, and mine, can also prove the faithfulness of God, for the promise comes to us, that if we will believe on the Lord Jesus Christ, His blood will keep on cleansing us from all our sins. And then as Christians, if we confess our sins after being unfaithful, God in mercy will be faithful. He will forgive us (1 John 1:9). Divine forgiveness comes not so that we can sin more, but so that God can be declared righteous. To be in Christ, is to be in a place of privilege.

The Pitiful Charge against the Apostle Paul: Romans 3:5-18

By way of review, the Apostle Paul has found it necessary to anticipate rhetorical questions of objection to his teachings. Four main concerns are responded to. The first objection, is that if the Jews and Gentiles stand in disgrace before God together, what advantage then hath the Jew? The answer is that there is a place of privilege for the Jews. God has honored them in many ways. But most of all they have been given the oracles of God, which are the Scriptures of the Old Testament (Acts 7:38). The Jews have been given the types, promises, and prophecies that relate to Christ and the gospel so that they are without excuse for failing to keep the Law.

Because of the failure of the Jews to understand, appreciate, and appropriate by faith the great privileges that had been entrusted to them, the question arises as to whether the unbelief of the Jews will lead God to be unfaithful to His promises. Since the Jews broke the covenant, will God also not fulfill His part of the covenant promises? To this thought the Apostle Paul is startled. He is shocked and abhorred by the very concept and cries out in Romans 3:4, *"God forbid! The infidelity and obstinacy of the Jews could not invalidate and overthrow those prophecies of the Messiah, which were contained in the oracles committed to them. Christ will be glorious, though Israel be not gathered (Isaiah 49:5). God's word will be accomplished and all of His purposes performed though there be a generation that by their unbelief go about to make God a liar."*

Matthew Henry

This strong reaffirmation of the goodness and graciousness of God leads to the third thought which Paul felt he must challenge, for the charge could be made that people should be encouraged to sin. Why? Because sin or unrighteousness seems to commend or manifest the righteousness of God (Romans 3:5). That is the argument in the mouth of the ungodly, who desperately want to justify evil. Once more Paul is sickened at such deductive thinking and cries out again, *"God forbid!"* (Romans 3:6). But the sinful religious philosophers will not be silent and press the argument (Romans 3:78) that sin really promotes the glory of God.

According to this line of thinking, the liar should not be punished for lying; homosexuality should be considered an alternative lifestyle and not an abomination before God, and all murderers should be understood, not punished. In fact, the more heinous the sin of a soul, the more God should be glorified when He justifies the sinner (Psalms 52:1). If this concept is not bad enough, the whole discussion becomes more complicated; for upon hearing the philosophical argument made by the ungodly that sin is good, conservatively religious minded Jews, opposed to salvation by grace alone, charged that Paul himself must be teaching that people should practice evil that good may come.

A modern day discussion taking place in the Christian community parallels what Paul was up against. Consider the debate that rages between those who believe in eternal security and those who believe that man can lose his salvation. Those who believe that salvation can be lost are charged by those who believe in the final preservation of the saints of embracing a system of salvation by works, thereby taking glory from Christ and His redemptive work. The basis of salvation then becomes faith, plus good works, instead of salvation by grace alone. The response to this theological attack is to argue that those who believe in eternal salvation for the saved are really teaching that a person can go out and do whatever they want, and live in whatever manner they chose without fear of condemnation.

> *"Free from the Law,*
> *O happy condition,*
> *Sin as you please,*
> *For there is remission!"*

Because of these types of verbal attacks people fail to communicate, division comes, and each side feels slandered. Paul believed that he was being slandered or literally, blasphemed when he was charged with teaching that people could live in a constant state of sin and still be justified according to faith. *"It is no new thing for the best of God's people and ministers to be charged with holding and teaching such things as they do most detest and abhor; and it is not to be thought strange, when our Master Himself was said to be in league with Beelzebub. Many have been reproached—as if they had said that the contrary of which they maintain: it is an old artifice of Satan there to cast dirt upon Christ's ministers. Lay slander thickly on, for some will be sure to stick."* (Matthew Henry)

Paul never taught that people should practice evil so that good could come out of bad (Romans 3:8). Paul taught that the damnation of all mankind is justified. Paul taught that the Gentiles are worthy of condemnation because they had deliberately violated the Law of Conscience. Paul taught that the Jews were worthy of God's wrath because they had broken the Law of the Lord. Paul taught that it can be said of all of humanity in bold letters that, *"There is none righteous, no not one."* To prove his case against any cry of protest, Paul levels specific charges against humanity that is unconverted to Christ. The Apostle brings all of mankind before the bar of divine justice and officially issues eight counts of indictments.

- Mankind does not seek after God (Romans 3:11). This charge is supported by quoting Psalms 14:3. *"They are all gone aside, they are all together become filthy: there is none that doeth good, no, not one."*

- Mankind does not do anything that is good (Romans 3:12).

- Mankind possesses deceitful tongues (Romans 3:13).

- Mankind has a mouth full of cursing and bitterness (Romans 3:14).

- Mankind engages in collective murder (Romans 3:15).

- Mankind loves destruction and misery (Romans 3:16).

- Mankind does not know the way of peace (Romans 3:17).

- Mankind has no fear of God (Romans 3:18).

If these charges seem to be too broad in scope and unfair, then two thoughts need to be realized. First, all of mankind's human good is considered nothing but raw sewage in the sight of God when it is offered to Him as a basis of salvation. Those who are in the flesh will never be able to please God, or be acceptable in His sight.

Second, while individuals do many acts that might be considered good, God looks at the source of all good and sees that it all springs from a corrupt heart. It is this heart; it is this unregenerate soul that needs to be changed. The evidence abounds that nothing less than a new heart, a new mind, and a new will bestowed by God upon individuals will ever suffice to stop the slide toward eternal self-destruction, and for good reasons.

- **The unregenerate soul does not seek after God.** Whenever this declaration is made, the question springs to some minds, *"What about all the temples to be found in pagan lands?"* The Biblical answer is that all these people are not seeking after God but the devil. *"The things which the Gentiles sacrifice, they sacrifice to demons, and not to God"* (1 Corinthians 10:20). Behind all of the world's false beliefs is the god of this world (2 Corinthians 4:3-4), the devil. If a person ever comes to faith in Christ, it is because the Good Shepherd has come to seek and to save that which is lost (Luke 19:10).

- **The unregenerate do not do any good.** The problem with all of the so-called *goodness* of the unregenerate is that their motive is all wrong. The goodness of the unregenerate is to make self feel good. That others are helped is glorious, but the motive is selfish. The truth of the matter is that God looks at not only what is done, but also why things are done. Jesus warned that in the Day of Judgment people would come to Him and point all that has been done in His name. But He will say, *"Depart from me ye workers of iniquity, I never knew you. You have not done any real good for all of these deeds were not done with the proper motive of love for God."*

- **The unregenerate have deceitful tongues.** Like a snake with the fangs pulled in, individuals are ready to lash out, and strike with venomous words, when crossed, angered, or offended.

- **The unregenerate have mouths, which are full of cursing** and bitterness reflected in the profanity of the movies, the vileness of common conversation, and even the sick humor of popular comedians, which finds targets of opportunity to ridicule in the name of political correctness. In the nightclubs of the world, the Church is very often the object of ridicule and bitterness all in the name of entertainment.

- **The unregenerate are swift to shed blood.** When the history is written of life in the 20th century, the evidence will declare that it was the most violent and bloody in all of human history. The divine indictment is not overstated. Man loves to kill his enemies in the most bloody and violent way possible. At the Nuremberg War Crime Trials, following World War II, Justice Jackson, in opening the case for the prosecution, described the rise of the Nazi party to power, and then went on to tell of the crimes they committed against the Jews.

"The most savage and numerous crimes were planned and committed by the Nazis...The ghetto was a laboratory for testing repressive measures. Extermination of the Jews enabled the Nazis to bring a practiced hand to similar measures against Poles, Serbs, and Greeks." Sixty percent of the Jews in Nazi controlled Europe were exterminated. *"History,"* he said, *"does not record a crime perpetrated against so many victims or ever carried out with such calculated cruelty."*

- **The heart of the unregenerate is bent upon provoking destruction and misery.** Any local news program will verify this truth on a daily basis.

- **The unregenerate know nothing of making peace**. If this accusation were not true, then the United Nations would be the most powerful and useful organization on planet earth. But the United Nations has not stopped, and cannot stop the bloodshed and carnage that rage around the world.

- **The unregenerate do not fear God**. The human heart would rather be damned, than concede that God has the right to rule His creation.

Mankind stands guilty of the charges leveled against it. There is too much evidence. What can be done? There is only one hope for the unregenerate and that is to call upon the name of the Lord for salvation. Paul has gone to great lengths to try to silence the tongue of the Jew. Paul has gone to great lengths to try to silence the tongue of the Gentile. Paul has gone to great lengths to silence the tongue of all men so that they might hear the gospel of redeeming love. Yet it is the very gospel that men reject.

"The last place to which a sinner ever betakes himself for relief is to Jesus Christ," said Charles G. Finney. *"Sinners had rather be saved in any other way in the world. They had rather make any sacrifice, go to any expense, or endure any suffering than just throw themselves as guilty lost rebels upon Christ alone for salvation... It cuts up on their self-righteousness, and annihilates their pride."*

Only when we capture a sight of ourselves through the eyes of God can we begin to see the desperate condition of fallen humanity. May God grant us grace to see the natural depravity of the human heart and then seek a Savior, in the person of Jesus Christ.

The Free Grace of a Righteous God: Romans 3:19-24

The Apostle Paul has finally proved his main points concerned with sin and mankind. Paul has argued that the Gentile world is guilty before God and therefore is in need of a Savior. The Gentiles have violated the Law of the Lord and cannot deny it. In like manner, the Jewish world is also guilty before God. The Jews have broken the holy ordinances and cannot deny it. Therefore, every mouth in humanity should be stopped from efforts of self-defense and self-justification. The entire world is guilty before God. All of mankind is guilty of open disobedience and willful rebellion. There stirs within the soul of man a surging restlessness, stronger than the waves of the sea, to do what it wants to do.

The Law of the Lord says, *"Thou shalt not have any other God before me."* But the world produces many glittering toys, and the heart covets them. Strong impulse made stronger by repetitive behavior leads to consumer debt that in the sight of God is a great sin. Why do we grab for things we cannot afford and more often than not, have no need of? The Biblical answer is sin. And I am guilty. The Law of the Lord says, *"Thou shalt not murder,"* yet how easily this sin is committed in spirit. Someone offends our reputation or someone we care for, and we discover hatred in the heart.

If the opportunity were given to kill, and not be punished, the hand might quickly pick up a powerful weapon and strike with passion and force the object of anger. That more and more people are beating, and hurting others is commonly reported in the news. As a result, new terminology is being created to accommodate societies' aberrant behavior. For example, the term *"road rage"* has been coined in recent years to refer to angry people in cars. Then there is *"spousal abuse"* and *"domestic violence."*

The root of this violence is murder in the heart of man. The Ten Commandments (Exodus 20) reveal that men are guilty of breaking the Law of God. Not only are men guilty, but they have been caught and convicted. The voice of the Lord can be heard calling out, holding individuals to a high level of accountability. But men run from the Lord. They run to their sins with the hope of being able to continue in bad behavior despite the fact that the conscience condemns their behavior. Men are guilty. Individuals do not want to fellowship with the Lord. God knows too much. And every heart shares the knowledge of sin (Romans 3:20). This knowledge comes by the Law. The Law says not to do certain things. The Law was broken.

What is broken cannot heal. What is broken cannot help. What is broken cannot make whole, which is why the deeds of the Law shall never be able to justify, or declare righteous a man in the sight of God. The Law condemns. The Law accuses. The Law convicts, but it can never convert. All the Law can do is to expose and accentuate the great chasm between man's behavior and God's holiness. Cain tried to keep the Law only to be exposed by it as a murderer. The Pharisees tried to keep the Law only to have the Law reveal the pride and arrogance of their heart. So the Law cannot save the soul or secure an eternal place in heaven for the heart that longs to go there. Upon realizing this, a person may despair. If there is no salvation by keeping the Law, how then shall anyone be saved? If the attempt to perform righteous religious duties will not avail any merit or favor with God, how shall the soul be saved?

If the hope of eternal life, based on the performance of good works is removed, then on what basis can man be justified, or deduced righteous in the sight of God? The good news is that there is an answer to these questions. The good news is that there is an alternative to the Law. The first hint we have of hope is found in the words *"But now."* How precious these words are, *"But now."* Whatever my life has been up to this part, no matter how many sins have been committed, no matter how many attempts at spiritual renewal may have been attempted with a view to keeping the Law, there is something else. *"But now,"* Now, the righteousness of God is manifested.

Of course, the righteousness of God was manifested in the Law, but it was a judicial righteousness. It was a righteousness that condemned, convicted, sentenced, and executed. It was a righteousness that was high and holy, stern and inflexible. *"But now, the righteousness of God is manifested without the Law."* This does not mean that God changed, nor does it mean that He reduced His standards of holiness to accommodate the frailties of fallen man. It does mean that God found a way to satisfy the righteous demands of the Law, and still show mercy to men. God found a way to save souls, and still be righteous.

That news is good news indeed. Concerning this righteousness of God without the Law, Paul says that it has been manifested, and made crystal clear, to the point that the prophets testified to it

(Romans 3:21). The Law and the Prophets testify to this facet of Divine righteousness by way of anticipation, for the Scriptures foretold of a Messiah who would come. When the Messiah came, He would make war against the Devil (Genesis 3:15; Galatians 4:4). He would fulfill all the demands of the Law perfectly. He would be born of a virgin (Isaiah 7:14; Luke 1:26, 27, 30, 31), and die a substitutionary death for His people (Isaiah 53:3; John 1:11).

He would rise again from the grave (Psalms 16:10; Mark 16:6), and live to rule and reign forever and ever (Isaiah 9:7; Luke 1:32, 33). In a perfect Person the Law would find satisfaction. Now, the righteousness of God that has been made clear by the Law and the Prophets can come to men by faith in Jesus Christ. Unto all, and upon all that believe, is the righteousness of God given. But individuals must believe in Christ. Sadly, most of mankind still does not believe in Christ. Therefore, most people do not have the righteousness of God upon them, which means that they will continue to try and establish their own righteousness. Some will do this by trying to keep the Law like the Pharisees of old. There are legalists who go about to establish their own salvation apart from grace. Some will try to establish the righteousness of God by reinterpreting the Scriptures.

Here is the irony. Even those who are engaged in the most despicable lifestyle want to be considered righteous in the sight of others. Not fearing God, they at least want to be viewed as righteous in the sight of man. But there is no righteousness of God upon anyone who is outside of Christ. Nevertheless, for all that are in Christ, for all that believe on Jesus Christ as Lord and Savior, the righteousness of God has descended.

And there is no difference if one is a Jew or a Gentile. Salvation is found in Christ, and the righteousness of God comes upon both. For there is no difference, *"all have sinned and come short of the glory of God"* (Romans 3:22, 23). All who embrace Christ will enjoy the righteousness of God. It is not a national Israel in the Middle East for whom Christ died; He died for the Church (Ephesians 5:25), which is also considered to be a spiritual nation (1 Peter 2:8).

Christ loves His Bride and He rules His spiritual nation as King. Jewish political Zionism has managed to find a western ally in the teaching of Dispensationalism that in principle overthrows the unity of the Church. In Biblical theology there is no dramatic distinction between a Jew and a Gentile who met together at the Cross to form a new spiritual nation called the Church. Upon them both the righteousness of God is given so that both are freely justified by God's grace through the redemption that is in Christ Jesus.

The justification of man is without cost. No one has ever been able to earn salvation. No one has ever been able to purchase salvation. No one has ever been able to deserve salvation. It is freely given by God's grace. Justification comes to men because of free grace. Justification comes because of God's grace. John Newton understood something of this grace of God and was amazed by it. Moved with love, he took up a pen one day and wrote:

> *"Amazing grace, how sweet the sound,*
> *that saved a wretch like me.*
> *I once was lost, but now am found,*
> *Was blind, but now I see."*

While the grace of God is amazing and free, it was not free to God, for it cost Him the purchasing price of the blood of His Son, Jesus Christ. We can rejoice in the free grace that came to us while we were yet sinners, justified us, and caused blind eyes to see. We can be grateful that our redemption is in Christ (Romans 3:24). Are you in Christ? Has grace been freely given to you so that you believe on the Lord Jesus Christ? Do you value the redemption that was purchased at Calvary? And most of all, do you realize that God is righteous in forgiving sinners because the penalty for sins was paid by His dear Son?

The Basis on Which to Boast: Romans 3:23-30

Romans 3:23 is perhaps one of the most familiar texts in the entire Bible. Little children memorize it and theologians study it. The verse teaches what is universally acknowledged: *"All have sinned and come short of the glory of God."* To sin is to break the Moral Law of God. To sin is to miss the mark established by Divine righteousness. To sin is to be rebellious. To sin is to be willful. And all have sinned. By sin, all of mankind has come short of the glory of God. The glory of God refers to the fullness of the Godhead.

The glory of God refers to anything and everything that could be and should be said about Him. It can be stated that God is omnipotent, and thus His glory is declared. By His power the universe was created and by His pleasure alone it is sustained. It can be said that God is omniscient so that again His glory is revealed. The wisdom of God is amazing. His knowledge is incomprehensible.

One day, when mankind has finally reached the end of the universe, and created all of the wonderful inventions that helps him to understand this world, God will change it. There will be a new heaven and a new earth with new Laws to explore, and the glory of God will be enhanced once more. It can be argued that God is omnipresent, and so He is able to communicate with His creation. Men once marveled at the printing press and how it helped people communicate and be closer. Then came the telegraph. Man was amazed when the transatlantic cable was laid and two continents were united. They stood breathless before the wireless and the radio. Then there came the television putting pictures and sound together. Today, we have satellites in outer space and dream of a communication expressway on the Internet.

As glorious as all of these inventions are that seem to make us a global home, they pall into insignificance when compared to God, for His presence permeates the universe. God does not have to transmit Himself or go somewhere, for He is everywhere. He is at the bottom of the sea. He is in the depths of the cave. He will be found on the most distant planet in the universe. In all of this, His glory is displayed. Many other attributes of God make Him altogether glorious. And man has fallen short of His glory; that means in part that man has failed to meet God's approval. Long ago in the Garden of Eden the hour of approval or disapproval based upon a test came. Man failed the test.

He chooses to sin rather than to submit to the Sovereign. In the failure man came short of being confirmed in righteousness. God could have approved him. He could have enhanced his created state of holiness. How glorious that would have been. How happy the elect angels would have been. But we see man eating of the forbidden fruit and falling further and further away from God. We look again, and we see that the light that clothed Adam and Eve is now gone. Now Adam and Eve realize that they are naked. Their nakedness was not the nudity of the skin, but the absence of the glorious brilliance and splendor of righteousness that surrounded them (Genesis 3:7-11).

Left in moral, intellectual, and spiritual darkness, Adam rushed to replace their glory with fig leaves, only to discover that those things too, would perish, for the glory of Creation was lost with the glory of man. Their history was united according to divine design. All human resources to cover the sin of man proved inadequate. This falling short of the glory of God was illustrated down through centuries time and again when the Tabernacle was built. There was the brazen altar to which men had to go with their sacrifices, but then they could go no farther.

From the point of the altar the priests or High Priest had carry on the work of intercession and worship. No one could go into the Holy Place or the Holy of Holies unless divinely appointed. So men stood outside the sphere where the glory of God dwelt. They came short of the glory of God. Many a heart longed to look within the sacred veil and to know something of God's glory once more. One day, the prophets of Israel began to appear and teach that the longing for the glory of God would one day be realized. The gospel message declares that

> *"There is a way for man to rise*
> *To that sublime abode:*
> *An offering and a sacrifice,*
> *A Holy Spirit's tender energies,*
> *An advocate with God.*
>
> *These, these prepare us for the sight*

> *Of holiness above;*
> *The sons of ignorance and night*
> *May ever dwell in the eternal light,*
> *Through the eternal love."*

The gospel declares that one day God would find a way to reveal His glory to mankind once more. One day God would be able to justify men freely by His grace through the redemption that is in Christ Jesus. In this redemption, He would be absolutely righteous. Having established the righteousness of God to forgive sins, and having proved that God is just to justify those who believe in Christ (Romans 3:26-27), the Apostle comes back to the question of the Law. Can a person boast in having the Law? No. All boasting is excluded.

On what basis? Did the Law exclude itself? No. The Law would never do that. The Law could freely encourage boasting if kept. And that is what happened. Those who tried to keep a portion of the Law felt smug and superior to all others who did not have the Law or felt no need to try to keep any part of it. So Paul had to show these people that they should not boast, for to break one part of the Law is to break all the Law, and to remove any basis for boasting of moral superiority.

If a person is going to be saved, the qualification will not be because of keeping the Law. If a person is ever going to be saved, it must be because of faith. It is faith that pleases God. But man has no natural faith that is acceptable to God for he is flesh and all that are in the flesh cannot please God. How then is it possible to have the type of faith that will please God? The Biblical answer is that God gives the very faith that is needed to believe so that salvation will be all of grace (Ephesians 2:89). Saving faith is contrary to the fallen nature of man, who is declared to be dead in trespasses and sin. These thoughts lead Paul to a firm conclusion. *"A man is justified by faith without the deeds of the Law"* (Romans 3:28).

For a person to be justified by faith was a shocking concept to the Jews. It is a shocking truth when presented plainly today, for the thought immediately comes that such a gospel will teach individuals to be lawless. But that is not the case. The evidence of a holy life is essential for salvation. However, the root or ground of justification is faith. Now, the Bible speaks of several types of faith. First, there is a faith that does not save. This was the faith of the Gentiles as they put their trust in idols. Second, there is the faith of religious philosophers who create a god of their own imaginations. Such gods are far different from the God of revelation. The god of man's imagination is usually limited as the god of the Mormon's who is just man. The god of the Jehovah Witnesses is an exalted angel. The god of the Hindus is the god of nature. The god of the New Age movement is man deified.

To embrace any of these *gods* so-called is to embrace a sure damnation. The God of the Bible is the God of power and wisdom, mercy, truth, and justice. He is the God who is sovereign over sin. It is this God who has revealed Himself in the person of Jesus Christ. To believe in Christ by faith is to be declared righteous. Who may be declared righteous? The Jews only? No. God can justify both Jews and Gentiles (Romans 3:29). In all of this the Law of God is not made void, but is established in the life of Abraham and David, illustrated in Romans 4.

A Brief Review of Romans 2-3

By way of review, Paul has made a number of important statements in chapters 2 and 3 dealing with certain theological truths. He has also raised several rhetorical questions, so that he could come to some other logical conclusions that may be stated.

1. People cannot condemn others for breaking the Law while doing the very same thing, and escape God's just judgment.

    - Romans 2:3, *"And thinkest thou this, O man, that judgest them which do such things, and doest the same, that thou shalt escape the judgment of God?"*

2. People can despise the goodness of God's grace by not realizing that the long-suffering of God is designed to bring repentance.

- Romans 2:4, *"Or despisest thou the riches of his goodness and forbearance and long-suffering; not knowing that the goodness of God leadeth thee to repentance?"*

3. People cannot teach others without teaching themselves.

    - Romans 2:21, *"Thou therefore which teachest another, teachest thou not thyself?"*

4. A person can preach against stealing, and then steal.

    - Romans 2:21, *"thou that preachest a man should not steal, dost thou steal?"*

5. A person can preach against adultery, and then commit the same.

    - Romans 2:22, *"Thou that sayest a man should not commit adultery, dost thou commit adultery?"*

6. A person can denounce idols, and then worship them.

    - Romans 2:22, *"thou that abhorrest idols, dost thou commit sacrilege?"*

7. A person can boast of having the Law of God, and at the same time dishonor God.

    - Romans 2:23, *"Thou that makest thy boast of the Law, through breaking the Law dishonourest thou God?"*

8. People who do not have the sign and seal of the covenant mark on their body may still be righteous in the sight of God, if they do that which pleases the Lord.

    - Romans 2:26, *"Therefore if the uncircumcision keep the righteousness of the Law, shall not his uncircumcision be counted for circumcision?"*

9. Those who are outside the sphere of saving faith may justly condemn those who boast of being in the sphere of faith and yet live in sin.

- Romans 2:27, *"And shall not uncircumcision which is by nature, if it fulfill the Law, judge thee, who by the letter and circumcision dost transgress the Law?"*

10. Despite their failures, racial Jews have advantages.

    - Romans 3:1, *"What advantage then hath the Jew? Or what profit is there of circumcision?"*

11. The faithlessness of man will never cause God to be faithless.

    - Romans 3:3, *"For what if some did not believe? Shall their unbelief make the faith of God without effect?"*

12. God never intended that a person's sins should be the basis for more sin.

    - Romans 3:5, *"But if our unrighteousness commend the righteousness of God, what shall we say?"*

13. God is never unjust for exacting justice.

    - Romans 3:5, *"Is God unrighteous who taketh vengeance? (I speak as a man.)"*

14. God has a basis on which to judge the world, and that is the basis of absolute righteousness, which is exacted from each person either directly or by way of a substitute.

    - Romans 3:6, *"God forbid: for then how shall God judge the world?"*

15. Men would like to use the glory and grace of God to promote sin by arguing that since God is so good to forgive, then men should sin much for to sin much means to be forgiven much.

    - Romans 3:7, *"For if the truth of God hath more abounded through my lie unto his glory; why yet am I also judged as a sinner?"*

16. Good men will often be charged with teaching the very thing they spoke against.

    - Romans 3:8, *"And not rather, (as we be slanderously reported, and as some affirm that we say,) Let us do evil, that good may come? Whose damnation is just."*

17. No Jew is better than the Gentile is, and no Gentile is better than a Jew in the sight of God.

    - Romans 3:9, *"What then? Are we better than they? No, in no wise: for we have before proved both Jews and Gentiles, that they are all under sin."*

18. Because sin is universal, there is no basis for boasting in the Law or human morality of men. If individuals are to boast, let them boast of salvation by grace through faith.

    - Romans 3:27, *"Where is boasting then? It is excluded. By what Law? Of works? Nay: but by the Law of faith."*

Doctrine of Grace

> *"The grace of God is love freely shown towards guilty sinners, contrary to their merit and indeed in defiance of their demerit. It is God showing goodness to persons who deserve only severity, and had no reason to expect anything but severity."*
> —J. I. Packer

1. The first mention of grace in the Bible is found in Genesis 6:8, where we read that *Noah found grace in the eyes of the Lord.*

2. As used in the Old Testament, grace often has the sense of special favor being held, based upon a high estimation of someone by another person. Joseph, for example, found grace in the eyes of Potiphar, and Ruth found favor in the eyes of Boaz (Genesis 39:4; Ruth 2:10).

3. In the divine economy, grace is what God is freely able to do, and indeed what He does do for those for whom Christ has died. Mercy, the compassion of God, and love, the motive of God, unite when expressed to manifest grace that is undeserved favor.

4. The grace of God rules out human merit for salvation (Romans 3:24; Ephesians 2:8-9).

5. Grace perfects forever the salvation of the elect in the sight of God.

6. Grace removes condemnation, and brings peace between God and man forever (Romans 5:1; 8:1; Colossians 2:9-10).

7. Grace removes any obligation to gain favor with God by legal duties (Romans 4:14; 6:14-15).

   - Once man was in Adam, but now he is in a state of saving grace. He has been baptized into Christ, dead unto sin, but alive unto God (Romans 6:1-10; 5:2).

   - Saving grace is a free gift of God (Romans 5:15; Titus 3:7).

   - Grace can abound, or be diminished (Romans 5:20).

   - There is the reign, or ruling principle of grace under the New Testament economy (Romans 5:20).

   - Grace can be abused (Romans 6:1).

   - The election to salvation is based upon the principle of grace (Romans 11:5).

   - Paul never ceased to marvel that he was the object of God's redeeming grace (Romans 12:3; 12:6; 15:15; 1 Corinthians 15:10; Galatians 1:15).

- The grace we receive from God should be desired for others (1 Corinthians 1:3; 2 Corinthians 1:2).

- In times of personal tribulation, God's grace is sufficient (2 Corinthians 12:9).

- It is possible to fall from the sphere of grace if dependency is made upon salvation by good works, or if there is excessive sin in the life, which testifies to a lack of genuine conversion (2 Corinthians 5:17; Galatians 5:4; Jude 1:4).

- Praise should be offered to God for His great grace (Ephesians 1:6; Colossians 3:16).

- Gracious words should characterize the speech of a Christian (Colossians 4:6).

- There is a throne of grace before which the Christian is to pray (Hebrews 4:16).

- More grace is given to the humble (James 4:6).

- Christians are to grow in the sphere of grace (2 Peter 3:18).

Establishing the Law: Romans 3:31

Having concluded that a person is justified by faith without the deeds of the Law (Romans 3:28), the question arises whether the Law has been made void. Does faith abolish, or destroy the Law? Does faith make the Law ineffectual? A patriotic Jew would want to know, for several reasons.

- **Economical**. A tremendous amount of money was associated with organized religion. Animals were bought and sold for sacrifices. The Temple had to be kept up and repaired. The priests had their livelihood associated with the rituals of the Temple. All of this could be destroyed.

- **Social.** Religion has always held societies together. Every warlord has realized that by destroying the faith of a people, they are more easily conquered. The first action the Communists take when they come to power is to attack the Church, and persecute the Christians. They do not want a rival God.

- **Traditional.** Great comfort is associated with traditional ceremonies. They do not, and should not disappear too easily.

- **Theological.** The Jewish people were taught that eternal life and fellowship with God were based upon a strict keeping of the Law. They really believed that if they did certain things they would live. Therefore, the Jews did not want Paul teaching that the Law was meaningless or somehow void, after all of these centuries. And on this point the Apostle is in agreement. *"God forbid such a thought!"* says Paul. *"May it not be considered!"*

Paul is very emotional about this matter. He loves the Law. He respects the Law. He has studied the Law at the feet of one of the greatest Rabbis of the Jewish world. Paul has been zealous to keep the Law. Paul has a very high regard for the Law. He does not hold it in contempt. He does not diminish its value. Rather, Paul believes that the gospel of faith establishes the Law. The gospel causes the Law to stand, for the Law is established in several ways.

First, the Law is established as an expression of the holiness of God. Without the Law, we could never fully appreciate the holiness of God. In page after page, and in story after story in the Scriptures, noble principles are set forth of honesty, integrity, justice, truth, purity, virtue, equity, and loyalty, and separation from sin.

In Genesis 6 we read of the wickedness of mankind. Evil had become so bad that it was said that the imaginations of the hearts of men were only evil continually. While God knew about the thoughts of men, He himself was without sin. He was, and is, beyond sin. He was, and is, altogether holy and lovely. No wonder the seraph veil their faces as they fly crying, *"Holy! Holy! Holy! is the Lord of hosts"* (Isaiah 6:3).

As the Law reveals the holiness of God and the un-holiness of man, so it establishes His righteousness. Sometimes God is accused of being unrighteous, unfair, and unjust. Men get angry with God for creating the universe the way He has, and for allowing sin to mar His creation. Whenever we see a loved one suffering, or whenever we see little children crippled and crushed for no apparent reason, the heart is tempted to cry out against God. But then we read the Bible and are reminded that God can do no wrong. God is not the agent of or the actor of evil. Sin is the culprit. If angels and men chose to be unrighteous and sinful, then they must pay the penalty without shifting blame upon God.

God has always done what is right to His creation and for His creation. And beyond that, He has found a way to reverse the power and pollution of sin so that individuals can one day enjoy His presence with joy and peace. One day there will be no more sorrow and no more sin. One day there will be a new heaven and a new earth. One day there will be no more disease or death. Until that day comes, God is still righteous to judge those who break His Law. He is also free to deal with individuals in holiness according to His righteousness. Not only does the Law establish the holiness and righteousness of God; the Law is the revelation of the sinfulness of man. In Exodus 20, Ten Commandments are given. The Lord in two commandments has summed up these Ten Commandments, *"Thou shalt love the Lord thy God with all thy heart, and with all thy soul, and with all thy mind. This is the first and great commandment"* (Matthew 22:37, 38).

But who has ever loved the Lord in such a manner? Who is willing to stand and to say, *"I have loved the Lord my God with all my heart, and with all my soul, and with all my mind. This is the first and great commandment"*. No sane person would ever make such a boast. Why? Because we know the moral code of God. The Law has established sinfulness. By the Law is the knowledge of sin. The Law is well established when men concede their sinfulness. Furthermore, the Law is fully established when the verdict it demands is executed.

For example, in the desert one day a man was found gathering up sticks to make a fire on the Sabbath day. Now the Law had said, *"Ye shall kindle no fire throughout your habitations on the Sabbath day."* How then was this Law to be established? By letting the Lawbreaker off? No. By securing his promise to keep the Law in the future? No. By finding someone who had kept this commandment and letting his obedience be reckoned to the Lawbreaker? No.

How then was the Law established? The Bible tells the answer. All Israel was commanded by the Lord to stone the man to death. We read, *"And they that found him gathering sticks brought him unto Moses and Aaron, and unto all the congregation, And they put him in ward, because it had not been declared what should be done to him. And Jehovah said unto Moses, The man shall surely be put to death: all the congregation shall stone him with stones without the camp. And all the congregation brought him without the camp, and stoned him to death with stones; as Jehovah commanded Moses"* (Numbers 15:33).

In this way, and only in this way, was the commandment of the Lord established by the execution of the penalty. As soon as the Law is executed, and the penalty for sin is applied then the Law is established; truth has prevailed, and justice has been made triumphant.

Now listen to the good news of the gospel. At Calvary, in the Person of Christ, the Law was fully satisfied. At Calvary, truth prevailed. At Calvary, justice was made triumphant. At Calvary, the Law was established. But then something else happened, for as soon as the Law was satisfied, grace and mercy was free to flow. God could now righteously save sinners. How? By attributing the work of Jesus to their account. This great transaction was accomplished, by faith.

So then, faith does not void the Law; it establishes it. Faith says that the Law is holy, just, and good. Faith acknowledges that the Law is right to condemn sin and sinners. Faith declares that the Law is righteous, to demand death for the soul that sins. Faith concedes that the Law should be kept. But faith also says that Christ did keep the Law. Faith says that Christ, being made under the Law, judged it. And though the Law could not find Him guilty of sin, the Law accepted the guilt of others placed on Him, so that when He died, they died.

When Jesus was executed, it was as if those who are in Him were executed. When Jesus bore the sins of His people, under the Law, it was as if they were there. All of this was in accordance with prophecy and divine design, for in the New Testament, Christ announced that He came to give His life a ransom for many (Matthew 28:28; Mark 10:45). Because of these things, there was no need for Paul to ever preach that the Law was ineffectual, outdated, or made null and void. However, he was accused of this. In Acts 21:28, a Jewish mob in the temple in Jerusalem cried out, *"Men of Israel, help! This is the man that teacheth all men everywhere against the people, and the Law, and this place: and further brought Greeks also into the temple, and hath polluted this holy place."* But Paul never did say what he was accused of saying. In reality it was his accusers who had disestablished the Law. It was his false accusers who had made the Law ineffectual through sin, specifically, the sin of hypocrisy. The Jews of Jerusalem pretended to be keepers of the Law.

Yet, there they were, willing to spill innocent blood. Here they were, full of murder and malice, hatred and hostility. The Jew had no real regard for the Law except as a club to kill Paul. The same thing is happening today. There are those who have no respect for the Law, or for its meaning. There are those who believe that all men have a spark of the divine within them. Individuals talk about the natural good that is in a man with the result being that they have no use for the condemnation of the Law, the penalty it demands, or the atonement which satisfies it. Many years ago, an Englishman who is now dead published a book, *The Faith of a Quaker* (John W. Graham, MA, Principal of Dalton Hall, University of Manchester).

A bitter enemy of the atonement he wrote these words. *"The evangelical doctrine of Atonement, as I am using the word historically, ascribed the salvation of mankind here and hereafter to their annexing for themselves, even while yet sinful, the infinite merits of the crucified Redeemer, whose shed blood was regarded as the equivalent in the Divine sight for the sins of the world. This doctrine most people now find incredible, unspiritual, and even immoral."*

If some people find the doctrine of the atonement immoral, others do not. Christians believe that the atonement establishes the Law. The atonement is the greatest demonstration of the justice and the righteousness of God. Because of Calvary, souls can be saved and sinners can be declared righteous. Because of Calvary, love is free to be demonstrated toward men. In concluding the study of this section of Romans, consider some practical points of application.

- **The Law is to be loved**. The Law refers to the Old Testament in general, which includes the moral, social, and ceremonial codices.

- **The Law is to be studied**. All Scripture is profitable.

- **The Law is to be kept**, first, in the Person of Christ, and then in the power of the indwelling Holy Spirit. While the ceremonial parts of the Law have ended, the moral part has not. The Moral Law is repeated in the New Testament and amplified. The Christian is not to be lawless. He is to operate under a higher Law, the Law of the life of the Spirit in Christ Jesus. We are able to keep the letter of the Law and the spirit of the Law in as far as we are absolutely surrendered to the Spirit.

4

Romans 4

The Faith of Father Abraham: Romans 4:1-5

There are three key words being considered by the Apostle Paul: faith, works, and Law. These three words are the focus of two great ideas that are in conflict, as one central question is considered. The main issue is this: *"How is a person justified in the sight of God? How does anyone become righteous after sin?"* There are only two possibilities. Either a person is justified in the sight of God by works, or a person is justified according to faith. The Jews, in Paul's generation, believed that if they only kept the Law, they would ultimately be acceptable to God. The Law was studied and analyzed. Elaborate rituals and rigid rules were established. Religious experts got up early and stayed up late studying the Scriptures to try to determine exactly what the oracles of God meant and how they were to be applied to daily life. Eternal salvation was worth the effort. Conscientious Jews wanted to obey the Law. Men and women wanted to be saved. Every effort was made to keep the Law as best as possible.

Paul was one of those people who believed that if he prayed, and fasted, and celebrated the Feasts, he would be saved. He would earn salvation by good works. Paul once believed that if he loved the Law, and literally killed or opposed all that deviated from the Law, he would be saved. If ever a person were to be found worthy of salvation, it would be Paul. But then one day Paul had his spiritual eyes of understanding opened for he saw the resurrected Christ. Suddenly, Paul understood. The Law could not save. The Law was never designed to save. The Law was simply a schoolmaster to bring individuals to Christ. Jesus saves! Jesus is the Lamb of God who taketh away the sins of the world. Jesus is the Promised Messiah of the Scriptures. Christ is to be the object of love and devotion, for this is the work of God: that men believe on Him whom the Father has sent (John 6:29). Salvation does not consist in good works of the flesh, but the one good work of the spirit, that is to believe in Christ.

During his ministry, Dr. Donald Grey Barnhouse was witnessing to a man. He tried many arguments and many illustrations, but the man could not comprehend spiritual truths. Finally, in desperation, the man cried out, *"Dr. Barnhouse what does God want me to do? What is it that God wants?"* And Dr. Barnhouse, led by the Holy Spirit was able to answer, *"God wants to be believed."* God waits for people to believe that He loves them and that He has provided a way of salvation that is based upon free grace, apart from the will and works of man. God wants individuals to have a personal relationship with Him through faith. Jesus said, *"Verily, verily, I say unto you, He that heareth my word, and believeth on Him that sent me, hath everlasting life, and shall not come into condemnation; but is passed from death unto life."* (John 5:24) *"And this is eternal life, that they might know thee the only true God, and Jesus Christ, whom thou hast sent"* (John 17:3).

It took a miracle for Paul to realize that Moses never gave anyone eternal life. Moses never gave anyone spiritual bread from heaven that would sustain them spiritually. But the Father has given to the world the true Bread from heaven, in the Person of His Son, Jesus Christ (John 6:32). What Moses did give was death for by the Law is the knowledge of sin. With the knowledge of sin comes conviction, and condemnation, leading to a just execution. The Law slays.

These are the things Paul came to understand, with the result being that he had a burning passion that others might also understand: salvation is by grace through faith alone. So while he was in prison, Paul picked up his pen to persuade other Jews and Gentiles to look to Christ and live. This would not be easy because many centuries of teaching a system of salvation by works had become entrenched in the lives of the people of Palestine. In a thousand ways the conviction was confirmed that keeping the Law was the proper way to please God. A clever Jew would ask, *"Was not Abraham himself justified by works? Did he not hear the voice of God and obey Him by going to the land of Promise in Palestine? Does not the whole life of Abraham prove that his good works made him acceptable to God?"* That Abraham lived a good life is without question. All Jews would concede that he obeyed God, following his own conversion from idolatry. There is a wonderful Jewish legend associated with Abraham. It is said that he was an iconoclast.

This term is composed of two Greek words, *"eikon," "an image,"* and *"klaein," "to break."* Abraham was an idol smasher! The story is told that one day, Abraham's father, Terah, had to leave on a trip and left Abraham in charge of the family business of making idols for the people in Ur of the Chaldees. In Terah's absence, Abraham broke all the idols except one. By this remaining idol, he placed a large club. When Terah returned home, he was shocked at the sight that he saw. All the idols were broken. Once valuable statues lay in ruins. Terah asked Abraham what had happened. Abraham answered that the idol with the club rose up one night and broke all the other idols.

This seemed a very unlikely story, and Terah cried out, *"Abraham, what are you talking about? What kind of a story are you telling me?"* In the asking of the question, the answer was given. No idol can destroy another idol. And only the Living God can move men to forsake what is foolish. Now, asks Paul, in the forsaking of his idols, in the movement from Ur, in the crossing of the Euphrates River in search of a new land, in the offering up of his son Isaac as a sacrifice to the Lord, was Abraham justified by his works?

The answer is, *"No!"* and for this reason: If his works justified Abraham, then he had a basis on which to glory. For time and eternity Abraham could boast by saying, *"I was an old man but I found God. I was a devil worshipper, but I got tired of that and decided to destroy all the idols. I was wise. I was wiser than other people. And I was more brave than they, for I took my family into a foreign country, etc."*

If his works justified Abraham, then he would have room for boasting, but not before God. God does not consider men doing right to be anything more than their duty to their Creator. God is not impressed with good deeds that are done by sinners so that self can boast. But God will honor faith. *"What saith the Scriptures? Abraham believed God, and it was accounted to Him for righteousness"* (Romans 4:3).

Doctrine of Belief

1. A main Greek word for belief is *"pisteuo"* which means, *"to have faith"* (in, upon, or with respect to a person or thing). By implication the word also means, *"to entrust"* (especially with one's spiritual well being).

2. A main Hebrew word for belief is *"aman"* (awman) which means, *"to build up or support, to foster"* (as a parent or nurse will help a little child or a patient). Figuratively the word means, *"to render"* (or be) firm or faithful. It means, *"to trust or believe"*; to be permanent or quiet; morally to be true or certain.

3. Belief is foundational to any relationship. When Moses was told to go to the people of Israel and speak as one sent from God, he was afraid that he would not be believed (Exodus 4:1).

4. To confirm that Moses had received his commission from God and to cause people to believe his words, the Lord gave to Moses three signs of confirmation: a staff that could turn into a snake; a hand that would turn leprous; and the ability to turn water into blood (Exodus 4:5; 4:8–9).

5. The Lord promised to appear to Moses in a special way so that the children of Israel would overhear and believe in Moses forever (Exodus 19:9).

6. God was provoked to anger with the children of Israel, and wondered how long it would be before they believed in Him, despite all the signs and wonders He had performed in their midst (Numbers 14:11).

7. Prior to his death, Moses reminded the children of Israel of their unbelief (Deuteronomy 1:32).

8. During the days of Ahaz, king of Judah, the prophets of God charged the nation with failure to believe in the Lord their God (2 Kings 17:14).

9. In the desert of Tekoa, the 35-year-old King Jehoshaphat (c. 875-850 BC) stood to exhort Judah to believe in the Lord God, in order for the nation to survive (2 Chronicles 20:20).

10. It is hard for people who are suffering to believe in God (Job 9:16).

11. Some people are not worthy of being believed (Proverbs 26:25).

12. God wants people to believe some specific things.

    - That He exists (Hebrews 11:6).

    - That there are no Gods beside Himself (Isaiah 43:10; Jeremiah 12:6; James 2:19).

    - That His power is great (Habakkuk 1:5).

    - That He loves us (1 John 4:16)

13. Jesus Christ wants people to believe some specific things.

    - That He has power to heal the sick (Matthew 9:28; Mark 5:36; 9:23).

    - That children believe in Him (Matthew 18:6; Mark 9:42).

    - The gospel (Mark 1:15).

    - That there is power in prayer (Mark 11:23; 11:24).

    - That He alone is the way of salvation (John 1:7; 1:12).

    - That Jerusalem would one day be destroyed (John 4:21).

    - That God sent Him into the world (John 6:29; 11:42).

- That people will perish who do not receive Him (John 8:24).

14. Two specific entities Christ does not want people to believe: false prophets (Matthew 24:23, 26; Mark 13:21) and every spirit (1 John 4:1).

15. Sometimes God will not give individuals the power to believe (Luke 8:12).

14. Belief which is not rooted in God can vanish from the heart (Luke 8:13).

15. The heart of man, by nature, does not believe spiritual truths concerning sin, salvation, and the Savior (Luke 22:67; 24:25; John 3:12; 4:48; 5:38; 5:44; 5:47; 6:64; 7:5; 9:18).

16. The heart of man, by nature, cannot believe (John 10:26; 12:39).

17. Sin keeps men from believing in Christ (John 16:9).

18. Wonderful things happen to those who believe.

    - Individuals are justified in the sight of God (Genesis 15:6; Romans 4:13).

    - Individuals are saved (Acts 16:31; Romans 1:16; 10:9; 1 John 5:1). There are remission of sins (Acts 10:43) and the privilege of baptism (Acts 8:37).

    - There is divine protection from harm's way (Acts 27:25).

    - The righteousness of God is given (Romans 3:22).

    - The soul receives eternal life (John 3:36; Romans 4:24; 6:8; 1 Timothy 1:16).

    - There is divine power imparted (John 12:44; Ephesians 1:19).

- There is the hope of a future resurrection (John 11:2526; 1 Thessalonians 4:14).

- There is joy and peace (Rom 15:13; 1 John 5:13).

- There is a rest to enter into (Hebrews 3:18).

- There is some knowledge of divine love (1 John 4:16).

- Signs and wonders may follow those who believe (Mark 16:17).

- Confidence of salvation (1 Timothy 1:12).

- No more shame (Romans 10:11; 1 Peter 2:6).

- A distinction between the saved and the lost (2 Corinthians 6:15).

- New confidence in God (1 Corinthians 13:7).

- The right to be identified with other believers in the Church (Acts 3:32; 5:14; 1 Timothy 4:12).

- The gift of the Holy Spirit (Acts 19:2).

- The privilege of leading others to Christ (Acts 18:8).

- The deliverance of a nation from destruction (Jonah 3:5).

19. Terrible futures await those who do not believe God, Christ, or the gospel.

- a certain and fearful damnation (2 Thessalonians 2:12).

- a just condemnation (John 3:18; 12:44).

- no eternal life (John 3:36).

- a possible premature death (Hebrews 11:31; Jude 1:5).

- The heart of the unbeliever will be susceptible to the lies of Satan (2 Thessalonians 2:11).

- It will be blinded to the truth (2 Corinthians 4:4).

The Delight of David: Romans 4:6-8

Having proved that Abraham was justified by faith, the Apostle Paul appeals to another important Jewish figure to teach the doctrine of salvation by grace apart from works. The personage Paul chooses to use is David, the greatest king in Israel's history. After examining the writings of David to discover how he thought, Paul reminds his audience that the Sweet Singer of Israel described the man with whom the Lord is pleased. David wrote of the blessed man unto whom God credits righteousness apart from works. Such a person is spoken of in Psalms 32:1, *"Blessed are they whose iniquities are forgiven, and whose sins are covered."*

The person whose iniquities are not forgiven is not blessed. The person whose sins are not covered is not blessed. Nor can such a person be truly happy, for sin places a heavy burden upon the soul. Sin robs the mind of fellowship with God and peace with mankind. When Adam and Eve sinned, their fellowship with God was broken and their marital harmony was destroyed. Adam and Eve turned on one another rather than accept personal blame and responsibility and seek God's forgiveness. Every descendent of Adam and Eve knows the agony of sin in the hour of accountability. When the spotlight of righteousness shines upon the soul, sin is no longer something to be desired. There is shame.

A holy God has been offended. A righteous God has been wounded. The Law of God has been transgressed. The happiness of the heart, based upon the principle of obedience has been lost. What is a person to do? Can future good works atone for the sins of the soul? As David considered his options, he realized how futile they all were in trying to regain righteousness. Can David offer sacrifices? Yes, but the whole concept of an animal dying, as a substitute for the sins of a human does not seem adequate. Man is guilty, and an innocent animal dies to atone for the sin.

Can David offer restitution? Yes, but restitution can never replace the original. A reproduction is never as valuable as the original work of the artist. A person may replace stolen money they steal, but basic honesty and integrity are lost. A husband may do many nice things for the wife he has cheated on, or abused, but all the acts of repentance and restitution can never replace the original trust and love that were once in place. Can David offer prayers of praise and worship God? Yes, but worship is a mockery to God unless there is a basis for fellowship. Giving glory to God, while offending Him at the same time, only compounds the ugliness of the situation. Now if sacrifices and acts of restitution and renewed efforts at worship do not bring a person into a state of blessedness, what will?

The Biblical answer is discovered in the concept of divine forgiveness. Blessed are they whose iniquities are forgiven. But who can forgive sins? Man cannot forgive himself. Man can do many things with himself and his sin. He can pretend that he has not done anything wrong. A lot of people have convinced themselves that they are innocent, by declaring that their motives were pure, or that there is no Law against their behavior. So good motives, and no compelling legal authority to condemn an act, justifies certain things. People say, *"I have done no wrong."*

Another way men handle sin is to simply defy righteousness, and accountability, and to say, *"So what?"* On the throne of Israel sat a king named Ahab. He was married to a clever woman named Jezebel. One day Ahab looked out his palace window and saw a vineyard. It belonged to a man named Naboth. So what? The king wanted it for himself. He told his wife, Jezebel. She knew that the Law of God stipulated that land inherited could not be sold. So what? Jezebel will take by force what she desired. The death warrant of Naboth was signed. Soon he was killed. The land became the property of the king. How did this outrageous event happen? It happened because Ahab and Jezebel defied the objective standard of righteousness, knowing full well that what they had done was wrong. In contrast to Ahab and Jezebel, there are people whose hearts are not hardened. They look at the Law of God, which has been violated, and tremble, knowing that it is a terrible thing to fall into the hands of the living God. But what shall be done with sin? What shall be done with the sensitive heart that has sinned? What shall David do?

Though David dealt in deceit with Uriah the Hittite, his heart could not maintain that level of activity. Though David was cold-blooded enough to send a loyal soldier to a deliberate death, his heart was not so hardened that it could not be broken by a simple story of an injustice being done. The prophet Nathan told the simple story. He stood before the king of Israel to remind him that there was a God in heaven who had seen what he had done. *"Stand up, David! Stand up! You are guilty of great sin. David, you are the man who has unlawfully desired another man's wife. David, you are the man who has committed adultery. David, you are the man who has tried to cover up his crime. David, you are a man with blood stained hands."*

As Nathan speaks, the heart of David begins to break. Pressing on God's videotape, we witness the following scene. We hear David speak. We listen as he confesses, *"I am the man. I have sinned against the Lord"* (1 Samuel 12:13). When God heard that honest confession, He had to make a decision. Would He make David pay for his sins? Was there a way to show mercy? The answer is that Divine omniscience, motivated by love, found a way to satisfy justice and extend grace.

There would be a Substitute who would bear the penalty of sin. This Substitute would not be an animal or a mere man but the Son of the Living God. He would die the death of the wicked. He would die for David's sins. With spiritual insight, David foresaw the Suffering Messiah. He believed that Christ would make atonement for His sins. The gracious provision of God was accepted by faith. The iniquities of David were forgiven. The blood of Christ covered the sins of David. They were not covered up by deceit. The Lord of Grace and Glory would not impute or charge sin to David's account. Nathan said it plainly, *"The Lord also hath put away thy sin; thou shalt not die."*

In all of this, it must be remembered, that God did not put away David's sin in an arbitrary way. The basis for God's decision was the righteousness of Christ imputed to David's account. David could adequately describe the blessedness of a man divinely forgiven, because he was such a man. He wrote of his own spiritual experience with the Living Lord.

Doctrine of Imputation

1. The word *imputation* refers to the act of setting to someone's account or reckoning something to another person.

2. In Romans 4:3 we read that Abraham believed God, and it was counted unto him for righteousness (Genesis 15:6). This means that God accepted Abraham because he trusted in the Lord rather than trusting in something that he could do.

3. Appealing to Psalms 32:13, Paul argues that only God can forgive sin. Those who are forgiven are not regarded as wicked any longer since the Lord does not impute, or charge them with iniquity. Instead, they are considered, or reckoned to be children of God (Romans 4:7 8, 11, and 23-24).

4. The imputation of divine righteousness to sinners lies at the heart of the Biblical doctrine of salvation.

5. The imputed righteousness is seen by God in all those who are in Christ, for it is His righteousness that allowed Him to purchase redemption.

6. God grants righteousness to those who have faith in Christ (Romans 1:17; 3:21-26; 10:3; 2 Corinthians 5:21; Philippians 3:9).

7. Not only is the imputation of God's righteousness to the believer taught in Scripture, but also taught is the concept that the sin of Adam has been imputed to all mankind (Romans5: 12-21; 1 Corinthians 15:21-22).

8. While all of humanity has been judged guilty as a whole race, each person has acted out his or her guilt so that no one is with excuse.

9. Because of the severity of the penalty of the guilty, it is impossible for individuals to be righteous in the sight of God apart from the gift of righteousness graciously granted by a merciful God.

10. This gift of righteousness is provided in Christ through the instrument of faith.

God Saves Sinners: Romans 4:9-11

The Apostle Paul continues to develop his thoughts about the origin of salvation in Romans 4:9. Paul is arguing that salvation is by grace through faith alone. Salvation is not conditioned according to human work, for man can never merit the merits of God. The life of Abraham and the life of David illustrate the concept of salvation apart from good works. Paul points out that David described the blessed man as one to whom the Lord does not impute sin.

That God has every right to charge all men with sin is without controversy. That God does not charge some men with sin is the testimony of time. If such grace were not shown to individuals no one would ever have fellowship with God. But on what basis does the Lord not impute sin to sinners? That is the great question of discussion.

How does this particular act of Divine grace come to individuals? Does saving grace come upon those who have received the sign of the covenant in their bodies? Does saving grace come upon the circumcision, or does grace also come to the uncircumcised (Romans 4:9)?

We would ask the question a little differently today. We would ask, *"Does the blessing of forgiveness of sins come only upon those who have been baptized?"* Or, *"Does Divine grace also come to the un-baptized as well?"* For a conscientious Jew, the life of Abraham offered the pattern. Looking to Abraham, the answer to the great question is that salvation does not come because of circumcision. One can almost hear the orthodox Jew take a deep breath in shock. But Paul is right. When Abraham first heard the word of the Lord, he was an uncircumcised devil worshipper. Yet he had faith, and it was faith that was accounted to Abraham for righteousness.

God came to Abraham when he was uncircumcised just as God comes to many today who have never been baptized. God reveals Himself to people apart from human merit, and apart from acts of Divine obedience. Because he was righteous, Abraham submitted to the ritual of circumcision just as professing believers submit to the ordinance of baptism in obedience to faith. By receiving the sign of circumcision after believing in God, Abraham became the father, or the pattern, of all that believe regardless of the act of circumcision. This means that even Gentiles, who have not done the good deed of being circumcised, can still be converted.

With these simple words, the Apostle Paul created a firestorm that has raged to the present day. For many Jews, circumcision had become a synonym for salvation. Today, baptism creates the same effect. The emotion that Paul generated came because he was asking people to look at salvation in a different way. It was not a new way historically, but it was a new way theologically. To draw a modern parallel, consider the impact upon people when they are told that the will is not free but is subject to the Sovereign of the Universe. In many places an argument immediately arises.

Consider how emotional some people become when cherished concepts are challenged, such as the autonomy of human decisions in light of Divine election. Look at the anger that is generated when the thought is set forth that the great tribulation of Matthew 24, Mark 13, and Luke 21 is a historical reality. Many issues can still create tremendous controversy among orthodox Christians when certain fundamental presuppositions are challenged. One of the great ironies in such discussions is that what are believed to be orthodox presuppositions are wrong.

The pre-suppositional thoughts are embraced as ultimate truth despite the fact that they are not rooted in spiritual logic or Church history. It is to logic, and to Church history, that Paul appeals for his illustration of salvation by grace through faith alone.

At one time, Paul was just as illogical and uninformed as his countrymen. He was called Saul of Tarsus then. Saul of Tarsus was among those who would have killed a teacher who insisted that the act of circumcision was not part of the process of salvation. How dare someone teach something that all the Rabbis and all the families of all the tribes of Israel believed and practiced! Paul knew what he was doing when he said that Abraham received the sign of circumcision as a seal of the righteousness of faith. Paul knew that he was challenging established beliefs and thinking. But Paul was willing to risk his life and his reputation for the sake of gospel truth. And the truth is that the sign of faith is not the same thing as saving faith. The seal of salvation is not the substance of salvation.

Salvation is by grace apart from human works of goodness. Salvation is a sovereign act of God whereby He does not charge man with sin. Salvation is God's imputing the righteousness of Christ to sinful men. Perhaps Paul's voice trembled a little as he spoke these words to the scribe who was writing this letter. In his imagination, Paul saw it all clearly: God Saves Sinners. R.K. McGregor Wright in his excellent work, *No Place for Sovereignty*, places great stress upon those three simple words.

- **God.** God, sovereign in eternity, wills or decrees (that is, He plans, intends, decides, and foreordains) to save some of those who are to be enslaved by sin through the fall of Adam. This means that it is God who initiates the program and process of salvation, rather than the sinner. Salvation is therefore by grace alone, since the sinner, being finite, does not have the ontological standpoint in eternity even to plan saving acts, let alone the sovereign power to affect them. On His own divine initiative from eternity, God interferes in history to initiate and consummate all that is necessary to save rebel souls. Salvation is a gift, and the sinner contributes nothing but the empty hand that reaches out to receive it.

Even this simple act of faith itself is by divine initiation, not by autonomous self-generation. Saving faith is itself a gift, not a natural capacity by which we simple decide to focus on Christ as an object of trust like we do with other objects (e.g., a chair, our parents, and the telephone). From the first feeble stirrings of a desire to know God in some vague sense, through all the steps necessary to link a soul savingly to God through Christ, and all the way to our final glorification in the presence of the Father, *all is of grace*. Salvation is of the Lord! (John 2:9)

- **God saves.** God does not merely do enough to make salvation possible, leaving it to us to work our way up, to *"merit the merits of Christ,"* to do our part to make the merely possible become the actual. Every link in the chain of redemption is forged on God's anvil from start to finish. Even God cannot achieve an end without a means. In order to secure the predestined end, he foreordains each step and causal link, sovereignly acting to see that each cause and effect occurs. God had to move the entire Roman military bureaucracy several years earlier to make certain that at the end of the Empire wide census, one particular pregnant girl was in the right town at the right moment just so the Messiah would be born in Bethlehem and not up north in Nazareth!

The entire Roman bureaucracy was predestined to keep in step with the body chemistry of one unknown Jewish girl in the far outer reaches of the first century Roman Empire.

As far as the atonement is concerned, in dying on the cross as our great High Priest, Jesus actually achieved and secured on our behalf the salvation of every one of His sheep, of every one of those that the Father had given Him out of the world, of all those upon whom He had set His electing love from before the foundation of the world. He had to secure every step in the process, every microscopic means, however detailed, to secure the end result intended. Nothing could be left to chance. There could be no chance in a created cosmos consequently none of His promises could fail (Joshua 23:14).

- **God saves sinners.** Sinners are rebels, averse to all good. They are slaves to sin, with darkened minds and unclean consciences, suppressing one part of the truth by the selective use of other parts, by playing off one truth of God against another. In short, sinners are practicing unrighteousness. And yet, in matchless marvelous grace, God saves sinners.

Doctrine of Circumcision

1. In Genesis 17:11 God established the ritual of male circumcision with Abraham as a sign of the covenant relationship.

2. Circumcision was to take place for all males on the eighth day after birth (Genesis 17:12).

3. Abraham was to circumcise his own children and descendants, any purchased slaves, and any proselytes.

4. The uncircumcised were to be considered as being *cut off* from the covenant of spiritual blessings.

5. Provisions were made for all that wanted to be part of a covenant relationship with God in that the poor and those outside the racial distinctive could be included. However, God had to be met according to His terms, and His terms included blood, suffering, humility, and a sacrifice of self.

6. In the Old Testament, the circumcision of the body was symbolic of the need for a spiritual circumcision of the heart (Deuteronomy 10:16; 30:6). The image is that the heart has become surrounded with the disease called sin. As a surgeon must cut away fatty tissue, or unnatural growth, so the heart must be spiritually circumcised. In particular, greed must be cut away; idolatry must be cut away; anger must be cut away, and hatred must be cut away.

7. The physical tool used to circumcise the body, is a sharp knife. The spiritual tool used to circumcise the heart, is the Word of God (Hebrews 4:12). *'For the Word of God is quick [alive] and*

powerful, and sharper than any two-edged sword, piercing even to the dividing asunder of the soul and spirit, and of the joints and marrow, and is a discerner of the thoughts and intents of the heart."

8. While human responsibility is involved (Jeremiah 4:4) the spiritual circumcising of the heart requires a Divine ability. God must circumcise the heart (Deuteronomy 30:6).

9. When the Lord circumcises the heart of His elect people, there will flow a natural love for God, and new spiritual life (Deuteronomy 30:6).

10. God never intended for man to forget that the physical act of circumcision was only a ritual to represent the spiritual circumcision of the heart.

11. The obedience of Abraham (Genesis 17:11), Moses (Exodus 4:25), and Joshua (Joshua 5:2, 4) to perform the bloody ritual of physical circumcision, reflected a spiritual heart of obedience, love, and devotion.

12. With the passing of time, people paid less attention to the spiritual dimensions of the act of circumcision and gloried only in the physical mark, which led Paul to argue against placing confidence in the flesh (Philippians 3:19).

13. In John 7:22 Jesus argued from the act of physical circumcision that it was right to perform miracles on the Sabbath. The point the Lord made was simple and powerful. If the Law allowed the cutting of the flesh on the Sabbath to symbolize the keeping of the covenant and minister to the soul, why should anyone become angry when someone was healed or made whole on the Sabbath?

14. With the resurrection of Christ, the ceremonial ritual of circumcision could be abolished, and emphasis focused exclusively upon the circumcision of the heart. Not everyone understood the transition that had taken place from the physical to the spiritual (Acts 15:5). Even the apostle Paul found the

transition from law to grace difficult, reflected in the fact that Timothy was circumcised while under his guidance. (Acts 16:1-3).

15. As Paul ministered more and more to the Gentiles, as the apostle understood the gospel more clearly, circumcision of the flesh gave way to the true spiritual circumcision of the heart whereby Paul affirmed that the Church consists of those who are of the true circumcision (Acts 21:21). We are the circumcision, which worship God in the spirit, and rejoice in Christ Jesus, and have no confidence in the flesh (Philippians 3:3).

16. In summary, circumcision is personal, it is not the basis of salvation, is an outward sign of an inward salvation, and it is a seal of the righteousness of faith.

In the Steps of Abraham: Romans 4:12

The Apostle Paul has latched onto a particular theological point like a hungry lion with a fresh kill. He will not let it go. As a skilled surgeon will cut away layer upon layer of fatty tissue to get to a vital organ, so Paul will cut away excessive thoughts until he gets to the vital truth that salvation is by grace through faith alone.

Paul has much fatty theological tissue to penetrate because error upon error had grown around the story of Abraham until the greatness of what God did for him was lost. Men had begun to emphasize what Abraham had done to make himself a great man of faith. The deeds of Abraham were rooted in a historical reality. What Paul wanted to question was the understanding of that historical reality. It was true that Abraham had been circumcised. It was true that Abraham had left the land of Ur. It was true that Abraham had begun to offer acceptable sacrifices to God. It was true that Abraham brought his family and servants into a covenant relationship with the Lord. It was true that Abraham moved to protect his property from thieves and robbers. It was true that Abraham rescued his nephew Lot from harm's way. It was true that Abraham did many good works and helped many people with the passing of time.

However, what was also true theologically is that none of these good works saved him. It is precisely that point that Paul is pressing home. Paul is arguing that even a lifetime of good deeds is meaningless in the sight of God apart from appropriate faith. What saith the Scripture? Abraham believed God, and it was accounted unto him for righteousness. A great chasm exists between good works as a result of proper faith and good works as a means of obtaining eternal life. While the distinction may not be clear or important to many, it is extremely important to God for He is a jealous God and will share His glory with no one.

The Lord God Almighty knows how easy it is for man's heart to be drawn away by false gods so that they do good deeds regardless of the proper object of faith. Consider the god of the Mormon. He is just an exalted man, yet many Mormons do good deeds for this false god. Why? Because they are not informed of the truth. Moreover, *"the god of this world"* has blinded their eyes so that they are not attracted to the true and only God of the Bible. We could take another example. The Hindu religion has many gods. As a deeply religious people, the Hindus perform many good works but they are not motivated by proper faith according to the Bible. Therefore, all of their religious deeds are unacceptable in the sight of the Lord.

Those who embrace the Jewish religion can say the same of the good deeds performed. They do many good works. They are zealous in their religion. They celebrate holy days and observe the Sabbath. They study the Scriptures. They say many prayers. They have a zeal for God, but it is not according to knowledge. Why? Because they have learned to worship a god called *"Good Works."* Historically, the most important expression of faith in this god of Good Works was the act of circumcision. At this point, the objection could be raised. Paul, how can circumcision be considered to be part of a false religion? Was not Abraham circumcised?

And the answer is this: *"Yes, Abraham was circumcised, but he was circumcised with the proper motive and understanding. Abraham did not receive the ritual of circumcision in order to be saved and to produce faith. He did not do this in order to merit favor with God. Abraham received the sign of circumcision as a seal of the righteousness of faith, which he already possessed. First he believed, and then he was circumcised."*

Here then is the Divine answer. Abraham never fell into the error of thinking that his works made him acceptable to God. And so by faith Abraham became the Father of the Circumcised who realize that salvation is by grace alone apart from works. The sign of the covenant was received because of the content of the heart that believed God. The critical point for Paul was when Abraham first believed in God. And the answer is that Abraham's faith was present while he was yet uncircumcised.

Those who have grown up in the Church and those who have reared their children in the Church can immediately see the spiritual implications that face those in the household of faith. There are great advantages to being in the sphere of faith but there are also great dangers. It is possible to repeat the errors of the Jews of old and come to believe that a life of religious activity, a life of good works, and a life of receiving the signs of salvation equals salvation apart from any true vital, living faith. Statistically, there are today a large number of people in the Church who have grown up with Bibles in their hand, prayers on their lips, and religious songs in their heads. But they have no real saving faith. They have yet to walk in the steps of Abraham. The forces of ritual and routine have carried them along, but they have not stepped out on their own. They have no personal relationship with the living God.

So what happens? Life goes along, taking the poor soul in one of two directions. One direction is marked Vanity Fair in the words of John Bunyan. In Vanity Fair are the bright lights and fast life of the world, the flesh, and the devil. Swiftly is the soul swept up with pleasures and passions. But soon the thrills become dull and routine. The heart opens itself up to every perversion and expression of depravity. The soul discovers pleasure in sin. The heart is open to experimentation with evil because the feet have never truly walked where Abraham walked, and that is in the paths of righteousness by faith.

Of course, there is another path that people may and do take other than the route marked *"Vanity Fair."* There are those who—for whatever reasons—are repulsed by gross sin and open immorality. They prefer to follow the road marked *"Destruction."* This road is chosen because the road sign is not believed. The path looks smooth; the lane is broad; and so many others are already, on the road. They have ignored the sign saying that it has no real meaning. It is just a marker and a clever word to start a conversation with. Surely, so many people on this broad road cannot be wrong. Just listen to the clever conversation. Bits and pieces of worldly wisdom can be overhead. Not all of it is uplifting, but it is loved. Listen as individuals say,

- *All roads lead to heaven.*

- *People are basically good.*

- *God is a merciful God; there is no hell.*

- *Love means never having to say you are sorry.*

- *I am a Christian. I was baptized as an infant.*

- *Of course I am going to heaven some day. I sang in the choir for thirty years. I was a Sunday school teacher for forty years.*

- *Every day and in every way I am getting better and better. I have great self-esteem now. Learning how to love myself has helped me a lot.*

Those who travel on this broad road marked *"Destruction"* engage in so many clever conversations and get involved in so many well-meaning activities that they are distracted. Like little children playing games on a nice playground, spiritual travelers are so intense they hardly notice that the light has faded and the road has declined steeply. Not until their feet slip out from under them and they start that long slide towards the gaping mouth of the open pit at the end of the road marked *"Destruction"* that they become alarmed. The mouth of hell has been enlarged with the passing of time, for more and more people are choosing to walk by sight and not by faith. They are willing to follow others who also ignore the warning signs and seek to prove that they have nothing to fear in the future no matter which road is traveled. And this happens because there is an unwillingness to walk in the steps of Abraham by faith.

It is only by the grace of God that some individuals who stand before the roads marked *"Vanity Fair"* or *"Destruction"* hesitate to begin life's journey. It is only by the grace of God that those who are on these roads realize that something is wrong and begin to turn back. They must turn around and they do. And in the turning, they discover Divine grace.

A third sign, which was not seen before, but it is clearly seen now, is marked *"The Narrow Way."* Something is different about this road. It seems to be much straighter. Not many people on it. Perhaps the few know something the many do not know. A mysterious imparted surge of faith suddenly moves the feet to step onto *"The Narrow Way,"* and the journey of a lifetime begins.

The journey seems a little frightening until the evidence appears that others have passed this way before. Telling signs and monuments mark important moments of historical people and places. The heart is glad to see these signs, for they tell a story. Men such as Abraham, Isaac, and Jacob have also walked this way. Peter and James and John have been here as well. The evidence abounds. And, oh, how wonderful it is to discover that one is walking in the steps of Abraham, after all. He is the Father of those who been circumcised. He is the Father of those who have not received the outward sign of the Old Covenant. For the promise, that he should be the heir of the world, was not to Abraham, or to his seed, through the Law, but through the righteousness of faith. The greatest act of self-evaluation that must be made is for the heart to determine if it has walked or is walking in the steps of Abraham. The steps of Abraham lead to a life of faith while the steps of the world, the flesh, and the devil lead to a lifetime of bondage and then ultimate damnation. Paul desperately wanted the people of Rome to walk in the steps of Abraham according to the faith that he had before he was circumcised, for that is the starting point. If the starting point is in error, then whatever happens afterwards is worthless.

This truth applies in the world of sports. A runner who moves out of the blocks too quickly, before the sound of the gun, is disqualified. It does not matter if he breaks all of the known racing records; he is still disqualified. In math, if even one number is miscalculated, then the whole answer is wrong. In spiritual matters the same principle applies. The starting point is significant. In God's economy, the starting place is faith. Without faith it is impossible to please God. The righteousness of faith is what God will honor, and that alone, for it is by grace through faith that the Lord is glorified, and man is humbled. Let us walk in the steps of Abraham, who walked by faith.

The World is Mine: Romans 4:13

In Romans 4:13, the Apostle Paul begins to take his logical argument a step further as he continues to prove that justification is by grace through faith alone. Paul has established that the blessings of God came to Abraham while he was yet uncircumcised. Before he had received the physical sign of the covenant, God blessed Abraham with the gift of faith. While he was still in the flesh, God revealed Himself to Abraham, justified him, declared him to be righteous, and then made specific promises to him. It was all of grace. Though Abraham had no Mosaic Law to live by, no ceremony of cleansing, and no sign in his body of a covenant relationship, the promises of God still came to him.

One promise in particular emphasized in Romans 4:13 is that Abraham should be the heir of the world. This concept of being heir to the world is a divine interpretation of the original promise. In Genesis 12:34 God had said that the families of the earth would be blessed. *"And I will bless them that bless thee, and make thy name great; and thou shalt be a blessing: And I will bless them that bless thee: and in thee shall all families of the earth be blessed."* Genesis 18 contains an amplification of the promise. The Bible says that God promised Abraham that he would be the source of blessing to the nations of the earth. *"And the LORD said, Shall I hide from Abraham that thing which I do; Seeing that Abraham shall surely become a great and mighty nation, and all the nations of the earth shall be blessed of him?"* (Genesis 18:17, 18)

In Romans 4:13, the discovery is made that the whole world will be blessed and that Abraham and his seed will be the heirs of the world! Here was a more precise thought for many. The plan of God was greater than the Jewish community imagined. God had determined to have many sons and daughters. God had made a promise not only with a man, but also with men. God had promised the seed of Abraham the world. But who is the seed of Abraham? The answer is twofold: First, all that have the faith that Abraham had may be considered to be his seed. Galatians 3:9 says, *"So then they which be of faith are blessed with faithful Abraham."*

Whether Jew or Gentile, all who have faith in God and in His Son will be blessed and made an heir of the world. Second, Christ is the seed of Abraham. Galatians 3:16. *"Now to Abraham and his seed were the promises made. He saith not, And to seeds, as of many; but as of one, And to thy seed, which is Christ."* As the seed of Abraham, and according to promise, Christ has already begun to inherit the earth. *"Ask of me, and I shall give thee the heathen for thine inheritance, and the uttermost parts of the earth for thy possession"* (Psalms 2:8).

"And Jesus came and spake unto them, saying, All power is given unto me in heaven and in earth. Go ye therefore, and teach all nations, baptizing them in the name of the Father, and of the Son, and of the Holy Ghost" (Matthew 28:18, 19).

Some are pessimistic about the future. The eye of fear looks upon the world's situation and sees nothing but chaos and darkness. Many people believe that the world is coming to an end. Even a Christian has been known to tell others that the world is such a bad place; children should not be brought into society. In contrast, the eye of faith laughs and says with Abraham and with Christ, *The world is mine.* This is to be understood in both a spiritual and literal sense.

Spiritually, there is a worldview that is distinct and belongs to the Christian. It is rooted in the belief that creation is not the product of time plus space plus chance. Creation is the act of a sovereign God. Though sin has darkened man's understanding, the day will come when the knowledge of the Lord shall cover the earth as the waters cover the seas. The Christian view will yet prevail against atheism, pantheism, and all the other false beliefs of the world. In addition, the Christian will possess the earth physically. Though this globe will one day be renovated by fire, in the new heaven and the new earth there will be righteousness as eternal life is enjoyed in glorified resurrected bodies. No eye has seen, no ear has heard, no tongue can tell what the future will be like, but it will be most glorious. The future belongs to those who are the heirs of salvation. The future belongs to the Christian. We can say with confidence, *"This world is mine."* Christ has purchased the future at Calvary. At the Cross, Christ became victorious over all the powers of sin.

Death is a power of sin. And Christ has conquered death (1 Cor 15). Judgment is a power of sin. And Christ has come to remove the judgment (Romans 8:1). Addiction is a power of sin. And Christ has come to set the captives free (Matthew 1). A wicked heart that deviseth wicked imaginations is a power of sin. Yet, if any man be in Christ he is a new creation (2 Corinthians 5:17). The way that Christ was able to win the strategic victory over sin at the Cross-came through the fact that He was judged. But how was that justified? Jesus had never done anything wrong. How could He be judged when He was never guilty of any transgression? The answer is this: Jesus was judged as a substitute; He took the place of others.

But then that raises another problem. In order for Jesus to be judged on behalf of others, He had to get to the place of judgment on a legal basis. Something had to happen, according to the Law of God, to make Jesus guilty of violating the Law so that a just judgment could take place. And something did happen. What transpired was this. Christ was made a curse by allowing Himself to be hung on a tree (Galatians 3:13). This is a legal point but very important in the Divine economy. Christ was Himself morally sinless but externally the Law found something to judge Him on, and that something was that He allowed Himself to be hung on a tree. The Bible says that, *"Christ hath redeemed us from the curse of the Law, being made a curse for us: for it is written, Cursed is every one that hangeth on a tree"* (Galatians 3:13).

The Law of God pronounced a curse upon one who died in a certain way as per Deuteronomy 21:22-23. *"And if a man have committed a sin worthy of death, and he be put to death, and thou hang him on a tree: His body shall not remain all night upon the tree, but thou shalt in any wise bury him that day; (for he that is hanged is accursed of God) that thy land be not defiled, which he Lord thy God giveth thee for an inheritance."* By being placed on a tree, Jesus became a technical violator of the Law. And it was upon this ground that God was able to justly judge Christ, allow Him to be a suitable substitute, and pour out the entire weight of His wrath upon His Son so that the sins of the elect were judged.

In this way it can be said that Christ was made sin for us (2 Corinthians 5:21). He did not sin, but He became sin in our place so that He might secure the redemption of many and make them heirs of the world. The salvation of souls is a reality only because of the fact that in matchless grace God the Father and God the Son found a plan of redemption. In eternity past, God the Father and God the Son entered into an agreement or a covenant relationship.

Writing in modern legal language, Dr. Donald Grey Barnhouse has suggested that the covenant or contract may have been along these lines:

"Whereas God alone is holy, and whereas there is no good in man that could ever satisfy God, it is now therefore divinely decreed that God the Father, hereinafter called the party of the first part, covenants and agrees with Abraham and Jesus Christ, hereinafter called joint parties of the second part, to redeem and to justify any member of the human race who will turn his faith, hope, and trust away from man or anything in man, and put that faith, hope, and trust in the Word of God about Jesus Christ, especially that Word concerning the person of Christ, that He is very God, and in the work of Christ, that He did by His death provide the perfect satisfaction which the justice of God was required to demand of all sinners. It is moreover decreed that nothing in this covenant and agreement shall be voided by any failure, positive or negative, in one of the parties of the second part. And it is finally decreed that any person who would enter a claim to the benefits of this covenant and agreement must, a priori, abandon all claims to worthiness in himself, and that any such claim to worthiness, under whatever heading, shall thereby constitute full grounds of exclusion of that person from any of the benefits of this covenant and agreement."

Here then, are the terms of the New Covenant based upon the promise received by Abraham through faith; *"not...through the Law"* which was still 430 years in the future. If being heirs to the world were dependent on obedience to the Law, then no one would ever be saved for no one has ever kept the Law. Though the Law is holy, just, and good, no one can keep it (James 2:10). No one! This means that there are no moderate sinners. There are no partial sinners. There are no pastel sinners. All have sinned and come short of the glory of God. Because of the love of God, Divine omnipotence has found a way to redeem individuals from the power, pollution, and penalty of sin.

5

Romans 5

Six Truths about the Gospel: Romans 5:1

The word *"therefore"* in Romans 5:1 points the reader back to all the arguments in Romans 14 that have been set forth so that a logical conclusion can be drawn. *"Therefore, being justified by faith, we have peace with God through our Lord Jesus Christ."* Paul has no doubt that he has proved the doctrine of justification by faith. In Chapter 14 of Romans, Paul has set forth the legal case the Sovereign Creator of the Universe has with His creation. The case is being argued in the Moral Court of Divine Justice.

Inside the courtroom is the Court Reporter (Romans 1:1-17), the former Saul of Tarsus. He is a servant now of the Lord Jesus Christ and, he is called an apostle. Saul has seen the resurrected Christ (1 Corinthians 9:1; 15:8, 9). He has been called by God into special service (John 6:70; Acts 9:15). Of course, only God can call a man to preach. No person should ever presume to enter the ministry unless the Lord calls Him to such service (see John 15:16; Matthew 9:38; Hebrews 5:14; Jeremiah 23: 21; Ezekiel13: 46, 10; Jeremiah 1: 15; Luke 1:15). And once called, no person should ever turn back. As a called servant of the Savior, Paul was a separated soul in three ways. First, he had been separated from the kingdom of Satan at his birth (Galatians 1:15). Second, he had been separated on the Damascus Road for salvation (Acts 9:15, 16). Finally, at Antioch, Paul was separated for spiritual service (Acts 13:1, 2). As the servant of Christ, Paul was to proclaim the gospel that is explained in Romans 1:25. Six observations can be made about the gospel.

- **The gospel is not new.** Whatever the gospel may be, it is rooted in the story of redemption as set forth in the Old Testament. In

Romans, Paul will quote the Old Testament sixty one times and appeal to fourteen books. A familiar adage says, *"If something is new, it's probably not true, and if it is true, then it is not new."* The gospel is not new. It is as old as the Garden of Eden.

- **The gospel is about Jesus**. The gospel is not about social justice, self-esteem, psychology, or how to be a financial success. The gospel is about Christ.

- **The gospel was manifested through the incarnation**. Christ was born of a virgin, and of the seed of David, according to promise. He is *"God with us."* Christ is true humanity. He grew as other children (Luke 2:40, 52; John 4:9; 20:15). The Lord knew hunger (Matthew 4:2) and thirst (John 19:28). He grew weary (Mark 4:38; John 4:6), and wept (John 11:35; Luke 19:41). At Calvary Christ suffered, bled, and died (1 Peter2: 21; John 19:34; Matthew 27:50).

- **The gospel is declared through the resurrection**. The Greek word *"declared"* (Romans 1:4) is *"horizo"* (from which we get the word *horizon*), and means, *"to mark out by sure signs."* People can look at Christ and clearly see a marked difference between Him and all others, for Jesus is very God of very God.

  He is called God in Titus 2:13. He is declared to be eternal in Revelation 1:8, 18. As God, He is unchanging (Hebrews 13:8). The Lord Jesus possesses all power (Hebrews 1:3), and all knowing. (Colossians 2:3) He is ever present (Matthew 18:20).

- **The gospel demands service from those who are saved** (Romans 1:5).

- **The gospel is received by faith** (Romans 5:1; Ephesians 2:8, 9).

As Paul reflected upon the gospel of redeeming grace, his heart overflowed with thanksgiving (Romans 1:6-15). He believed that he owed a great gospel debt to everyone (Romans 1:14; 2 Kings 7:9) and so was ready to give his life for the sake of the gospel (Romans 1:15). When Paul preached, mobs tried to kill him (Acts 21:31; 22:22, 23).

He was mocked at Athens (Acts 17:32), and he was martyred in Rome (2 Timothy 4:6). Despite his many travels, trials, and tribulations, Paul never lost confidence in the gospel (Romans 1:16, 17). Paul believed in the power of the gospel to change lives (Romans 1:16) and to produce righteousness (Romans 1:17). It is this faith that inspired and motivated Paul against all odds. Paul's faith in the power of the gospel to change lives is important to realize, for it is possible to lose faith. Without faith in the capacity of the gospel to produce righteousness, witnessing ceases, prayer is not offered, services are set aside, study of the Bible is neglected, and little effort is made to honor Christian standards.

But let there be faith in the power of the gospel to change lives and dynamic things begin to happen. A search for souls will begin. The woman at the well immediately witnessed to the men in the city. She believed the gospel. It had changed her, and it could change others. Again, let there be sincere faith in the power of the gospel, and there will be a longing for holy standards. A popular myth teaches that a person who does not have boundaries is happier in life. That is not true. While staying within the rules can be confining, time testifies to the greater burden that having no boundaries brings. In the absence of rational rules that are enforced, life seeks the lowest level of disintegration. Chaos results. Righteous people are glad to have good rules; and when the gospel is believed, the righteous will ask once more for the Moral Law of God to live by. When the power of the gospel is believed, vigorous prayer will be offered, and religious services will be desired. The Church must ask God to give back her faith in the power of the gospel to change lives and produce righteousness.

Because Paul's own sinful life had been changed by the gospel, he was in a position to present the Court Record against all of humanity (Romans 1:18-4:25). Three defendants are summoned to the bar of Divine Justice: The Pagan (Romans1: 18-32); the Moral Hypocrite (Romans 2:1-16); and the Religious Hebrew (Romans 2:17-3:8). The charge against each is the same: spiritual treason against the King of all creation (Romans 3:23). The world watches and waits to hear what the Presiding Judge will say. The decision is handed to the Court Recorder who reads the detailed indictment. A sick feeling rises in the stomachs of the sons of humanity. God's fierce wrath is revealed against all ungodliness and unrighteousness. This wrath is manifested at the Cross of Calvary (Matthew 27:46; 1 Peter 3:18). The Divine fury is justified because the sins of mankind are many.

- Mankind suppresses the truth (Romans 1:18).

- Mankind does not honor the knowledge of God (Romans 1:21).

- Mankind manifests a spirit of not being thankful (Romans 1:21).

- Mankind engages in foolish speculations (Romans 1:21).

- Mankind engages in a willful darkening of the heart (Romans 1:21).

- Mankind is prideful (Romans 1:22).

- Mankind prefers the creation to the Creator. The Greeks worshipped the body. The Assyrians bowed before birds. The Egyptians honored cows and crocodiles. In America, self is exalted as a god. In all of this, devolution, not evolution, is the story of man.

- Mankind abandons the body to sexual perversion (Romans 1:26, 27).

- There is the saturation of the soul with unrighteous acts (Romans 1:29-32).

What makes these sins all the more heinous, is that men and women, and young people who commit such practices continue in them, and even encourage others to join (Mark 14:10; Revelation 11:10). What will the righteous Judge do? He will give souls over to a reprobate mind, a mind incapable of rational judgment (Proverbs 1:24-31;

Romans 1:24, 26, 28). He will also call people into account by the Law (Romans 2:12) for the deeds done in the body (Romans 2:6).

As the court proceedings continue, the three Defendants offer a defense to the Supreme Judge. The defense of The Heathen is presented first (Romans 1:18-32) in summary form. The argument is made that the heathen should be acquitted on the grounds of ignorance. The plea is immediately refuted, for all men have both the witness of conscience (Romans 1:19) and the witness of nature (Romans 1:20; Isaiah 40:26; Psalms 8:3; 19:13; Acts 14:17; 17:29) to remind them of what is right and what is wrong. God has not kept secret what His will is for all men. The Hypocrite hopes to do better than The Heathen in arguing his case. The plea is entered that The Hypocrite should be acquitted on the grounds of comparison. He is not as bad as the pagan. This plea is also immediately refuted. The Hypocrite is shown that he does the same things that he accuses the Heathen of doing, much like David, who condemned a rich farmer, because he stole from a poor one.

While David grew angry at the idea of a man taking the last sheep of another, he, as a powerful king, had taken the wife of one his most faithful and loyal soldiers (2 Samuel 11,12). The problem with all self-righteous people is that they misunderstand the height of God's Law and they underestimate the depth of their own moral conduct. They desire the fruit of righteousness without the root. While the Religious Hypocrite underestimates the knowledge of God to look into the heart (Romans 2:1), God knows all the facts. God knows the number of the stars (Psalms 147:4), and calls them by name. God knows the thoughts of man and even his very words (Psalms 139:1, 24, 23, and 24). God knows the number of hairs on a man's head (Matthew 10:30). God knows the past, the present, and the future (Acts 15:18). God also knows what might have been (Matthew 11:23).

Despite this tremendous knowledge, the Religious Hypocrite despises the goodness and forbearance of God (Romans 2:4). The Religious Hypocrite disdains God's forbearance, or His act of holding back His wrath. *"If there is a God,"* said Sinclair Lewis in public, *"I will give him fifteen minutes to strike me dead."*

The Religious Hypocrite disdains not only God's forbearance but also His goodness and all His expressions of grace. The open hand of God is slapped away with a clenched fist. The Religious Hypocrite does something else. He assumes that his morality will excuse him from judgment. Sometimes people do escape judgment.

But with the Just God, there is no escape (Hebrews 2:3). All men will be judged according to their thoughts (Romans 2:16), words (Matthew 12:36), and deeds (Revelation 20:22). In the Day of Judgment, there will be no respecter of persons (Romans 2:11; Deuteronomy 10:17; Acts 10:34; James 2:1, 9; Ephesians 6:9; Colossians 3:25). Only those who are found to be in Christ will have any hope of being justified in the sight of God.

The Courtroom Drama of Redemption: Romans 5:1

Remaining in the Courtroom of Divine Justice is the Hebrew Defendant. He has heard the plea of The Pagan (Romans 1:18-32), and the Moral Hypocrite (Romans 2:1-16). Now, the Religious Hebrew (Romans 2:17-3:8) will try to persuade the Righteous Judge of the Universe that he should be acquitted on the grounds that he knows the Law of God and is able to teach it to others. The Judge is not impressed and immediately reminds the Religious Hebrew that his defense is what provides the basis for his condemnation. Why? Because the Religious Hebrew does not practice what he preaches! The Religious Hebrew claims to know the Law, but the Law which he knows establishes his guilt (Romans 2:17-24).

The Religious Hebrew is guilty of violating the Law of God, perverting his knowledge of God, and being a terrible witness to the Gentile world (Romans 2:24; Genesis 34:30; Ezekiel 36:17, 20). While the Religious Hebrew is proud of possessing the external Law, God judges him for not performing the spirit of the Law (Matthew 21:13; 23:36; Acts 15:10). As the Law could not save the Hebrew, neither could the physical act of circumcision save him (Romans 2:25-27). This was a shocking thought to many who had come to believe that the ritual of circumcision corresponded to the reality of saving grace. There was an interesting teaching that Abraham, the first to be circumcised, stood at the Gate of Hell to make certain that no circumcised Jew would ever enter there. While circumcision was the seal of God's covenant, the source of blessing was inward faith (Deuteronomy 10:12, 16; 30:6). There was more bad news for the Hebrew. After being told that the Law could not save him, and circumcision would not save him, he was next told that his birth could not save him (Romans 2:28, 29). Salvation is not based upon geographical location, racial identity, or external markings in the body. Salvation is by grace (John 8:39, 44). The case against all of Israel is summarized by the Court Reporter (Romans 3:18). Specific points are made.

- Even though the Jews had a practical advantage over all other nations, for unto them were given the oracles of God (Romans 3:2), they had no spiritual advantage.

- Even though the Jews had failed to live by the gospel, God would not fail to advance the gospel (Romans 3:3, 4; 2 Timothy 2:13).

- Israel would be judged along with the uncircumcised Gentiles.

After the Court Reporter summarized the case against both Jews and Gentiles, after the defendants had been allowed to speak, after their plans had been silenced, the ultimate verdict was read: *"Guilty!"* Guilt was charged to both Jews and Gentiles for *"all are under sin"* (Romans 3:9-20). The Bible says that, *"None are righteous, no not one."* None have ever sought out God (Genesis 3:9; Isaiah 1:18; 55:1). All have become unprofitable.

Man has become defiled, as milk sours, meat rots, and bread grows moldy (Isaiah 1:6). Man is altogether unrighteous, unresponsive, and unrepentant. Man is found to be depraved in every facet of his soul. His speech is found to be full of conversation that stings like a serpent, and smells like the stench of a sepulcher. Murder and immodesty characterize man's conduct (Romans 3:5-18). Therefore, the whole world is guilty before God (Romans 3:19). The religion of the Heathen is perverted. The religion of the Hypocrite is pretentious. The religion of the Hebrew is powerless. The Divine sentence on all religion: *Death!* Spiritual death marks the soul. Spiritual death involves a separation from God forever, and suffering in the Lake of Fire (Romans 6:23; Revelation 20:11-15).

At this point in the legal proceeding, the Judge should rise from the bench, render the defendants over to the magistrates of the court, gather up the gavel, and Law books, and retire. But none of that happened. Instead, the Judge rises, takes off his judicial robes, and goes toward the defendants. They will not be led away. He will go in their stead, and receive in His own body what they so justly deserve. He will do this, and more, that the wretched souls might be justified or declared righteous before the Law. The demands of righteousness will be carried out at Calvary (Romans 3:25), and they were. The Law and the Prophets went to Calvary as silent witnesses (Deuteronomy 19:15). The Law and the Prophets watched, as the execution of the Court was carried out.

The great day arrived. The heaven could not bear to watch, and so darkness covered the earth. But the execution proceeded according to plan. Jesus Christ purchased redemption. Now, all boasting is over on the part of those who will be saved (Romans 3:24, 27). Certainly, the Pagan (Romans 1:18-32) cannot boast. The Moral Hypocrite (Romans 2:1-16) cannot boast. The Religious Hebrew (Romans 2:17; 3:8) cannot boast. Salvation is all of grace, *that God might be just, and the justifier of all who believe in Jesus* (Romans 3:26). But what about all who live, before Christ? Will their sins be dealt with according to gospel terms? And is any remission of sin possible for people who lived during the Old Testament era? And what about those who will be born in the future? Will the forbearance of God continue so that they can be saved? The Divine answer is, *"Yes!"* for the sacrifice of Christ accomplished specific objectives.

- The death of Christ propitiated, or satisfied all the demands of the Law (1 John 2:2, 4, 10; Hebrews 10:11, 12).

- The death of Christ redeems all those whom the Father had given to Him (Romans 3:22, 24), and sets them free from the power, and pollution of sin (see Galatians 3:13; 4:5;

Ephesians 5:16; Colossians 4:5; Luke 24:21; Titus 2:14; 1 Peter 1:18).

- The merits of the death of Christ are bestowed upon all them that believe (Romans 3:22).

- Those who avail themselves of the merits of the sacrifices of Christ will be redeemed, just as Abraham was saved. Abraham was saved not by a physical act of circumcision, not by a life of good deeds, but by faith. *"For what saith the scriptures? Abraham believed God, and it was counted unto him for righteousness"* (Romans 4:3; Genesis 15:6).

Three great imputations are spoken of in the Bible. First, is the imputation of Adam's sin to the human race (Romans 3:23; 5:12; 1 Corinthians 15:22). Second, is the imputation of the sins of the elect upon Christ (Isaiah53: 5; Hebrews 2:9; 1 Peter 2:24; 2 Corinthians 5:14). Third, is the imputation of God's righteousness to all who believe (Philippians 3:9). Abraham believed (Romans 3:5 with Genesis 16:16).

He was justified by faith, fourteen years before he was circumcised, at age ninety-nine, so that he might be the father of all who believe.

- Genesis 17:24, *And Abraham was ninety years old and nine, when he was circumcised in the flesh of his foreskin.*

- Romans 4:11, *And he received the sign of circumcision, a seal of the righteousness of the faith which he had yet being uncircumcised: that he might be the father of all them that believe, though they be not circumcised; that righteousness might be imputed unto them also:*

A reward was promised to Abraham and to his posterity: a land, physical Canaan, and spiritual heaven; a seed: physically, Isaac, spiritually, Christ and the Church; righteousness, by faith, resulting in peace with God.

Five Great Results of Having Peace With God: Romans 5:1-11

Having reviewed the Doctrine of Justification, in chapters one through four, the Apostle Paul proceeds to the results of being justified by faith. Five major blessings are declared.

First, being justified by faith, we have peace with God (Romans 5:1). According to Paul's arguments, the legal battles are over; the Law has been satisfied; and the arms of hostility have been laid down. The result is peace with God, leading to the peace of God that passes all understanding. Peace with God, refers to the believer's legal position before Him, while the peace of God, refers to fellowship with Him.

Second, being justified by faith, allows access to God (Romans 5:2). The believer is free to approach God on the basis of a new sphere of existence. The believer has a standing, and state, before the Lord. The reference to one's standing, again, refers to the believer's legal position in Christ. This position or standing of the believer never changes (1 Corinthians 15:1; 2 Corinthians 5:17) for the Christian. The Christian will always be a priest. The Christian will always be a child of God. The Christian will always be part of the body of Christ. The Christian will always be a citizen of the kingdom.

However, the believer's practice and state of existence may certainly change, for it is affected by the world, the flesh, and the devil. The state of the believer may change for better, or for worse. On the negative side, the Christian may act in a selfish way, as Jacob. The Christian may revolt against authority, as did Saul. The Christian may sin grievously, as did David. The Christian may vacillate, as did Peter. The Christian may lie, as Abraham. Or, the Christian may move from glory to glory illustrated in the life of Paul. First, he was a convert. Then, he was a disciple. Next, Paul was an apostle. Finally, he was a martyr for the cause of Christ.

Spiritually, the state of the believer in the New Testament era allows an access to God that was not possible in the Old Testament economy. Under the Old Covenant a Gentile was barred at the gate of the Temple; a Jewish woman could not go beyond the court of women, a non-Levite could not enter the inner court; and the High

Priest could go into the Holy of Holies once a year, on the Day of Atonement. He had to pass behind the veil, which no one else could penetrate. Then came Calvary. Calvary has opened this separation between God and man by tearing the veil in two (Matthew 27:51; Hebrews 10:19).

A third positive result of being justified by faith is assurance from God (Romans 5:3,4). Many people have no assurance of salvation, for several reasons.

- People have been taught that they can lose their salvation. To many people, it makes sense to believe that salvation can be lost. However, God's ways are not man's ways. And if man is unfaithful, God is not.

- People do not believe the Scriptures, even though they are plainly written.

- People do not feel worthy of salvation that leads to a subjective concept of redemption. But salvation is not subjective; it is an objective reality. A man may not always feel married, but he is, if the vows have been taken. When a man has no assurance of salvation, his heart will be unstable; he will experience no inner peace; he will feel a nagging apprehension; and he will grieve the heart of God. What father wants his children to doubt the family relationship?

- Soul-winning power is lost. How can people preach the gospel effectively, who are not confident of their own salvation?

It is better to believe in justification by faith, and enjoy assurance from God, even when a measure of suffering is associated with the Christian experience. Paul reminds believers that *"tribulation worketh"* patience.

- **Patience.** Patience, during difficult days, refers to maintaining a calm disposition. Christian patience is not karma, nor is it fatalism. Rather, it is a profound assurance of the goodness of God (Hebrews 10:36; James 1:3).

- **Experience.** Patience, in turn, brings experiences that are beneficial to the soul (see Psalms 94:12; 2 Corinthians1:35; Galatians 4:19; Ephesians 4:14, 15). Not all experiences are pleasant, but they are all designed to produce a spiritual response, and move the believer toward maturity.

- **Hope.** From the unity of patience and experience comes hope. An earthly hope consists of three requirements. It must concern the future; it must concern something good in the future; and it must concern something possible in the future.

The hope of the Christian fulfills all three requirements. Every Christian believes in eternal life; every Christian believes in a future resurrection from the dead. All believers believe that they will see their loves ones from the past, the saints of the ages, and the Savior Himself. That is hope. The Christian can hope for these coming events, because of the resurrection of Christ. If Christ were not raised from the dead, then there is no basis for hope. But because Christ is raised, then there is confidence in the future, according to gospel terms. A fourth result of being justified by faith is that the soul is indwelt by the love of God. *"The love of God is shed abroad in our hearts by the Holy Ghost which is given unto us"* (Romans 5:5). There are several distinct words for love in the original language.

- *Storgos.* This word refers to a natural, gravitational love; an instinctive concern for one's offspring. It is found in both animals and man. Only the negative form *"astorgos,"* is used in Scripture (Romans 1:31).

- *Philos.* This word is described in Romans 12:10 as friendship love.

- *Agapeo.* This word is used 320 times in the New Testament, and clearly embraces the love of God for men (Romans 5:5; 11:3, 5; John 3:16; Ephesians 5:25).

Another result of justification by faith is that the saint is preserved in God (Romans 5:6-11). The preservation comes because of the Lord's past work on Calvary's cross, where Christ died for the ungodly (Romans 5:6). Christ died while we were yet sinners and enemies (Romans 5:6, 8, 10; Ephesians 2:1, 11, 12). He shed His own blood for us. It was innocent blood (Matthew 27:4, 19, 24). It was spilt blood (Matthew 26:28). It was cleansing blood (Matthew 27:25). Christ died to manifest the love of God (Romans 5:8). Christ died to save men from the wrath of God (Romans 5:9). Christ died to intercede for His own (Hebrews 1:3; 6:18-20; 7:25; 9:24). Therefore, the blood of Christ must not be despised, nor must its value be diluted. By faith in His blood work at Calvary, we are justified in the sight of God.

Peace for the People of God: Romans 5:1 with Matthew 11:28-30

The former Presbyterian minister, Dr. Donald Grey Barnhouse, liked to preach a sermon in his youth, with the rather long title, *"What Is The Most Sought After Thing In The World?"* The sermon had a simple structure. The question was asked, *"What is the most sought after thing in the world?"* and then various things were suggested that people spend their time in seeking, such as money, love, pleasure, power, and education. Of course, countless folks can testify that the acquisition of these things will bring no lasting satisfaction, or inner peace. Such is the testimony of Art Monk.

Art Monk once held the National Football League record for the most career catches, 934, and the most consecutive games with a catch, 180. As a Redskin, he went to three Super Bowl championship games. But half way through his remarkable career, Art Monk says, *"I began to feel a lot of emptiness and loneliness. I had everything I wanted and yet still felt something was missing. I started going to some Bible studies in 1987 and, upon doing that, all the things I had been taught by may parents and by the Church...came flooding back."* Art knew then, that he needed Christ. He came across these verses from Paul's letter to Timothy (Romans 1:15-16). Christ Jesus came into the world to save sinners, of whom I am the worst. But for that reason I was shown mercy, so that in me, the worst of sinners, Christ Jesus might display his unlimited patience as an example for those who would believe on him, and receive eternal life.

Art Monk gave his life to Christ, and his life changed. He testified, *"The emptiness and loneliness just kind of went away."* Art is fortunate. Many have not found the peace they are looking for; and so they keep seeking for something that eludes them, like a butterfly, moving just beyond the reaching hand. Napoleon once said, *"What a bore life is! What a cross!"* The possession of ultimate power, the acquisition of education, fame, wealth, and success, do not bring individuals what they want. This is reflected in the high number of suicides, and the continuing struggles, after one's goal has been attained.

Perhaps what people really need is peace with God. Then life will be satisfying. It is possible to have peace with God, for the Bible teaches that God is the God of peace. It is a title He has given Himself. But some problems must be overcome if one is to experience peace. The first difficulty is the fact that many do not realize they have no peace with God. It is possible to live without knowing that a state of war exists between the human heart, and the holy heart of the God of heaven, but the Bible is clear on this truth. The natural heart, the unconverted heart, the sinful heart is hostile to God.

Romans 8:7-8 expresses the situation vividly. *"Because the carnal mind is enmity against God: for it is not subject to the Law of God, neither indeed can be. So then, they that are in the flesh cannot please God."*

Here is the practical problem: A state of hostility exists between God and man, but man will not acknowledge the chasm that exists. As a result, the tension builds. God did not create the tension. The situation itself created the state of apprehension. Sin has its own dynamics. A protest against inappropriate actions may manifest tension, but the cause of any negative emotion is the initial behavior itself. So there it is. Many people will not acknowledge that they are not right with God. Why?

To do so would mean an admission that the reason for the conflict is a clash of wills. The heart of man wants its own way; the heart of God demands another way, the way of truth, justice, holiness, and kindness. What happens? Individuals smile, and pretend to be doing no wrong. Meanwhile, self-destructive, and other destructive behavior is practiced. Life offers a daily diet of this situation. Some people are concerned. A letter to the editor of a conservative Christian publication, *Expression Magazine*, crystallizes the situation (July 1998). Part of the text reads [as modified],

"Our nation is no longer just sliding down the slippery slope. Under the current administration, we are now in a cultural crash dive of catastrophic proportions. Many Christians contend that the President's stand on bringing intrusive government into every aspect of our lives, and the catering to the homosexual agenda, abortion rights advocates, and the many other disgruntled special rights groups is taking a heavy toll on our nation. However, as the master of spin, and in order to maintain the population's cooperation, [The President] denies that he is anti-Christian. Why, he exclaims, I am a Christian...I even go to Church...Then...he continues to wreck havoc on our nation, with hardly a whimper from the population, many of whom are Christians."

As long as the swirl of activity is clever, and legalistic, in defending the indefensible, the soul will resist righteousness. All of this happens because there is a desperate desire for an outward display of tranquility and control. That is understandable. But there is no peace, says my God, to the wicked. Conflict will come. Tension will arise in the home, at work, on the way to work, and with every chance encounter of strangers. God will not be mocked. *"Whatsoever man soweth that shall he also reap."*

Those who sow to the flesh will reap the corruption of the same. It may take a while, but a just reward will come. The house of cards will fall. In contrast to the way of those who transgress the Laws of the Lord, there is peace for all who will keep their heart focused upon Jehovah. When the heart cries out for God, He moves to be merciful. So listen to Christ Himself, as He says, *"Come unto me, all ye that labor and are heavy-laden and I will give thee rest"* (Matthew 11:28-30).

The word *"come"* is one of the great words in the Bible. It is a word of invitation to draw near. Jesus did not say, *"go there"*, or *"do that"*, or *"go away"*. He said, *"Come."* Again, the word *"come"* is a word of earnest entreaty. *"Come."* There is Divine pleading in that word. There is holy passion. There is no reason not to come, and every reason to come to Christ. In gospel language, the hounds of hell are snapping at the sinner's heels. Death is stalking the soul. The carcasses will one-day fall, for it is appointed unto men once to die. Satan, like a hungry lion, is roaring about the wilderness of this world, seeking whom he may devour. It is into this mess of madness, that the voice of grace can be heard calling, *"Come unto me!"*

Some of those who are young might think that they should delay coming to Christ until they have eaten of forbidden fruit. Many have gone to questionable things seeking pleasure and passion, only to find themselves ensnared with a surprising addiction. Jackie Robinson was a great baseball player. He was the first black man to play in the Major Leagues. He had a son named Jackie Jr. Jackie Jr. grew up and answered the call of his country to serve in Vietnam. But while in the service, he got hooked on drugs. He became an addict He sought pleasure and comfort, and found an addiction that became more of an enemy than the one he faced on the field of military conflict.

And yet, to all those who are addicted and burdened with any form of sin, Jesus says, *"Come unto me".* It does not matter how heavy the load of guilt and shame may be. Christ has omnipotent strength. The blood of Jesus Christ, God's Son, cleanses from all sin. So come. Abraham lied to the king of Egypt; still, he may come. Jacob cheated his brother and blinded father yet he may come to Christ.

David committed adultery; the woman at the well had five husbands; and they may come. Saul of Tarsus always remembered the blood dripping from his hands following the stoning of Stephen, and yet he heard Jesus saying, *"Saul! Saul!"* or, *"Come! Come!"*

Karla Faye Tucker remembered the pick ax she left in the lifeless form of her butchered victim in 1983. However, by many accounts, she came to another fountain to be washed from all of her guilt and stain. She was forgiven for her sins. Karla Faye Tucker came because the invitation is open to all: *"Come unto me all ye that labor and are heavy laden and I will give you rest."* So go and tell someone who is burdened with sin that they may come to Christ. Jesus still invites the vilest of the vile. William Booth, founder of the Salvation Army, had as his slogan, *"Go for souls, and go for the worst."*

For all that come to Christ, there is the promise of rest. The rest that is spoken of is the rest that comes when a vanquished foe accepts the sovereignty of his superiors. That is important to understand. There is a peace that is imposed, and a peace that is accepted. On the deck of the battleship Missouri, after World War II, the Allies imposed the terms of peace; the Japanese accepted them. A person who comes to Christ must accept the terms of peace imposed. When they are, all is well. According to the Bible, the gospel terms are these: Jesus Christ must be accepted as both Lord and Savior. He is both Divine Deliverer and Sanctifier. Sin is not to rule over the soul.

These gospel terms must be understood. Some have come to Christ, but they have never received peace in their hearts. Why? Because they have never fully accepted the gospel. They do not honor His Lordship of their lives. As soon as a passage in the Bible is read about holiness that challenges an unwholesome lifestyle, rebellion takes place. There are those who do not want to give up an improper relationship. Others do not want to give up a secret sin. And so Christ is not wanted as Lord. But for those who say, *"Yes"* to Christ in all areas of life, for those who are willing to be fully surrendered, a peace is given. The heart will want to sing,

"All to Jesus, I surrender,
All to Him I freely give.
I will ever love and trust Him,
In His presence daily live.

All to Jesus, I surrender,
Humbly at His feet I bow,
Worldly pleasures all forsaken,
Take me, Jesus, take me now.

All to Jesus, I surrender, Lord,
I give myself to Thee;
Fill me with Thy love and power,
Let Thy blessing fall on me."

The Surrendered Life finds that the yoke of Christ is easier to bear than the superficial shackles of the world that glitters with gilded gold. The yoke of Christ will bring peace, when properly worn. This peace is like the satisfying sigh of the farmer who turns and looks at the field he has plowed after a long day of toil. This peace is like the comforting cooing of a mother, who knows that all the children are tucked into bed after a busy day. This peace is the thankful heart that knows, after an hour of worship, there is no condemnation to those who are in Christ Jesus. Christ invites all to come to Him, and learn of Him, for He is meek and lowly in heart. The implication is that those who come to Christ should be meek and lowly as well.

Doctrine of the Glory of God

1. In Exodus 16:10, God's glory is spoken of for the first time. It is manifested in a visible way in a cloud. The power of God was displayed to provide a new form of food for the children of Israel. Power is associated with God's glory.

2. In Exodus 24:16, the physical manifestation of the glory of the Lord is said to have rested upon Mt. Sinai. The sight of this Divine glory was like a devouring fire on the top of the mountain (Exodus 24:17). Fire produces purity, and so the connection is made: purity is associated with God's glory.

3. In Exodus 29:43, God promised to meet with the children of Israel, and sanctify the newly constructed tabernacle by His glory. Holiness, or separation, is associated with God's glory.

4. In Exodus 40:34, the glory of God is inherent in His presence. There is no place where God is that His manifest, glorious presence is not (1 Chronicles 16:27).

5. According to Number 14:14, miracles are associated with the glory of God.

6. Divine protection is associated with the glory of God (Numbers 16:41-45).

7. Divine provisions are associated with the glory of God (Numbers 20:68).

8. The Exodus generation never forgot, it once saw the glory of God manifested in its midst (Deuteronomy 5:24).

9. In poetical language, the glory of God is like the first bullock, which means that there is great strength associated with God's glory (Deuteronomy 33:17).

10. Sometimes, the glory of God will depart from the midst of His people leaving people without a visible manifestation of the Lord. While some may not care, others will want to weep and tremble (1 Samuel 4:21).

11. When God's glory fills a place, people cannot stand in His presence (1 Kings 8:10-11; 2 Chronicles 5:14; 7:2).

12. The glory of God is to be declared among the heathen (1 Chronicles 16:24). Every Christian has a responsibility to witness.

13. Those buildings that are associated with God have Biblically, and traditionally, reflected the glory of God by their beauty (1 Chronicles 22:5).

14. The prayer language of glory is reflected by David in 1 Chronicles 29:10-13.

15. Prayer will bring forth the glory of God (2 Chronicles 7:1).

16. God is aware of His own essential glory (Job 40:6-10).

17. When God moves to protect His own, His glory is manifested (Psalms 3: 3). The Christian should be sensitive to these moments of spiritual Divine protection from harm, and give the Lord honor.

18. God values His glory (Psalm 8: 1).

19. The heavens declare the glory of God (Psalm19:1), as does all of creation (Psalms 29:9).

20. The salvation of souls declares the glory of God (Psalms 21:5).

21. The praise and worship of the Church bring forth the glory of God (Psalms 24:7), if the assembly is conscious of it (Psalms 24: 8-10).

22. The rulers of the Earth are commanded to give glory to God (Psalms 29:12). They do not at their peril.

23. When God speaks, He reveals His glory (Psalms 29:34). And God has spoken: through the prophets (Luke 24:25); through His Son (Hebrews 1:2); through the apostles (1 Corinthians 4:9); through miracles, creation, and providence (Hebrews 2:4); and through the recorded scriptures (2 Timothy 3:16).

24. God receives glory through the songs of the saints, and the instruments they play (Psalms 30:12).

25. In the day of spiritual warfare, the glory of God is revealed (Psalms 45:3).

26. The heart of the Christian is jealous that God receive honor and glory (Psalms 57: 5, 11; 115:1).

27. The passionate plea of the Christian is to know something, and to see something, of the power and glory of God (Psalms 63: 2).

28. One day, the whole earth shall be filled with the glory of God (Psalms 72:19). No den of the devil, no pit of hell, no human barrier shall be able to shut God out. He will come with great force, and take hold of the whole earth.

29. God will sometimes surrender His glory into the hand of the enemies of the Church as a form of discipline (Psalms 78:59-61).

30. When God is not a stranger in the Church, neither is His glory (Psalms 85:9).

31. God alone is the glory of the Christian's heart (Psalms 89:17; 105:3).

32. The glory of God is to be declared to all the nations. The Church must be missionary minded (Psalms 96:3).

33. The Church should find as many ways as possible to give glory to God (Psalms 96:7, 8).

34. The glory of God, manifested in the life of the Church, will cause the unconverted to fear God (Psalms 102:15).

35. When the Church is built up, God shall appear in His people (Psalms 102:16).

36. The glory of the Lord shall endure forever (Psalms 104:31).

37. Even heaven itself cannot contain the glory of God (Psalms113: 4; 148:13). Great is the glory of God (Psalms 138:5).

38. Every work of God is designed to bring Him honor and glory (Psalms 145:11).

39. While it is the glory of God to conceal a sin (Proverbs 25:2), the glory of God is associated with His righteous judgment (Isaiah 2:19, 21).

40. One day God shall purify His Church, and it shall be glorious (Isaiah 4:26; 58:8; 60:1, 2, 7, 13). God has always meant for the Church to be glorious (Ezekiel 20:6, 15).

41. The whole earth is full of the glory of God (Isaiah 6:3; Ezekiel 3:23), and shall ever be (Isaiah 66:18, 19; Ezekiel 43:25; Habakkuk 2:14; 3:3).

42. One day the Church will fully honor the Lord of Hosts, and He shall be their crown of glory (Isaiah 28:5; 40:5).

43. When God makes the earth to bloom in desert places, it reveals His glory (Isaiah 35:2; 42:11-12).

44. The glory of God is revealed when He uses His Church as an instrument of judgment (Isaiah 41:16).

45. God will never give His glory to anyone else (Isaiah 42:8; 48:11).

46. The Church was created for the glory of God (Isaiah 43:7; 45:25; 46:13).

47. It is the wisdom of man to fear God's glory (Isaiah 59:19).

48. One day, the glory of God will replace sin (Isaiah 60:19).

49. Heaven is filled with the holiness and glory of God (Isaiah 63:15; Ezekiel 1:28).

50. When the Church repents, and lives close to the Lord, recognizes God's glory (Jeremiah 4:2; 14:21).

51. The glory of God is not static but dynamic (Ezekiel 10:18, 19; 11:22, 23).

General Notes on Glory

1. The full glory of God cannot be seen by natural men and live (Exodus 33:18, 32).

2. Some individuals have special manifestations of the glory of God such as Moses (Exodus 3:16), Isaiah (Isaiah 6:14), and the Exodus Generation (Numbers 16:19).

3. The glory of God will appear in the midst of people according to sovereign choice (Leviticus 9:6, 23).

4. When the glory of God is manifested sin, ceases (Psalms 79:9), judgment is present (Numbers 14:10), people are humbled (2 Chronicles 7:3), individuals grow afraid with holy fear (2 Chronicles 7:3), and hearts are opened in praise (1 Chronicles 16:8-15).

5. When sins are not hidden and confession is made, God is given glory (Joshua 7:19).

6. It pleases God to give glory to the poor (1 Samuel 2:7, 8) and lowly.

7. Men rob God of His essential glory when they seek after idols (1 Samuel 6:5).

8. The glory of the Lord must be consciously sought (1 Chronicles 16:10, 11) and remembered.

9. The Church is to find specific ways to give glory to God (1 Chronicles 16:28, 29).

10. When God delivers His people in a special, spiritual way, they are to give Him glory (1 Chronicles 16:35).

11. When God desires to test His people, He will often strip them of the very honor and glory He has bestowed upon them (Job 19:9). Then, let the heart say, *"He must increase, and I must decrease."* Then, let heaven hear, *"Though He slay me, yet will I trust Him."*

12. The ungodly will try to turn the glory of the saints into shame by mocking God, by demeaning standards of holiness, and by enticing others to sin (Psalms 3:2).

13. Man, as the crowning act of creation, has been bestowed with intrinsic value and glory (Psalms 8:5).

14. When sin is resisted, the glory of man is enhanced (Psalms 16:79).

15. Sometimes, when God's glory is revealed in material prosperity, it is almost too much to bear (Psalms 49:16, 17).

16. There is no ultimate glory for the Christian outside of God (Psalms 62:7).

17. There is glory for the Christian who will remain steadfast to God (Psalms 63:11). This glory is according to promise (Psalms 64:10).

18. Heaven is filled with God's glory, and so, it is to heaven that the Christian prays to go (Psalms 73:24).

19. God is able, and willing, to give grace and glory to the righteous (Psalms 84:11).

20. God will remove the glory of the enemies of the Church (Psalms 89:44).

21. The Church must pray that the next generation will know something of the glory of God (Psalms 90:16).

22. It is possible for every person to see something of the glory of God (Psalms 97:6).

23. The gracious provision of God causes the Church to glory in its spiritual inheritance (Psalms 106:5).

24. It is possible, for the Church to act in such a way, as to change its essential glory to the level of an animal (Psalms 106:20).

25. The desire of the Church is to return all glory to God (Psalms 108:1, 5).

26. Let the saints be joyful in glory (Psalms 149:5).

27. The wise shall inherit glory (Proverbs 3:35).

28. Wisdom shall give glory to those who will be instructed (Proverbs 4:9).

29. Age is associated with glory (Proverbs 16:31).

30. The glory of children is their fathers (Proverbs 17:6).

31. The glory of young men is their strength (Proverbs 20:29).

32. There is a spiritual glory of grace in passing over a fault (Proverbs 25:2).

33. It is not good for men to seek for personal glory (Proverbs 25:27).

34. The righteous rejoice when there is great glory (Proverbs 28:12).

35. Men are commanded to fear the glory of the majesty of God (Isaiah 2:10).

36. It is possible for men to provoke the eyes of the glory of God (Isaiah 3:8).

37. The glory of the unrighteous shall be cast into hell (Isaiah 5:14).

38. The rulers of the earth enjoy a temporal glory (Isaiah 8:7; 20:5; Ezekiel 25:9).

39. Apart from God, men have no glory (Isaiah 10:3). He can easily take it all away (Isaiah 10:12, 16, 18; 13:19; 16:14; 17:14; 21:16; 22:18; 22:24; Jeremiah 48:18; Ezekiel 24:15).

40. The final resting-place of man's earthly glory is the tomb (Isaiah 14:18).

41. In the day of Divine visitation in wrath it pleases the Lord to stain the pride of man's glory (Isaiah 23:9).

42. There is a glory of association when men are righteous (Isaiah 24:16).

43. The Church shall one day triumph over all her enemies (Isaiah 61:6) and their glory. In that day, the glory of the Church will be recognized (Isaiah 62:2, 3). The Church will provide nourishment for the nations (Isaiah 66:10-12).

44. It is possible for the Church to lose her essential glory (Jeremiah 2:11).

45. The wise man shall glory in no one, and nothing, but God (Jeremiah 9:23).

46. Though God desires glory for the Church, it sometimes turns away (Jeremiah 13:11).

47. The Church is warned to give glory to God (Jeremiah 13:16-18).

48. When God moves in judgment upon men, the Church is sometimes commanded not to pray for their former glory (Jeremiah 22:18).

49. The Church delights in the fact of God's glory (Ezekiel 3:12).

50. The glory of God must fill the Church (Ezekiel 9:4; 9:3; 10:4; 44:4).

51. The Lord is able to manifest glory in the land of the living (Ezekiel 26:20; 39; 21).

The Importance of the Doctrine of the Atonement: Romans 5:11

In the movie *"The Longest Day,"* the story is retold of June 6, 1944, when the Allied forces invaded Normandy during the fateful days of World War II. One of the characters in the movie tells another soldier to remember the date, because, *"People will talk about it long after we are dead and gone."* Of far greater importance, is the death of Jesus Christ, and the day He died.

- The Atonement is the central fact of Christianity. Any system that leaves out the Atonement is not true Christianity. The importance of the death of Christ is reflected in the fact that it was accompanied by supernatural events. The earth shook, and darkness covered the land. Graves were opened and the veil of the Temple was torn in two.

- The Atonement was the subject of the first promise to man in Genesis 3:15. It was anticipated, and described by the Old Testament prophets (Psalms 22).

- Christ said, *"To this end was I born, and for this purpose came I into the world"* (John 18:37). The Lord knew that it was the Father's will that He come to die (Isaiah 53:10; Zechariah 13:7).

- The Atonement is that on which man's salvation depends, which is why Paul declared that he was determined not to know anything else except Jesus Christ and Him crucified (1 Corinthians 2:2). Whoever makes light of the Atonement, makes light of his own and the world's salvation. *"The Atonement made by the Son of God, is the beginning of the ransomed sinner's hope, and will be the theme of his exultation, when he shall cast his crown before the throne singing the songs of Moses and of the Lamb"* (James Haldane).

Terms Defined

To understand the doctrine of the Atonement certain terms must be understood, with discrimination.

- **Atonement.** It is easy to understand this term by studying the Old Testament sacrifices. The Law demanded that certain sacrifices be made for various sins. When the blood of a sacrifice was poured out, it became a covering for the sins of the one who offered the sacrifice and thus the Law was satisfied. Satisfaction is the basic meaning of the word *"atonement."* When Christ shed blood at Calvary, He covered our sins and He satisfied the penal demands of the Law, but Christ did something else. He satisfied the obedience that the Law made upon men as well. The Law said, *"Do this and live."* Christ did all that the Law required and so satisfied its obedience and then He did more. He became a substitute to satisfy the Law's penalty for disobedience, which was death. When you think of the word *"atonement,"* think of the word, *"satisfaction."*

- **Guilt.** A satisfaction for sin was needed because man has been found *"guilty"* of sin. The word guilt expresses two things: *"blameworthiness,"* pollution, moral turpitude, criminality; and *"liability for punishment"* or *"penalty."* The Bible tells us that man is guilty of breaking the Law of God. *"There is none righteous, no not one."*

- **Expiation.** Since man is guilty of sin, his sin needs to be expiated. Expiation means purging out, washing away, covering, making reparation or satisfaction; especially by suffering a penalty such as expiating a crime. The sacrificial rites of the Old Testament show how penalty was exacted, and remission and forgiveness declared. Leviticus 1:4 *"And he shall put his hand upon the head of the burnt offering; and it shall be accepted for him to make atonement for him."*

This placing of the hand on the head showed the transfer of the guilt by the one offering the sacrifice. When that act was completed, sin was purged out. In like manner, the Atonement of Jesus was expiatory. Christ paid the penalty of sin, fulfilled the Law, satisfied justice, and secured remission for sins.

- **Propitiation.** Once sin is removed there is propitiation, which means to appease or render favorable one who has been offended. The Atonement of Christ propitiates God, renders Him favorable or gracious; and reconciliation is effected between God and man.

  - Romans 5:1, *"Therefore being justified by faith, we have peace with God through our Lord Jesus Christ:"*

  - Romans 5:9, *"Much more then, being now justified by his blood, we shall be saved from wrath through him."*

- 2 Corinthian 5:18, *"And all things are of God, who hath reconciled us to himself by Jesus Christ, and hath given to us the ministry of reconciliation."*

- 2 Corinthians 5:19, *"To wit, that God was in Christ, reconciling the world unto himself, not imputing their trespasses unto them; and hath committed unto us the word of reconciliation."*

- 2 Corinthians 5:20, *"Now then we are ambassadors for Christ, as though God did beseech you by us: we pray you in Christ's stead, be ye reconciled to God."*

- Colossians 1:21, *"And you, that were sometime alienated and enemies in your mind by wicked works, yet now hath he reconciled."*

- **Vicarious.** The Christian must never forget that God would never have been propitiated apart from the vicarious death of Christ. Vicarious means substitutionary. A vicar is a substitute or one who takes another's place. The Atonement was vicarious. John 1:29 *"The next day John seeth Jesus coming unto him, and saith, Behold the Lamb of God, which taketh away the sin of the world"* Matthew 20:28. *"Even as the Son of man came not to be ministered unto, but to minister, and to give his life a ransom for many."*

- **Reconciliation.** Reconciliation means bringing into harmony or agreement.

- **Imputation.** Imputation means to charge to one's account. Romans 4:3. *"Abraham believed God and it was counted to Him for righteousness."* At Calvary our sins were imputed to Christ and His righteousness was imputed to us. Thus, in the Atonement a vicarious sacrifice expiates guilt, propitiates God the Father, and reconciles God and man. And what must never be forgotten is that it was God Himself who did this. *"God, to show His love to us, showed Himself God in this: that He could be God and go so low as to die"* (A Puritan named Sibbes).

Summary

- The Atonement was sacrificial for Jesus was the Lamb slain.

- The Atonement was expiatory as it purged sins.

- The Atonement was vicarious for Jesus took the place of sinners.

- The Atonement was the satisfaction of justice.

- The Atonement was sufficient to save all those who will come to faith.

- The Atonement was propitiatory as God was satisfied.

- The Atonement brought reconciliation for man was brought into fellowship with God.

The Purpose of the Atonement

- **To glorify God**. Either God will be the Savior of man if man is ever to be saved, or man will save himself. The problem is that men write and speak in very eloquent language about more virtue, self-esteem, and innate ability, none of which is possessed. Covered over is a heart desperately wicked and without any ability to do well in the sight of God. We read in our *Declaration of Independence* that, *"All men are created equal..."* Our minds are thrilled at the noble concept of justice, freedom, and equality under the Law. Yet the hand that penned these tremendous words held other men and women in chains of bondage and probably kept one slave woman as his mistress (Sally Fields). We make a mistake to admire the virtuous sentiments of individuals who deny the need of a Savior and hate the doctrine of the Atonement preferring a more enlightened view of redemption.

- **To humble man.** As Christians, we remember that we are saved by the death of another humbles us. One day, Christ stood in our stead. He took our hell to give us His heaven. The day Christ died is a day to remember.

- **To secure the happiness of God's elect for time and for eternity**. Even in heaven we will sing the praises of Calvary (Revelation 5:12).

How Can We Understand the Atonement?

Apart from Christ's giving understanding, no one cannot begin to hope to appreciate this doctrine (John 3:27). *"Great is the mystery of godliness"* (1 Timothy 3:16). However, a look back into the Old Testament era and especially the Day of Atonement will be very instructive.

The Day of Atonement According to Leviticus 16:3 and Numbers 29:7-11

The Day of Atonement was a special day for Israel, for on that day the sins of the people were confessed, and forgiveness was found. The Day of Atonement was observed on the tenth day of Tisri (October), and was called *"Yom Kippur."* On this day the high priest was to bathe himself and offer a bullock for the sins of himself and his family. The sacrifices began with the daily offerings. The daily offering included the following: a yearly lamb for a burnt offering, a tenth deal of flour for a meal offering, and twelve fresh loaves of shewbread.

To these sacrifices were added: a bullock for a sin offering, a ram for a burnt offering, for the priesthood; two goats for a sin offering and a ram for a burnt offering on behalf of the people. This was followed by one young bullock, one ram, seven lambs, for burnt offering, flour mingled with oil, three deals for bullock, two tenth deals for ram, and one tenth deal for each lamb, for a meal offering, one half hin wine for bullock, one third hin wine for ram, and one quarter hin wine for each lamb, for a drink offering.

The Doctrine of the Atonement

Atonement refers to man being reconciled to God, by the substitutionary death of Jesus Christ on behalf of sinners. Atonement, in the Old Testament economy, was recognized by the satisfaction, or payment made by animal sacrifices (2 Samuel 21:3), the offering of prayers, suffering, or acts of emotional repentance for wrongdoing or an injury. In the New Testament economy, the focus of attention on atonement is upon that which has been accomplished through the suffering of the God man, the Lord Jesus Christ. Man is reconciled to God by the death, burial, and resurrection of Jesus Christ (Romans 5:11).

Charles Spurgeon and Definite Redemption

"We are often told that we limit the atonement of Christ, because we say that Christ has not made a satisfaction for all men, or all men would be saved. Now, our reply to this is, that, on the other hand, our opponents limit it: we do not. The Arminians say, Christ died for all men. Ask them what they mean by it. Did Christ die so as to secure the salvation of all men? They say, No, certainly not. We ask them the next question, Did Christ die so as to secure the salvation of any man in particular? No. Christ has died that any man may be saved if and then follow certain conditions of salvation. Now, who is it that limits the death of Christ? Why, you. You say that Christ did not die so as infallibly to secure the salvation of anybody. We beg your pardon, when you say we limit Christ's death; we say, No, my dear sir, it is you that do it. We say Christ so died that he infallibly secured the salvation of a multitude that no man could number, who through Christ's death not only may be saved, but also are saved and cannot by any possibility, run the hazard of being anything but saved. You are welcome to your atonement; you may keep it. We will never renounce ours for the sake of it."—Predestination, Loraine Boettner

The Death of Christ and the Atonement

1. The atonement refers to the act by which God restores a relationship of harmony, and unity, between Himself and human beings. The word can be broken into three parts, which express this great truth in simple, but profound terms: *atonement*.

2. Through God's atoning grace and forgiveness, we are reinstated to a relationship of atonement with God, in spite of our sin.

3. Human Need. Because of Adam's sin (Romans 5:18; 1 Corinthians 15:22), and our own personal sins (Colossians 1:21), no person is worthy of relationship with a Holy God (Ecclesiastes 7:20; Romans 3:23).

4. Since we are helpless to correct this situation (Proverbs 20:9), and can do nothing to hide our sin from God (Hebrews 4:13), we all stand condemned by sin (Romans 3:19).

5. It is human nature (our sinfulness), and God's nature (His holy wrath against sin), which make us *"enemies"* (Romans 5:10).

6. God's Gift: Atonement. God's gracious response to the helplessness of His chosen people, the nation of Israel, was to give them a means of reconciliation through Old Testament covenant Law.

7. This came in the sacrificial system where in the death, or blood of the animal was accepted by God as a substitute for the death (Ezekiel 18:20), which the sinner deserved: *"For the life of the flesh is in the blood, and I have given it to you upon the altar to make atonement for your souls"* (Leviticus 17:11).

8. The Law required that the sacrificial victims must be free from defect, and buying them always involved some cost to the sinner.

9. But an animal's death did not automatically make people right with God in some simple, mechanical way. The hostility between God and man, because of sin, is a personal matter.

10. God, for His part, personally gave the means of atonement in the sacrificial system; men and women for their part personally are expected to recognize the seriousness of their sin (Leviticus 16:29-30; Micah 6:6-8).

11. They must also identify themselves personally with the victim that dies: *"Then he shall put his hand on the head of the burnt offering, and it will be accepted on his behalf to make atonement for him"* (Leviticus 1:4).

12. In the Old Testament, God Himself brought about atonement, by graciously providing the appointed sacrifices.

13. The priests represented Him in the atonement ritual, and the sinner received the benefits of being reconciled to God in forgiveness and harmony.

14. Although Old Testament believers were truly forgiven, and received genuine atonement through animal sacrifice, the New Testament clearly states that during the Old Testament period, God's justice was not served, *"For it is not possible that the blood of bulls and goats could take away sins"* (Hebrews10: 4).

15. Atonement was possible because, in His forbearance, God had passed over the sins that were previously committed (Romans 3:25).

16. However, God's justice was served in the death of Jesus Christ as a substitute *"who not with the blood of goats and calves, but with His own blood He entered the Most Holy Place once for all, having obtained eternal redemption"* (Hebrews 9:12). *"And for this reason He is the Mediator of the new covenant"* (Hebrews 9:15).

17. Our Response. The Lord Jesus came according to God's will (Acts 2:23; 1 Peter 1:20*) "to give His life a ransom for many"* (Mark 10:45), or for all (1 Timothy 2:6).

18. Though God *"laid on Him the iniquity of us all"* (Isaiah 53:6); (2 Corinthians 5:21; Galatians 3:13), yet Christ has loved us, and given Himself for us, an offering and a sacrifice to God (Ephesians 5:2), so that those who believe in Him (Romans 3:22) might receive atonement and *"be saved from"* [God's] *"wrath"* (Romans 5:9) through *"the precious blood of Christ"* (1 Peter 1:19).

19. No believer who truly understands the awesome holiness of God's wrath, and the terrible hopelessness that comes from personal sin, can fail to be overwhelmed by the deep love of Jesus for each of us, and the wonder of God's gracious gift of eternal atonement through Christ. Through Jesus, God will present us *"faultless before the presence of His glory with exceeding joy"* (Jude 24).

Objections to the Atonement

Not all men love the Atonement. Many objections have been raised against it, for *"The preaching of the Cross is to them that perish foolishness, but unto us which are saved, it is the power of God"* (1 Corinthians 1:18).

1. **The Atonement represents God as** unmerciful, cruel, vindictive, and bloodthirsty if He requires a sacrifice of a life to appease His wrath.

    - **Answer.** It was an act of mercy to mankind to permit a substitute. It was a greater act of mercy that God permitted a substitute, but also provided one, and He became that substitute. Since the Law of God could not be annulled, or lowered, and since sin could not go unpunished, God Himself in the person of His Son, submitted to the penalty in order to set man free. That act was mercy in superlative. *"God so loved the world that He gave His only begotten Son."* No man can deny God's mercy after reading John 3:16.

2. **There is no need of Atonement.** This is a very prevalent objection at the present day. It is said that all that is necessary is for the sinner to repent, and for God to forgive Him on the ground of His repentance.

    - **Answer.** This is not God's view of this matter. God has taught us something very different in His Word. From end to end, the Bible teaches that salvation is only by a vicarious sacrifice. Christ must go to Calvary.

- Mark 8:31, *"And he began to teach them, that the Son of man must suffer many things, and be rejected of the elders, and of the chief priests, and scribes, and be killed, and after three days rise again."*

- Luke 24:7, *"Saying, The Son of man must be delivered into the hands of sinful men, and be crucified, and the third day rise again."*

- Luke 17:25, *"But first must he suffer many things, and be rejected of this generation."*

- John 3:14, *"And as Moses lifted up the serpent in the wilderness, even so must the Son of man be lifted up."*

- John 12:34, *"The people answered him, We have heard out of the Law that Christ abideth forever: and how sayest thou, The Son of man must be lifted up? Who is this Son of man?"*

- Acts 4:12, *"Neither is there salvation in any other: for there is none other name under heaven given among men, whereby we must be saved."*

- Acts 17:3, *"Opening and alleging, that Christ must needs have suffered, and risen again from the dead; and that this Jesus, whom I preach unto you, is Christ."*

- Hebrews 9:23, *"It was therefore necessary that the patterns of things in the heavens should be purified with these; but the heavenly things themselves with better sacrifices than these."*

Special Note. It is God's place to state the conditions on which man may be saved. It is man's business to accept the conditions as God has laid them down. Man is not wiser than God. Since God has provided a vicarious sacrifice, it is not for man to say there is no need of it. That is inexcusable presumption. It is teaching for doctrines the commandments of men.

3. It is unjust to punish the innocent for the guilty.

- **Answer.** This objection, as most of the others, proceeds from the standpoint in making an absolute distinction between the offering, and the one making the offering. If God had laid the penalty on some innocent being, without his consent, that act would have been an injustice; but if God Himself assumed the penalty, it was no injustice to man, and no injustice to him who voluntarily assumed it; but rather the expression of divine, and infinite love.

4. **If sin is punished, it cannot be forgiven; and if forgiven it cannot be punished.** This objection is illustrated in this manner: If a murderer is pardoned, he cannot be hanged; and if hanged, he cannot be pardoned.

    - **Answer.** If a murderer is pardoned, the Law is simply set aside, and true justice is not exacted. But God's Law is not set aside. Rather, His justice and mercy are exhibited in the Substitute who bore the penalty at Calvary to secure the remission of sins. Justice and mercy met in a divine atonement for sins.

5. **Christ could not suffer the penalty of sin without enduring remorse and eternal death.**

    - **Answer.** Christ's infinite dignity and worth gave to His sufferings an infinite value, which was a full legal equivalent for the sins of a race; and more than sufficient for all the penalty due to the whole race, for all the sufferings of the race would be only finite at most.

How Sin Entered into the World: Romans 5:12

The presence of sin is a great mystery. It has provided critics of religion opportunity to question both the existence and the goodness of God. The effort to vindicate God's goodness and justice despite the existence of evil is termed theodicy (Gk. *theos*, *God* and *dike*, *justice*). While conservative theologians rightly rise to defend the character of God, the Bible makes no attempt to justify Him or His actions. Rather, there is a simple affirmation that God is absolutely sovereign and that He has willed into existence both good and evil for His own glory. While God cannot be the actor of evil, He has ordained all things that come to pass. One instrument in the Divine plan to fulfill His purposes is man. *"Wherefore, as by one man sin entered into the world"* (Romans 5:12). The sin of man brought immediate and tragic results including death. There was Spiritual Death as fellowship with God was lost. *"Having the understanding darkened, being alienated from the life of God through the ignorance that is in them, because of the blindness of their heart"* (Ephesians 4:18). And there was Physical Death as the body was to force to separate from the soul.

What a tragedy death was. It reversed all the glory and goodness of God. Death was the opposite of what creation was intended for—life and fellowship with God. The strength of death was strong. But wait. Death is not the final word on the matter of sin and its consequences. There is hope. The gospel message comes to reveal the power of One who can change the role of death. His name is Jesus Christ. According to Romans 5:1-11 it is through Christ that individuals are justified. Through Christ peace with God can be found. Through Christ reconciliation with the Father can take place. Through faith there is the certainty of salvation from the power, pollution, and presence of sin. But that is not all. Romans 5:12-21 reveals that there is more good news. The grace of God not only nullifies the effects of sin, but also gives life everlasting to all who believe!

The Point of a Parenthetical Thought

In setting forth these truths, Paul becomes excited and almost elliptical in his writing. He has so much to say that he feels he must break in upon himself. Words tumble forth in the narrative. Paul begins a sentence but does not finish it. He begins to describe the entrance of sin into the world in Romans 5:12 but does not complete the statement until Romans 5:18. In between Paul begins to expand upon the universality of sin (Romans 5:13-17).

"In Adam's fall, we sinned All"

There is confirmation for the universality of sin in the fact that death reigned from Adam to Moses. Even prior to the giving of the Law from Sinai death reigned. Death manifested its power over those who had not transgressed by violating a specific command as Adam did (Genesis 2:16, 17). As Paul considers this point he anticipates a logical problem. Was it fair that death reign prior to the giving of the Law to mankind for *"sin is not imputed where there is no Law?"* The apostle would answer in the affirmative and for this reason. There was a Law at work. It was not the Law of Moses but the Law of Federal Representation. God viewed all of mankind as being *"in Adam."* And since *"in Adam"* all men fell, death justly reigned.

Adam: A Negative Figure of Christ

Having established the position that all people are *"in Adam"* Paul declares that Adam is the *"figure of him [Christ] that was to come"* (Romans 5:14). The figure will be negative as three contrasts are made between the first Adam and the Last Adam (Romans 5:15-17).

1. While the sin of Adam caused many to die, the free gift of God's gracious salvation in the person of Christ will cause many to live (Romans 5:15).

2. While the sin of Adam brought judgment and condemnation, Christ brings justification, where by sinners are declared righteous (Romans 5:16).

3. While the sin of Adam produces a reign of death, the righteousness of God brought forth a reign of life (Romans 5:17).

4. While the sin of Adam is extended to every person as a member of the human race, the righteousness of Christ is extended to those who are part of His spiritual race, even the elect.

Closing a Parenthetical Thought

Having proved the universality of sin and having enlarged upon it, Paul returns in Romans 5:18 to his interrupted thought of Romans 5:12. Once more, Paul is setting forth the centrality of salvation's being found in Christ. He is doing this, by establishing Adam as the Federal Head of the human race. Not only was Adam the Federal head, he was the Seminal Head as well. In seed (seminal) form, the entire human race existed within Adam, just as Levi was said to have existed in the loins of Abraham when he met Melchizedek (Hebrews 7:10). Therefore, embodying all of humanity, and acting as its Federal Representative, Adam made a decision that involved and committed all of his posterity.

The Federal Headship of Adam is reflected by the government of many nations. In the United States when the members of Congress vote to go to war, as the legitimate representative legislative body of the people, legally, it is as if each person in the country has voted for war. And so it is true, that when Adam disobeyed the Lord and transgressed, *"many were made sinners."* You were made a sinner, and I was made a sinner, ere we were born. Adam transgressed, and judgment came upon all. Therefore, each person is born into this world physically alive but spiritually dead, and under a just judgment.

Then Came Christ

The good news of the gospel is that Christ has come to act as the Federal Representative of a spiritual race, so that all who are *"in Him"* will know something about the imputation of righteousness (Romans 5:18); justification (Romans 5:18); righteousness (Romans 5:19); the abounding grace of God (Romans 5:20); and eternal life (Romans 5:21).

- **The Imputation of Righteousness.** The word for *"impute"* (Gk. *ellogeo*) means *"to reckon"* or *"to attribute."* The imputation of sin initially took place when the transgression of Adam was charged to the account of every person (Romans 5:12-13). Individuals do not sin and so become sinners. At birth and by nature individuals are sinners, so they transgress the moral laws of God.

The imputation of the sin nature to Adam's posterity is just in the Divine economy because it was so decreed to be just by the sovereign God who does all things according to His will. The value of this Divine judicial arrangement is reflected in the fact that the merits of Christ are also freely imputed or charged to the account of all who believe in Him as personal Savior (Romans 5:21).

- **Justification.** The Biblical meaning of justification (Gk. *dikaioo*) is *"to pronounce, accept, and treat as just."* When a person is declared just in the eyes of the Law, there is no liability of a penalty, while there is entitlement to all the privileges due to a person who has kept the Law. Justification, then, is a forensic or legal term, that speaks of a judicial act of administering the Law. In the case of salvation, the sinner is justified, or declared righteous, thereby coming out from under the condemnation of the Law. *"But how is it possible that the holy God of the universe can justify or declare righteous those who are obviously flawed and defiled?"* The answer is not to be found in the creature, but in the merciful plan of the Creator. The answer is not something inward in the soul of man but outward, in the person of a Savior. According to Scripture, justification takes place according to the following process.

  ➤ Christ has been appointed the One through whom God would *"judge the world in righteousness"* in *"day of wrath and revelation in the righteous judgment of God"* (Acts 17:31; Romans 2:16; John 5:27ff).

  ➤ At the appropriate place, and time, at Calvary, God the Father exacted the full retribution of an outraged holiness in the person and work of Christ.

  ➤ Those who are found to be *"in Christ"* by faith have thus been judicially judged as well, for Christ acted as a Federal Representative of all who shall be saved.

➤ Those who are outside Christ must still be judged so that God can *"render to every man according to his works"* (Romans 2:6). We are saved by grace but judged by works. In the day of ultimate accountability, *"the secrets of men"* will be revealed (Romans 2:16). And there will be no mercy for those who are not in Christ.

➤ In the Divine economy, final mercy is manifested only to those who have been given to Christ. Only the elect will enjoy the pardon, remission of sin, and righteousness of Christ. Only those who know Christ will be reconciled to God so that His severity and wrath are satisfied and turned away. (Acts 13:39; Romans 4:6; 2 Corinthians 5:19; Romans 5:9ff) Only those who are covered by the blood of the Cross- of Calvary will enjoy the privileges and blessings associated with the just (Romans 8:14ff; Galatians 4:4).

- **Righteousness.** In the New Testament the Greek word *"dikaios"* is usually translated *"just"* or *"righteous"*. This term conveys the sense of something being *"equal, right,"* or *"fair." "The Holy and all-powerful God who created the universe will not act unfairly toward His creation. Shall not the Judge of all the earth do right"* (Genesis 18:25).

As the ultimate source of justice, all that God does, may be trusted as being just (Deuteronomy 32:4; Romans 9:14). And since the verdict that God passes on all matters is right or fair then the righteousness of man may be looked at in relation to the judgment that God renders upon his condition. The righteous person is the one whom God has declared just while the unrighteous person is the one whom God condemns.

The judgment God administers is impartial (Amos 5:15, 24), for *"there is no respect of persons with God"* (Romans 2:11). God is absolutely free to render a just judgment. The first judgment God rendered was upon the righteousness of man. He said that it was *"very good"* (Genesis 1:31), but then something happened. Man rebelled and lost his innocence, and his righteousness. God passed another judgment upon man and declared Him unrighteous, and sinful. Retribution was inflicted, as a manifestation of the righteousness of God (Isaiah 61:2; 2 Thessalonians 1:6). However, in mercy, God found a way to restore man to fellowship. The sin issue was dealt with in the Person of Jesus Christ, for His righteousness was imputed to those who are to be the heirs of salvation. This imputed righteousness is a free gift (Romans 5:18) and reigns through Jesus Christ (Romans 5:17).

- **Grace.** The word used most often in the New Testament for *"grace,"* is the Greek word *"charis."* It speaks of a joy, and appreciation of things, or of people. This sense of joyful appreciation on the part of the recipient of grace is a proper response to the unmerited favor being freely bestowed.

  In mercy, God has freely poured grace upon His own. They have never earned or deserved His loving kindness or mercy (Exodus 33:13; Jeremiah 31:3; Deuteronomy 7:12) and never will. In the matter of personal salvation from the power, pollution, and presence of sin, that too is dealt with according to grace (Ephesians 2:8, 9; Romans 11:6; Ephesians 2:7; Romans 5:20). God, who is for the sinner, offers him free grace. While men may boast of free will, the Bible teaches the free grace of a free gospel bestowed upon the unrighteous that are unworthy of anything but the just judgment of an outraged holiness.

- **Eternal Life.** Three words are translated *"life"* in the New Testament: *"zoe, bios,"* and *"psyche."* *"Zoe"* refers not only to physical life (e.g. Romans 8:38; 1 Corinthians 3:22; Philippians 1:20; Acts 17:25) but also to a quality of life that has its source in God. *"Zoe"* is characteristic of Christ and of those who come to God through faith in Jesus. It sets forth the blessedness of God and the blessedness of the creature in communion with Christ (Trench).

  Eternal life is derived from Christ (John 1:4) and is imputed to those who are in Him. (Romans 6:4; 1 John 5:12) *"Zoe"* penetrates the realm of time to touch eternity. (2 Corinthians 5:4; 2 Timothy 1:10) In summary, *"zoe"* speaks of a *quality* of a spiritual relationship with God in the life of the believer. *"And this is life eternal, that they might know thee the only true God and Jesus Christ whom thou hast sent"* (John 17:3).

The Purpose of the Law

Once more, there is a dramatic pause in the writing. Paul anticipates a question about the Law. *"If sinners can be justified in the sight of God, if righteousness is a free gift of sovereign grace bestowed upon the unworthy, if righteousness reigns by the work of Jesus Christ, of what purpose is the Law?"* The answer is this: *"The purpose of the Law was to magnify the hideous nature of sin"* (Romans 5:20). The purpose of the Law was not to save but to slay. The purpose of the Law was not to convert, but to condemn.

The purpose of the Law was to expose the arrogance of man, and announce that by the deeds of the Law shall no man be justified (Romans 3:20). And yet, while this is true, as terrible as sin is, there is no sin too great for the grace of God. Though sin reigned, as a powerful principle even unto death, the grace of God found a way to triumph over death, so that righteousness can once more reign, and bring eternal life to all who believe. And the One, who has made the reign of righteousness possible, is Jesus Christ our Lord.

6

Romans 6

A New Theme: Romans 6:1-14

In Romans 15, the apostle Paul has presented men (saints) as sinners being saved from the *penalty* of sin. He has argued that men are guilty in the sight of God, and are under a just judgment of eternal wrath. They need to be justified. They need to be redeemed by the blood of the Lamb (Romans 5:9). They need to be under the reign of grace, through righteousness (Romans 5: 21). And they are.

Now in Romans 6, Paul sets forth individuals (saints) who have been saved from the *power* of sin. He is eager to argue that sin, as a dominion in the life of the Christian, has been broken (Romans 6:3, 6, 9, 12, and 14). Salvation leads to sanctification. The soul that has been justified and restored to life, and fellowship with God will move on to sanctification, and the restoration to spiritual health. The Christian is much like Lazarus, who came forth from the tomb by the power of the words of Christ. The Christian needs the old grave clothes to be taken off and discarded, and they will be.

The Conduct of the Christian

Several major views of the Christian life suggest how the ethics of salvation can be manifested.

- **Antinomianism.** Historically this term was used by Martin Luther to describe those who believed that they were free from all aspects of the Law of Moses, including the moral provisions of the Ten Commandments. They were against (*anti*) the Law (*gnomes*). In more recent days the term must also include those who believe that a person can live happily and consistently in a state of carnality, and still be saved. Romans 6:1 challenges such a concept, as does 1 John 3:7-10. The Bible is clear. The behavior of the true believer will conform to the character of his father. If the devil is the father of a person, then a life of wickedness will be manifested. If God is the Father, then sin shall not be practiced, for a measure of sanctification will be experienced.

- **Sinless Perfection.** Those who advocate Perfectionism to be part of the normal Christian life do take seriously the concept of sanctification, and for that they are to be commended. However, the practical problem in seeking a *Second Work of Grace*, subsequent to salvation whereby sin is eradicated in time is that it is contrary to Christian experience, and challenges the Word of God (1 John 1:8-10). Another problem is that sin is redefined, and minimized to cover ordinary indiscretions of word, thought, and deed.

- **Non-continuation of the Power of Sin.** The Biblical view of the Christian life, is that the believer is an individual with faults and limitations. However, the Christian is also one with great confidence that ultimate sanctification will one day take place, because the present power and reign of sin has been broken.

The Precept of Perfect Deliverance

The journey to spiritual recovery from the pollution of sin for the child of God begins with the precept of deliverance, that is declared to be knowledge (Romans 6:6). God wants His children to know something, and for a good reason: The secret of the happy Christian life is the knowledge of the doctrines of that life. Knowledge of specific doctrinal truths will result in a changed life. Behavior follows belief. The challenge for every believer is to know just what to believe, for it is very easy for a gospel truth to be misunderstood. The teaching of Romans 6 is a perfect illustration as Paul realized. The apostle anticipated a corruption of the gospel message, for a simple reason: Salvation by grace through faith goes counter to the dictates of the natural heart.

Anticipating an Argument

Paul has been preaching that men are justified by faith, and not by the deeds of the Law (Romans 3:20). Paul has argued persuasively, that salvation is the result of what Christ has done apart from human merit. But Paul also knows that the pharisaic heart does not want to hear that truth, so an argument is made. *"Paul, you have been teaching that the Law stirs up sin to show men they need a Savior. Well, if that is the purpose of the Law, why not sin all the more so that the Law can give greater condemnation and so that the glory of God can be revealed to a greater degree."* To such a suggestion Paul cries out, *"God forbid!"* The Christian life is not a life that allows for licentiousness. Sanctification is the natural outworking of salvation, and the Christian must know this principle. The doctrinal position may be summarized.

- At Calvary, Christ died for, and with, respect to sin.

- Every believer dies in Christ (Romans 6:3, 4), who is the legal and covenantal representative of all who shall be saved.

- Because of the intrinsic identification with Christ in His death, burial, and resurrection, there has occurred a once and for all breach with sin. Justification is incompatible with non-sanctification.

- If a person is just, he *must* be in the process of being sanctified.

- Union with the Last Adam, by His death, has severed the believer from the dominion of sin (Romans 6:3). What a glorious truth this is. The believer may sin, but he may not be ruled by sin. Sin does not have dominion over him any longer.

Christ Curing Sin

Regarding the wonderful work of Christ at Calvary in the area of sanctification, Dr. Benjamin Breckenridge Warfield wrote, *"He cures our sinning precisely by curing our sinful nature. He makes the tree good that the fruit may be good. He eradicates our sinfulness by operating directly on us by His renewing action through the Holy Spirit."* It is a blessed truth that Paul presents. Because the penalty of sin has been removed, the Holy Spirit comes to complete the work of salvation through sanctification, so that everything may be of grace. Salvation is a work of grace, but so is sanctification. Salvation comes through the instrumentality of faith, but so does sanctification.

While *positionally* the believer has been freed from the dominion of sin, *practically* there is still a measure of human responsibility to be realized. The believer is not to allow sin to reign in his mortal body. Rather, the Christian is to yield himself unto God (Romans 6:13). This yielding of the body to God must be done on the basis of doctrinal understanding of the victory that Christ has won, and the freedom that He has provided.

Just Like Joshua

An event in the life of Joshua offers a wonderful illustration of this concept. Capturing five hostile kings, Joshua had them brought forth. Then he commanded the captains of the men of Israel to put their feet upon the necks of the subdued kings. Afterwards, Joshua slew them (Joshua 10:22-26). The military men did not slay their enemies, but Joshua did, and they were identified with him in his work. In like manner, our Joshua has slain our great enemy, sin. Since we are in Christ, we have slain the enemy too. Therefore, the victory has been won. There is freedom not to sin, and there is freedom to yield one's life to God, so that sin does not rule any longer.

Saved to Serve the Savior Romans 6:15-23

Having anticipated, and answered the first question concerning sin in the life of the saint (Romans 6:1), the apostle anticipates a second inquiry. *"What then, shall we sin because we are not under Law but under grace?"* (Romans 6:15) Paul has been teaching that the Christian is not under the Law of Moses as a ruling principle for salvation, or for sanctification (Romans 6:14). He has previously taught that the Law was to bring souls to the Savior. By identifying himself with Christ in His death, burial, and resurrection, the Christian enters into a new sphere of existence on the other side of the Cross. In this new state, the believer has a standing with God that demands holiness (Hebrews 12:14). The Christian cannot continue in sin as a way of life

(Romans 6:2). He cannot serve sin (Romans 6:6), be under the dominion of sin (Romans 6:14), be enslaved to sin (Romans 6:18), or bear the fruit of sin (Romans 6:22). The Christian has been saved to serve the Savior. Any person who practices sin, any person who enjoys sin, any person who makes provision for sin has a right and responsibility to examine the root of his righteousness (2 Corinthians 13:5). The salvation that Christ brings is the salvation that frees the soul from the reign of sin (Matthew 1:21).

Reckoning what is Real

The theological basis for believing that the rule of sin has been broken in the saint is rooted in the believer's union with Christ. The Christian has a *judicial union* with the Lord. When Christ died at Calvary, so did the Christian. When Christ was buried, so was the Christian. When Christ rose again from the dead so did the Christian (Romans 6:36). This death, burial, and resurrection with Christ, brought freedom from sin as a dominion over the soul (Romans 6:7). A new life is found on the other side of spiritual death with Christ. A new freedom is found on the far side of the Cross.

The responsibility of the saint to believe this doctrine and reckon it to be accurate because it is true (Romans 6:11). *"It is the truth,"* says Paul, to the Church of Rome, *"that you died with Christ. It is the truth that you were buried with Him. It is the truth that that sin does not rule over you. It is the truth that you are free from the dictates of the Law. It is the truth that you are now under the reign of grace."*

Battling Bias and Unbelief

Unfortunately, it is also true that the heart of the Christian is dull of understanding and slow to receive the good news of the gospel (Matthew 13:15; Luke 24:25). The heart of man does not easily let go of basic unbelief and so objections are raised. *"Paul, if what you have said is true, shall we continue to practice sin?"* (Romans 6:1). *"Shall we continue to sin in specific areas because we are now under the reign of grace?"* The answer to both questions is, *"No! God forbid!"* The Christian is not to sin as a practice, nor is the Christian even to engage in specific acts of sin. Granted, living a life of perfection is not possible. Nevertheless, in context, Paul is arguing against that mindset that concludes it is possible to sin as a practice—or at least it is possible to engage periodically in specific sins with heaven's approval. And the response is *"Good gracious, no! God forbid such a thought!"* Not only must the bent of the life be toward God, but also the daily behavior of the believer must have heaven in view as well and for this reason: to whomever the will is yielded, that entity is the master.

Made to be Mastered

According to the Bible, man was made to be mastered by someone. Though given dominion over the earth and the animals, man was still made subject to the Sovereign. Tragically, sin entered into the world, and man tried to rebel against God. The creature rose up against the Creator. But the insurrection did not succeed. Adam and Eve's only accomplishment when they ate of the forbidden fruit was to exchange one Master for another. Adam and Eve traded the reign of righteousness for the tyranny of sin. What Christ offers is for man to come back under the reign of righteousness.

The Sovereign Work of the Holy Spirit

In salvation the Holy Spirit comes to reverse what sin has done to the nature, will, and behavior of man. Since the Fall, the inclination of man's mind issues volitional decisions, which are manifested in sinful acts. When Eve saw the forbidden fruit, she was inclined to take it. Her inclination influenced her volition, resulting in the action of taking the fruit and eating it. Such is the pattern of sin in every soul: inclination → volition → action → Salvation redirects the inclination of the heart so that new decisions are made resulting in different actions (2 Corinthians 5:17). It is important for the Christian to know this truth.

The Agony of Ignorance

One reason why many believers remain in agony, wallowing in the mire of personal pollution of repetitive sin is that that they either do not know Bible doctrine, or do not really believe that what the Bible teaches is true—at least for them. This lack of faith is devastating because it is linked to selfish experience rather than spiritual reality. A person says to himself, *"I understand what Paul is saying doctrinally. I understand intellectually the union every Christian has with Christ resulting in positional sanctification. Still I sin in a certain area. I hate myself when I succumb to my weakness, and I hate the sin after it is indulged in. But I am so weak—and there is no hope."* But there is hope. That message is what Paul is trying to declare. There is hope for the soul struggling with a sinful addiction. Child of God, there is a spiritual road to recovery, but you must travel by faith the gospel path that includes knowledge (Romans 6:3, 16), reckoning (Romans 6:11), and yielding (Romans 6:13, 19).

The Mark of the Master

Paul teaches something else, which should encourage the heart of every believer struggling with sin. Sanctification will be part of the Christian experience. Paul says, *"But ye have obeyed from the heart that form of doctrine which was delivered to you"* (Romans 6:17). The word *"form"* in the Greek is *"tupos,"* and refers to a mark, or impression left by a die. As salvation is ultimately the work of God the Father, Son, and Holy Spirit, so is sanctification. Those who have the mark of the Master will obey the doctrine of the faith. Some may experience a long period of struggling with some facet of the world, the flesh, or the devil; but the victory will belong to Christ. *"Being confident of this very thing, that He which hath begun a good work in you will perform it until the day of Jesus Christ"* (Philippians 1:6).

Destined for Deliverance

Doctrine produces a mark on the soul when it is believed. Gospel doctrine teaches that the Christian has been made free from sin to become a servant of righteousness, with the result being spiritual fruit unto holiness, and everlasting life (Romans 6:22). The soul that Christ saves has been delivered from being a servant of sin that produces shame and everlasting death (Romans 6:23). Let every soul ask, and answer, *"Am I the servant of sin? Is sin my master? Does my heart have a loving inclination to unrighteousness despite the shameful fruit it produces and the eternal condemnation it earns?"* Again, let every soul ask, and answer, *"Am I the servant of the Savior? Am I the slave of righteousness? Though I sin, is my inclination to seek holiness? Heaven or hell rests upon the answer that is provided. Shall we continue in sin that grace may abound? God forbid! Shall we sin because we are not under the Law, but under grace? God forbid!"*

7

Romans 7

"In God's sight, there are two men:
Adam and Jesus Christ.
And these two men have all
others hanging at their girdle."
—Thomas Goodwin

Married to the Master: Romans 7:1-6

Using a different analogy, Paul returns to the doctrine of the believer's essential unity with Christ, and the results that brings in the area of sanctification. Admitting that his illustrations are imperfect (Romans 6:19), the apostle still struggles to teach that the Christian is no longer a slave to sin; rather, every believer is a slave to righteousness (Romans 6:18), which in turn leads to a life of holiness (Romans 6:22). And not only that but the believer who is freed from sin, and from its dominion (Romans 6:14), is actually married to the new Master, whom he serves in righteousness! What a glorious thought this is, for it reinforces the grand concept of union with Christ that is the general theme of this section of Scripture. The Christian is part of a Judicial Union with Christ (Romans 6:1-14), a Virtuous Union (Romans 6:15-23), and a Marital Union (Romans 7:16).

The Soul Set Free

In considering the Marital Union, several entities are set forth for consideration. Paul speaks of the husband, the wife, the Law, and death. The apostle observes that the Law hath dominion, or rule over a person as long as that person lives (Romans 7:1). On this point, as a general rule, no one would have disputed with Paul. The believers in the Church at Rome were familiar with Roman Law which forbade polygamy and polyandry, and they were also familiar with God's Law that exalted the marriage principle to be indissoluble according to Divine design (Matthew 19:6). Paul wants the point to be established that a marriage is important, for it speaks of a vital union and, for the sake of argument, there is only one sure way out of that union—death.

The Death of a Sinner

Once a death in the relationship took place, the living spouse was free to remarry. In spiritual terms, Paul teaches that a Christian is married to Christ and how such a remarriage took place. Simply enough, there was a death in the former relationship the Christian person had to another. Who died? The Christian person died. *"My brethren, ye also are become dead"* (Romans 7:4). This spiritual death took place at Calvary. In the sight of God every believer was in Christ at Calvary. When Christ died, the souls that leaned on Christ also died. When Christ was buried, every believer was buried with Him. And when Christ arose again from the dead, the Christian person shared in His resurrection.

With all this in mind, what Paul wants to convey is that there was a death of the sinner, and a resurrection to life of the same, but not as the same person, for a divine transformation took place in the essence of the soul. Every Christian can honestly say, *"I am not the person I used to be."* As a saint in the sight of God, as a holy, or set apart person, as one freed from the dominion of Law and the power of sin as a ruling principle, the Christian is no longer subject to the Old Man, which is the Old Nature, because a new marriage has taken place.

Victory by Vital Union

In summary, the following statements can be made.

- The Christian is married to the Master.

- This new marriage is legitimate because a death has occurred.

- No shame or spiritual adultery is involved in the process.

- The Christian died to all that ruled his life, and condemned him to death. The Christians died to the Law, the Old Adam, and sin as a ruling principle.

- The believer died in Christ, and so shares the victory by a vital union with Him.

The Results of Righteousness

Because of the work of Christ at Calvary, and its acceptance by the Father, because of the vital union that the believer shares in the work of Christ, the new life yields practical results beginning with new life. While married to the Law, while united with the Old Man, while under the rule of sin in the flesh, the impulses of sin had to be obeyed, even though the result earned nothing but just condemnation and death (Romans 6:23). However, marriage to Christ produces life in the form of spiritual offspring. This is normal. In a healthy marriage there is love and intimacy with the result being new life. Likewise, in spiritual marriage, the Divine design is to produce new heartfelt impulses, resulting in spiritual offspring, or works of righteousness (Romans 7:5, 6).

Struggling With Sin

To recognize that new life manifested in works of righteousness is the natural result of being married to Christ does not negate the real struggle that continues with sin. The reason Paul spends so much time on this section is the problems are associated with sanctification. The Word of God is realistic. The spirit may be willing to be holy, but the flesh is weak and struggles to do right. It is a constant warfare. What are needed are hope and assurance that the victory will be won. This hope comes in part by understanding the process of sanctification. God wants the Christian to *know* something. In particular the believer is to know a vital union with Christ. The believer is to know that he is married to the Master. This marriage has occurred because a death, burial, and resurrection have taken place in the Divine economy. If the believer can just know this, then a holy relationship with Christ can be cultivated, resulting in the spiritual fruit of sanctification. The soul that has been saved is not to serve the flesh (that is the old husband), but is to serve the Savior, to whom he has been wed.

> *"Free from the law o happy condition,*
> *Jesus has bled and there is remission.*
> *Cursed by the law and bruised by the Fall,*
> *Grace hath redeemed us once for all."*

Is the Law Sinful? Romans 7:7-12

As Paul continues to develop the doctrine of sanctification, he addresses the relationship of the believer to the Law, by which he means the Mosaic Law, summarized by its moral teaching in the *"Decalogue"* (lit. ten words). The teaching has been set forth that the Law, as a ruling principle has no more power over the Christian. The believer in Christ has died with respect to the Law so that he might be married to a new Master, Jesus Christ the Righteous One (Romans 7:4; 7:6). Having taught that, the apostle is concerned that others think that the Law is being denigrated, so he raises the rhetorical question, *"Is the Law sin?"* And the answer, *"God forbid!"* (Gk. *me genoito*, lit. *May it never be said!*) The phrase, *"God forbid,"* expresses Paul's strongest emotional reaction against something, which he will utter nine times in the epistle (Romans 3:4, 6; 3:31; 6:2, 15; 7:7, 13; 11:1; 11:11). So Paul has great respect for the Law, as must all Christians, for good reason. The Law was used by God to accomplish three specific deeds.

- **The Law was given to reveal sin** (Romans 7:7). Paul says, *"I had not known sin except the Law said, Thou shalt not covet."* That is an amazing statement because it provides an insight into the soul. It is within the power of individuals to say they have no sin despite obvious transgressions. One of the ancient controversies God had with Israel is that the people insisted on maintaining their innocence. (Jeremiah 2:1-37), so the Law was given to force into the open the issue of transgression.

- **The Law was given to stir up sin** (Romans 7:8). It is one matter to come to the conclusion that a person is a sinner in general; it is something else to be specific. Paul was specific about his sin when he finally felt it stirred up inside his soul. Paul realized he was a sinful man with a wretched heart. This sight of self probably came on the road to Damascus. Blinded by the glory of the resurrected Lord, Saul of Tarsus realized that he was a covetous man. He wanted the honor and glory of others. He wanted to be praised for persecuting the Christians. When he realized his own desire of covetousness, Saul realized that he was not a good man. He had broken the very Law he intended to keep, and assaulted others for not keeping.

- **The Law was given to reveal the presence of personal spiritual death** (Romans 7:9). When Paul finally found out the true status of his own soul by the Law he said, *"And I died."* Paul became a dead man walking. The Law slew him. Oh, what power the Law has. That which was designed ideally, and hypothetically to give life if honored perfectly, became the instrument of spiritual death (Romans 7:10).

The Strength of the Savior

Nevertheless, the Law remained holy, just, and good. And so the question of Romans 7:1 is answered. "Is the Law sin?" No. The Law is holy, just, and good; for by revealing sin, by stirring up sin, by bringing spiritual death, the Law serves to drive desperate sinners to the Savior, or to be saved by grace, through faith alone. Though the Law cannot save, though the Law cannot sanctify, though the Law cannot make alive, though the Law cannot loose the soul from sin, Christ can. Revelation 1:5 says that Christ loves (Gk. present tense, only time in Scripture) all who believe on Him.

"Unto him that loveth us" [lit. present tense] *"and washed us from our sins in his own blood"* (Revelation 1:6). By His blood Christ is able to make blind Bartimaeus see. He is able to raise Lazarus from the dead. He is able to set those who are captive to sin free. Christ is able to do what the Law could never do, and that is to save the soul from the power, pollution, and presence of sin. The story is told, that one day, the

eighteenth century Germany poet Heydrich Hiene, went to see the great statue Venus de Milo on display in Louvre, Paris. After gazing upon the stone figure for quite a while he exclaimed, *"But the goddess has no arms to help poor people like myself."* The Law is like that. While holy, just, and good, the Law could not help any poor sinner. It could only condemn. The strength of a Savior is needed. Jesus is such a Savior.

The Grievous Sins of the Saints: Romans 7:13-25

One of the easiest things for people to do in life, in a religious conversation is to confess that men, in general, are sinners. Even the non-churched will acknowledge that humanity is not all that it should be. Seneca referred to the *"universal madness of men."* Conversely, one of the most difficult realities for people is to be honest with self, and honest with God, and confess personal sins specifically (1 John 1:8-9). It is within the human heart to want to pretend that all is right with self. Others may do wrong, but not self. The Bible says that, *"All have sinned and come short of the glory of God."* And all keep on sinning even after salvation.

However, a fundamental difference exists between the sins of the saints, and the sins of the non-converted. The sins of the saints are more grievous to the soul. There is a new struggle in the saved soul to cease from doing that which is evil. Unfortunately, the battle to subdue the soiled soul is difficult. Some of the most grievous sins are to be found in the saints. David, the sweet singer of Israel, battled with lust, and lost. Abraham, the Friend of God, struggled with lying and lost. Moses had a violent temper that would burst forth suddenly. The heathen wives of Solomon turned his heart from the Lord so that the wisest man in the world could not overcome idolatry. And the list goes on and on. Christians sin grievously. Christians struggle with the presence of indwelling sin, as seen in the life of the apostle Paul, who one day cried out in anguish, *"O wretched man that I am! Who shall deliver me from the body of this death?"* (Romans 7:24)

A Page from the Life of Paul

Of course, not all-Biblical commentators believe that Paul writes as a Christian in Romans 7:13-25, but there are compelling arguments.

- **The general flow of the narrative favors the concept that Paul writes as a believer.** The teaching of the epistle is that men need to be justified in the sight of God, and they need to be sanctified. A work of grace needs to be done for the believer and in the believer as well. Since Paul has dealt with the issue of justification by grace through faith alone, he would logically progress to discuss how a Christian could be free from the presence of indwelling sin.

- **Paul uses the first person and the present tense in this part of the narrative.** He writes as if he is presently a wretched man struggling with sin.

- **Paul has a clear sight of his sinful condition.** The unsaved do not see themselves so clearly, nor do they diagnose themselves so carefully as Paul does here. All in all, it is the language of a saved man who struggles with the problem of indwelling sin and wants to be free. He knows that the Law is not the problem for the Law is holy, just, and good. He knows even that the Law does not bring about the death he will die though it does condemn. He dies because he has sinned. *"The soul that sinneth, it shall die"* (Ezekiel 18:4).

Hope for Habitual Sins in the Saints

Writing as a saved man, Paul confesses his inward struggle with evil. *"For that which I do I allow not* (lit. *do not approve of): for what I would, that do I not; but what I hate, that do I"* (Romans 7:15). Using the term *"I"* in a comprehensive sense to convey the person actuated by the new nature and sin, Paul acknowledges that as a Christian he struggles with being good and bad for he is both. He recognizes that there is a Law, a force of sin that still dwells in him (Romans 7:16, 17).

Most Christians have recognized this Law of sin, and some have found themselves powerless before it in a terrible way. Though all Christians struggle with the presence of indwelling sin to one degree or another, some fight against repetitive practices of besetting or habitual sins. The Puritans called these repetitive transgressions *"darling sins."* What is a *"darling sin"* or an unholy habit of the heart?

- **A habitual sin is a sin that brings private pleasure.** The pleasure may be physical or psychological or both. This sin is loved for the pleasure it brings. Often, the pleasure was first discovered in childhood.

- **A habitual sin is irresistible**. Something in the soul keeps going back to it over and over again in a fatal attraction. The question of why is never answered. Sin is a great mystery.

- **A habitual sin is a protected aberration of the heart**. Other sins may be conquered; other sins may be subdued; but this habitual sin is protected in the heart.

- **A habitual sin is habitual, and so is provided for**. If it requires money, as much as possible will be spent on it even at the expense of legitimate needs. If this sin requires time, an inordinate period will be given to it even if sleep is lost and job performance suffers. If this sin requires energy, strength will be found to perform it. No expense is too great, no time is too much, no strength is too demanding for the habitual sin.

- **A habitual sin is private**. The heart may fear public exposure, but the grip on the soul is so secure that self will risk acute embarrassment rather than have this sin finally put to death.

- **A habitual sin will bring spiritual anguish to the soul of the child of God**.

Despite the momentary perverted pleasure it brings, despite its power to enslave the soul, despite the fact that it is protected, despite the fact that the sin is still secret after many years from friends and family members, the single dominating sin of the soul still brings great pain to God's people. Peace of heart is destroyed, and assurance of God's love is questioned.

Generally speaking, after the dark deed is done, self-loathing and self-hatred, remorse sets in; shame is felt; sorrow is expressed; confession is made; vows are taken not to let it happen again and then the pattern starts all over.

> *"O that a man would arise in me*
> *That the man I am may cease to be."*
> —Tennyson

This is not to say that habitual sin is part of every Christian's life. Nor will every believer have the same problems with sin. However, many Christians would like to confess (though they dare not) that their religious experience has been a death struggle with habitual sin. Their soul longs to be set free from emotional conflict, for there is nothing but secret shame, repeated failure, and self-loathing when the deeds of darkness are done. At times, it seems that two people live in one body. One entity wants to do right; the other wants to do wrong. One part of the soul that is saved wants to love the Lord; the other part acts as a Master of meanness and debauchery. The habitual sin says with authority, *"Come!"* and the soul responds. The bodily parts are rendered servants to sin. The Sin Master says, *"Do this!"* and that which is wrong is performed. In the struggle for survival, sanctification, and spiritual deliverance, the professing Christian is tempted to think unworthy things. There is resentment, and desperate thoughts that the heart has not been truly converted, that God is not listening to prayers for help, that the gospel is not effective, and that the Holy Spirit does not care. Then time passes, and the impure passions subside.

During those periods of spiritual enjoyment when the habitual sin lies dormant, the professing Christian may studiously read books on sanctification, try all the techniques advocated by the Higher Life Movement, pray and agonize, and perform many other religious acts. But then one day, the Sin Master returns. It calls yet again, and the soul and body yields to its compelling influences. The terrible inner shame spills over the transgressing heart. Now, it may be that Paul did not have a besetting sin. But he did struggle with indwelling sin. In like manner, many Christian people—who really love Jesus Christ—cry out in the language of Paul, and scream in spiritual agony, *"O wretched man that I am! Who will deliver me?"* (Romans 7:24).

Some people in the Church know the language of Romans 9:24 but have yet to enjoy the language of Romans 9:25. To these struggling hurting hearts, a word of encouragement can be given by saying that Jesus Christ has come to set the captives free. The angels said, *"He shall set His people free from their sins"* (Matthew 1:21). Paul does not ask, *"What shall set me free?* But *Who will deliver me?"* And the answer is Christ. Only Christ can set the captives free, and the truth is established that the solution to sin's problem is not in self, but outside of self in another, even Jesus Christ. How then, will the wretched man find victory through Jesus Christ? How does Christ deliver souls that struggle with habitual sins?

- **Christ delivers through His death at Calvary.** That truth is the root of all righteousness. The problem is that while Christians have heard this gospel truth, the heart is hesitant to truly believe it fully. Experience seems to make a mockery of scriptural teaching. Nevertheless, the Word of God stands sure. *"Sin shall not have dominion over you!"* (Romans 6:14).

- **The Lord Jesus Christ delivers by His Word.** The Psalmist said, *"Thy word have I hid in my heart that I might not sin against you."* The hiding of God's word does not refer only to scripture memorization. Satan can quote the Scripture better than anyone else, but he can still sin. Most cult leaders, such as Jim Jones, have memorized scores of scripture, and then lead other people into sin by twisting the Word. To hide God's word is to make it a vital part of the soul by faith.

- **The Lord delivers His people through His Church.** Christian author Jay Adams has reminded the Church that it is competent to counsel. But counseling can only come when the heart wants heaven more than it wants the lust that rages in the soul and so there is a willingness to be accountable to the Church. Accountability demands three things: honesty, humility, and trust.

- **The Lord delivers His people through practical steps of gospel obedience.** The heart that wants to be set free might have performed some simple acts, such as throwing out ungodly material, blocking off selected television channels, moving away from the opportunities to sin, and most of all, going back to the basics of the Christian faith, to evangelical repentance which has distinct features.

- A person who truly repents in an evangelical way must see and know the horror of sin. A true sight of sin is a requisite to genuine repentance. One of the best ways to see sin is to take a long look at the Crucified One. Look at what sin has done to Jesus. That time of pondering will produce true mourning and sorrow. The more a person is able to see Christ wounded and bleeding, the more the heart will be pierced for sin committed (Zechariah 12:10-12).

- When true evangelical repentance is present, a person is grieved, and humbled by it, as the woman that anointed Jesus one night was grieved (Luke 7:37-38).

- As a person repenting must be grieved for sin committed, he must, and he will loathe himself; self loathing is requisite to evangelical repentance as per Ezekiel 20:41-43.

- A repenting person does not only loathe himself for his sin, but also experiences a shame of it; he is ashamed of his former evil ways (Ezra 9:6).

- Not only is a repenting person ashamed of his former evil ways, but as the opportunity comes, he will acknowledge his sins sincerely. Saul and Pharaoh acknowledged their sins insincerely, for they returned to their evil ways. David, and Peter, and others expressed true contrition.

- A repenting person labors to undo his sins, as the jailer ministered to Paul and Silas (Acts 16). For those who truly want to repent, three areas must be given great consideration: the sincerity of the heart, the matter of unbelief, and the time factor.

Hope does exist for habitual sinning saints: hope that the spiritual chains of bondage will be broken, hope that Christ will come and set the captive heart free, hope that the soul will one day be integrated and that God will be loved with all the heart, and all the mind, and all the soul. Perhaps God will be pleased to set some soul free from habitual sins in this very hour.

> *"Not enjoyment and not sorrow*
> *Is our destined end or way,*
> *But to live that each tomorrow*
> *Finds us farther than today."*
> —Longfellow

8

Romans 8

"If the Holy Scriptures were a ring,
and The Epistle to the Romans its precious stone,
Chapter Eight would be the sparkling point of the jewel."
—Spener

A Life of Liberty: Romans 8:1-4

The testimony of life, as well as the teaching of Scripture, is that every believer, including the great apostle Paul, struggles with indwelling sin. Romans 7:14-25 is an accurate description of the desperate struggle that rages in the soul of the saint. The apostle John said, *"If we say we have no sin, we deceive ourselves, and the truth is not in us"* (1 John 1:8). Even after salvation, sin remains as an indwelling presence and a great burden. The heart that longs for holiness cries out, *"O wretched man that I am!"* (Romans 7:24) The heart of the believer finds a new impulse to do all things well for Christ's sake. There is a desire for deliverance from the pollution of sin, all the while accepting responsibility for the darks deeds of the flesh.

In more recent years, a new self-esteem theology has arisen to assuage any sense of guilt due to inner conflict. The concept is now widely advocated even in evangelical circles, that self-love should replace self-judgment. But that is not realistic, for the soul does sin. There should be personal responsibility, despite the inability to change from within by one's own power. Charles Hodge is correct when he writes,

"Inability is consistent with responsibility.... As the Scriptures constantly recognize the truth of these two things, so are they constantly united in Christian experience. Everyone feels that he cannot do the things that he would, yet is

sensible that he is to blame for not doing them. Let any man test his power by the requisition to love God perfectly at all times. Alas! How entire our inability; yet how deep our self-loathing and self-condemnation.... The renewed man condemns himself, and justifies God, even while he confesses and mourns his inability to conform to the divine requisitions" (Commentary on Romans).

Besides mourning, the renewed man can do something else. He can believe that a life of liberty from sin is still possible, but only because of a source outside himself. He can begin, like Paul, to give thanks for the Divine Deliverer—Jesus Christ the Righteous One. *"Who shall deliver me from the body of this death? I thank God through Jesus Christ our Lord"* (Romans 7:25b; 8:1a).

A Glorious and Grand Promise

Because of the work of the Divine Deliverer at Calvary, the justified soul, though plagued with indwelling sin and afflictions while in the world, finds comfort in the promises of God being assured that, *"There is now no condemnation to them which are in Christ Jesus."*

Special Note. The latter part of Romans 8:1 is not found in many ancient manuscripts, though the words are found in Romans 8:4.

The word *"no"* is emphatic and deserves special attention. Paul is not teaching merely that now, or today, there is no condemnation, with the possibility that tomorrow things might be different. He is saying that there will **never** be any condemnation for those who are in Christ. It is because of a vital union with Christ that the Christian will have no ultimate judgment brought against him in the form of the Second Death (Revelation 20:6). Union with Christ brings justification, resulting in a life of sanctification through the Holy Spirit.

The believer has peace *with* God, by looking to the finished work of Christ at Calvary. He has peace with God, because the wrath of Divine justice has been satisfied by the substitutionary death of Christ. Now the peace *of* God can be known, by looking to the work of the Lord Jesus Christ, Who is seated on His throne in heaven, and Who has sent the Holy Spirit as a sign and seal of the continuing work of redemption in the hearts of believers. The Christian must not look to himself to find the strength to resist sin, and to be holy, but he must look to Someone outside himself. It is through the Spirit that sin is subdued. It is the Spirit's power that quenches the strong passions of the heart as He operates with omnipotent power with the force of Law. It is the Spirit who will finally achieve what the Mosaic Law could never accomplish, and that is to provide freedom from the rule of sin, and the penalty of death (Romans 8:2).

The reason why the Law of Moses could never deliver a single soul from the burden of sin, or the penalty of death, is that it was inherently weak through the flesh (Romans 8:3). The Law was powerful enough to reveal sin, stir up sin, and condemn those who committed sin; but it was never strong enough to stop sin. The Law itself was holy, just and good, but it could not give man the salvation he needed. So Christ came to save and the Holy Spirit came to sanctify men according to the will of the Father (Philippians 2:13; Colossians 1:29).

In the Likeness of Sinful Flesh

The Spirit is able to work His sanctifying grace because God the Father *"sent His own Son in the likeness of sinful flesh"* (Romans 8:3). While all who believe in Christ become the *sons of God* (John 1:12), Jesus remains His uniquely begotten Son, distinct in kind from all others. This unique Son of God came *"in the likeness of sinful flesh."*

- Paul does not say that Jesus came *in sinful flesh*. Modern theologians try to teach that Jesus Christ came in sinful flesh, though He did not yield to sin. No, the Lord came *"in the likeness of sinful flesh."*

- Paul does not say that Jesus came *"in the likeness of flesh."* That assertion is what the early Docetics used to say. The Docetics taught that Christ was a divine being who only *"looked"* or *"appeared"* (Gk. *dokeo, to seem*) human, but he did not really have a human body.

- Nor did Paul say that Christ came *"in the flesh,"* though that in and of itself was true.

Paul was careful to stress the coming of Christ, in precise language that freed Him of sinful flesh but maintained His true humanity. Jesus came in order to condemn sin in the flesh. And He did accomplish this feat by the life He lived, and the death of deaths that He died.

The result of His condemnation of sin is deliverance for all for whom He died. The Christian is not immune to sin, but he does not have to serve it any longer. The Christian is not married to sin any longer. He is not under sin's dominion any longer. And the stirrings of sin do not have to be succumbed to any longer, for the Law of the Spirit of life in Christ Jesus hath made him free from the Law of sin and death (Romans 8:2).

The Bent of the Believer

Now the purpose of a spiritual life of freedom is holiness (Romans 8:4). The soul is set free from sin, the Spirit operates sovereignly in the soul *that the righteousness of the Law might be fulfilled.* The Christian is not lawless. The Christian has been set free to fulfill the righteous moral facet of the Law. This is the bent of the believer.

Life in the Sphere of the Spirit: Romans 8:5-17

All genuine Christians have a vital interest in living out the ethics of the Christian life. Unfortunately, not all believers are in agreement as to how this is to be done. As a result, confusing, and conflicting concepts are contended for.

- Some Christians believe that the Christian life is to be very legalistic. Certain prohibitions are drawn up and adhered to, with the hope that if certain standards are honored, the result will be sanctification.

- Some Christians believe that the Christian life is to be lived pretty much as one pleases. The result is often a life of anti-nomianism, or lawlessness.

- Some Christians believe that life is to be lived by the power of the Holy Spirit—and, of course, they are correct. Nowhere does the Bible ever teach that sanctification is ultimately grounded in human works. The Bible says that, *the just shall live by faith* (Romans 1:17; Galatians 3:11; Hebrews 10:38). The redemptive work that God the Father has begun in the heart will be manifested in sanctification, because it is *God* which worketh in the soul to will and to do of His good pleasure (Philippians 2:13).

As the Bible opposes legalism as an expression of the Christian life, so it opposes anti-nomianism, or lawlessness. While the believer is not under the mandates of the Mosaic Law, the life that is lived in the Spirit will result in the righteousness of the Law (Romans 8:4). Dr. S. Lewis Johnson, for many years a professor at Dallas Theological Seminary, Dallas, Texas, liked to illustrate the Christian life, in the Spirit, by dogs. He talked about three types of dogs.

- The first type of dog has no liberty for a chain at all times when outside binds him with the master. Such is the bondage of legalism: no freedom to be spontaneous or deviate from taboos.

- The second type of dog has total liberty, and no Law. Such a status seems wonderful until the dog encounters the dogcatcher, or races out into the street and meets oncoming traffic. Suddenly, freedom is not so free, or preferable.

- The third type of dog has no chain, and total freedom in the presence of his master. But he is always looking at the master. This dog can run and jump and play, but he always comes back to the master because he is bound by invisible chains of love and affection. Ideally, the Christian life is to be lived with tremendous freedom—especially from the Mosaic Law—but with invisible chains of love, attached to the Spirit.

Reasons for a Life of Righteousness

There are some specific reasons why genuine Christians should, and will, live a life in the sphere of the Spirit.

♦ The Christian life is lived in the Spirit because there is a new inclination to do so. Salvation brings a new propensity to the heart, and that propensity is toward holiness (Romans 8:5).

♦ The Christian life is lived in the Spirit in order to avoid condemnation. To walk after the flesh is to walk in the path of death (Romans 8:6).

♦ The Christian life is lived in the Spirit in order to prove salvation. *"if any man have not the Spirit of Christ, he is none of his"* (Romans 8:9).

Results of Life in the Spirit

♦ **Righteousness.** The believer who lives life in the Spirit knows something about fulfilling the righteousness of the Law. *"That the righteousness of the Law might be fulfilled in us, who walk not after the flesh, but after the Spirit"* (Romans 8:4).

♦ **Life.** To be spiritual minded is life (Romans 8:6). *"And this is life eternal, that they might know thee the only true God, and Jesus Christ, whom thou hast sent"* (John 17:3).

♦ **Peace.** To be spiritual-minded is peace (Romans 8:6). Sin agitates the heart. Sin makes the mind unstable in all its ways (James 1:8).

♦ **Under authority.** To be spiritual minded is to be subject to the Law of God (Romans 8:7). The Christian life is not a life of lawlessness. Paul warned against that thinking in 1 Peter 2:16. *"As free, and not using your liberty for a clock of maliciousness, but as the servants of God."* Certain obligations are imposed upon the behavior of the believer. The many divine imperatives of the New Testament for the Christian are there because the spiritual life is not totally free from the presence of sin in time. Those who teach otherwise produce despair in the heart of genuine saints, who struggle with the flesh. However, the rules and regulations for believers should not lead to legalism or to a system of sanctification by works. No, the Spirit led life is by faith.

Christians are saved by faith, and are sanctified by faith. *"The just shall live by faith"* (Romans 1:17; Galatians 3:11; Hebrews 10:38).

- **Self-mortification.** Through the Spirit, the believer is to say no to sin, and the stirrings of the dark side of the soul. *"For if ye live after the flesh, ye shall die: but if ye through the Spirit do mortify the deeds of the body, ye shall live"* (Romans 8:13). *"Mortify therefore your members which are upon the earth: fornication, uncleanness, inordinate affection, evil concupiscence, and covetousness, which is idolatry"* (Colossians 3:5).

- **Sonship.** It is wonderful to be able to look back into one's lineage and find a notable ancestor, but nothing equals the privilege of being united to Christ, and to God Himself. *"For as many as are led by the Spirit of God, they are the sons of God"* (Romans 8:14). If any person wants to glory, let him glory as a child of the King of kings and Lord of lords.

- **Intimacy with the Father.** In the Garden of Gethsemane Jesus prayed, *"Abba, Father"* (Mark 14:36). And every Christian can also pray, *"Abba, Father"* thereby enjoying a measure of intimacy with the Father (Romans 8:15). The word *"Abba"* is a tender word of affection, much like the English word *"papa"* or *"daddy."* It is also a word associated with revelation and illumination. In the Jewish world, it was the father who was primarily responsible for taking the child upon the knee and teaching him the Law of the Lord. There was instruction in righteousness. So the Christian is reminded that there is no revelation or illumination, there is no ultimate instruction in righteousness, apart from the Lord Jesus Christ. But in Christ, by the Spirit, the believer can know intimately the Father and His will.

- **Assurance.** Evangelist D.L. Moody often said that he never knew an effective Christian who did not have assurance of their salvation. There is a reason for that. It is difficult to share the good news of saving grace, while unsure whether that grace has changed one's own heart. The apostle Paul teaches that the Holy Spirit Himself bears witness with our spirit that we are the children of God (Romans 8:16). The apostle John would agree that assurance of salvation is the privilege of every Christian, for he says, *"These things have I written unto you that believe on the name of* *the Son of God; that ye may know that ye have eternal life, and that ye may believe on the name of the Son of God"* (1 John 5:13).

- **Heirs of God and joint heirs with Christ.** The concept of an heir anticipates an inheritance. The inheritance of which the Bible speaks, is in the future, and consists of all the riches that every Christian will enjoy because of an association with Christ (Ephesians 3:18; 2 Timothy 4:8). Specifically, the inheritance of the saints includes a new name (Revelation 3:12), and a crown of gold (Revelation 4:4; 14:14). There are thrones to reign from (Revelation 20:4; 3:21) in a glorified resurrected body (1 Corinthians 15:49) in a new universe (2 Peter 3:13). And there is much more. For the Christian, the future is fantastic, because the Testator who bestows the gifts of divine grace is rich. All the silver and gold are His (Haggai 2:8). Every animal of the forest belongs to His domain, and all the cattle on a thousand hills (Psalms 50:10). In fact, there are no limits to His riches. No wonder the Christian wants to shout, *"Alleluia, what a Savior!"*

Sittin' Pretty

Dr. Donald Grey Barnhouse, former pastor of the Tenth Street Presbyterian Church in Philadelphia, liked to close his sermons from time to time, with a recitation of all that the Christian has in Christ, in respect to forgiveness of sins, and thus the freedom to walk in the Spirit. He liked to say that our sins have been forgiven, forgotten, cleansed, pardoned, atoned for, remitted, and covered. They have been passed into the depths of the sea, blotted out as a think cloud, removed as far as the east is from the west, remembered against us no more forever because they have been cast behind God's back.

One day, a little boy, who had been sitting near the pulpit in the balcony when this summary was stated, followed Dr. Barnhouse outside the Church where the pastor shook hands. As the people passed by, the little boy tugged at the great man's coat. Looking up at the tall man, Dr. Barnhouse was about six feet and two inches, said, *"Good sermon doc! Gee, we are sure sitten pretty."* And so we are. Life in the Spirit leaves us *"sitten pretty"* in Christ.

An Earnest Question and an Honest Answer

Are you in Christ? Do you know what it is to live in the Spirit? If you have never called upon the name of the Lord, if you have never renounced a sinful way of life, why not do so right now? Believe on the Lord Jesus Christ as your personal Savior. Having taken that step, please write to Mt. Zion ministries to let others know that Christ has saved you from the penalty, the power, and the pollution of sin. There will be a tremendous time of rejoicing with you. Others are waiting to encourage you in your faith; they are ready to help you grow spiritually, as you walk in the newness of life, in the Spirit, as a child of God.

Salvation's Mountain Range

Despite the great privilege the Christian enjoys as a child of God, despite being led by the Holy Spirit, despite being an heir of eternal riches, in time, the believer is still subject to suffering. Pain, and suffering shall always be part of the highs and lows of the Christian experience. It has been suggested that the Christian life might be viewed from Salvation's Mountain Range. As one looks over the spiritual landscape, majestic mountain peaks can be viewed. There are Mt. Justification and Mt. Sanctification. There are Mt. Heirship and Mt. Sonship. One of the most rugged peaks, and the highest to climb is Mt. Self-Mortification. At the end of Salvation's Range is Mt. Eternal Life. But then there are the valleys between the peaks. There is the Valley of the Shadow of Death. There is the Valley of Sorrow and Shame. There is the Valley of Suffering. These are the valleys of anguish that produce the agonies of grace.

Three Groanings for Grace and Glory: Romans 8:18-27

It is the consistent teaching of Scripture that the saints will suffer with the Savior. Sometimes the suffering is physical (Acts 8:1). Sometimes the suffering is mental and emotional. There is the suffering of misunderstanding. There is the suffering of reproach. There is the suffering of slander. There is the suffering that comes from family members, who do not understand the Christian faith. This suffering comes because the Lord has ordained that a coat soaked with blood and sweat will be worn by those who will one day be dressed in the glory of the robes of purity and righteousness. In context, Paul writes of the suffering saints. The Scriptures speak of the groans experienced by three entities: the Children of God, Creation, and the Comforter.

A Proper Response to Pain

The apostle begins with the groans of the Christian. Since suffering is inevitable, attention should be paid to a proper response. Paul *reckons* that the sufferings of time are insignificant when considered in light of eternity, and the coming glory that shall be revealed in the believer (Romans 8:18). These words do not minimize the severity of pain. Indeed, Paul himself has personally endured more than most Christians, according to an autobiographical account (2 Corinthians 11:23-33).

And yet, despite all the beatings that he endured, despite false imprisonment, Paul carefully concludes that the coming glory will overshadow the sorrows of time. By focusing attention on heaven, Paul encourages Christians to remember that a greater future is just ahead. All of creation waits for it.

While creation waits and watches for the grand climax of human history, it groans (Romans 8:19). With a voice of personification, creation screams in agony, for the creation was made subject to decay and destruction (Romans 8:20). This was not done willingly, but as a result of the rebellion of man. With the Fall, creation was cursed, as it became caught up in the affairs of the Sovereign, with His subjects.

But the story does not end there, for Paradise Lost, shall one day be Paradise Restored. The creation shall yet be delivered *"from the bondage of the corruption into the glorious liberty of the children of God"* (Romans 8:21). But until that day, creation groans, and travails in pain, like a woman about to deliver a child. Earthquakes shake the mountains. Volcanoes erupt spilling forth hot lava. Raging floodwaters break forth to destroy crops, and drown the innocent. Creation rages, until the time of rest. Creation rages, as it awaits a radical transformation.

And it will come. One day, there will be a restoration of the earth to its pristine glory. One day, the earth will deliver up its dead, and those who have died shall live again. For the Christian, the hope of the resurrection is a glorious hope. *"For we are saved by hope"* (Romans 8:30). Of course, if we could see our hope, if we could see the restoration of the earth, and the resurrection of the body, it would no longer be hope (Romans 8:25). Therefore, we must exercise patience, with quiet confidence that all that Scriptures says will come to pass, according to Divine revelation.

The Second Mediator

To encourage hearts that are waiting, according to promise, for the future glories of grace, the truth is revealed, that the agonizing Christian is not alone in the midst of a groaning creation. The Comforter has come to pray with, and for us. Three things characterize the ministry of the Comforter: pain, privacy, and power. First, there is pain. In the prayer ministry of the Spirit, there is agony, and intensity, as He makes requests according to the will of God. While the Father searches the heart, the Holy Spirit makes specific requests as a Second Mediator (Romans 8:34).

Two Sets of Sons

It is good to have this particular ministry of the Spirit, for what God the Holy Spirit requests, God the Father will honor. Just as the Father gave to the Son all that He asked, because the Son always pleased the Father (John 8:29), so the Father will answer the prayer requests of the Spirit.

Now several questions arise by way of personal application and self-examination, *"Does the Spirit help me in my infirmities? Does the Spirit groan on my behalf? When God the Father searches my heart, does He pause to listen to the pleas of the Spirit and then answer the prayers of the Spirit according to sovereign grace?"* These are not idle inquiries; for either a person is a Son of God (Romans 8: 14) with a glorious future of eternal life in a resurrected body suited for heaven, or a person is a Son of Disobedience (Ephesians 2:2; 5:6; Colossians 3:6) under the wrath of God and awaiting a fearful judgment (Romans 2:5). Come to Christ by faith and then tell others that redemption and thus the Redeemer, draweth nigh (James 5:8).

How Long, O Lord?

When the soul is in agony it is natural to wonder when the suffering will cease. The Psalmist cried, *"My soul is also sore vexed; but thou, O Lord, how long?"* (Psalms 6:3). The Christian can only hope that it will not be long before all pain and sorrow associated with time will be terminated. There is good reason to hope that the coming of Christ is near.

It is part of the birthing process that, when the labor pains become shorter between contractions, a child is about to be delivered. Perhaps the same is true spiritually. Prior to the coming of Christ, the earth will convulse more and more. Prior to the coming of Christ, the groans of the saints will intensify as renewed persecution sets in due to the convicting, and converting, ministry of the Holy Spirit (John 16:7-11). While the faithful community of the saints should not seek signs (Matthew 12:39), there should be a general awareness of the dawning of a new day and the meaning of the groaning for grace and glory by Creation, by the Christian, and by the Comforter.

The Ultimate Origin of Salvation: Romans 8:28-30

One of the most glorious passages in all of the Word is God, is this section in Romans 8, which deals with the ultimate origin of the salvation of the soul. The apostle Paul will teach, that the salvation of the soul is rooted in the divine act of predestination, and therein lies a problem. Not everyone understands, likes, or accepts the doctrine of predestination for many different reasons. As a result, this portion of Scripture has generated much concern and controversy. In fact, some students of the Bible wonder if the doctrine of predestination should even be openly discussed. John Calvin in one section of his *Institutes* addresses that thought with these words. *"There are others who, wishing to cure this evil, all but require that every mention of predestination be buried. Indeed, they teach us to avoid any question of it as we would a reef. Therefore, we must guard against depriving believers of anything disclosed about predestination in Scripture, lest we seem either wickedly to defraud them of the blessing of their God, or to accuse, and scoff at the Holy Spirit for having published what it is in any way profitable to suppress."*

No one should ever scoff at the Holy Spirit for teaching about those thing which the Father has revealed. Nor should anything that the Spirit has revealed be suppressed. That would be fundamentally wrong. John Calvin is correct when he writes elsewhere in the *Institutes*, *"Whosoever heaps odium upon the doctrine of predestination openly reproaches God as if He had unadvisedly let slip something hateful to the Church."* God is not foolish. While the secret things belong to the Lord (Deuteronomy 29:29), the things that are revealed belong to the Church. The doctrine of predestination is a gift of God, for the people of God. It is taught in Romans 8, and it is taught elsewhere in Scripture as a consistent theme of basic Biblical theology (Ephesians 1:45; 2 Thessalonians 2:13, 14). The doctrine of predestination is part of a strong chain of love that reaches from heaven to earth, to bind believers to God, and to encourage them during dark days of suffering. There are five links in the chain of love.

Five Golden Links

♦ **Foreknowledge.** To *"foreknow"* means *"to choose beforehand,"* or better, to *"forelove"*. Amos says, with reference to Israel, *"You only have I known of all the families of the earth"* (Amos 3:2). What did God mean? Only Israel as a nation had been chosen, and therefore Israel would be dealt with in a special way in grace and in judgment. Again, to *"foreknow"* means that a person has entered into an intimate relationship based upon a free choice.

The Bible says that Adam *"knew"* Eve (Genesis 4:1). Adam entered into an intimate relationship with Eve. Spiritually, God *"foreknows"* individuals. He chooses and enters into an intimate relationship with them based upon His own Sovereign choice.

♦ **Predestinate.** Predestination is a word that means different things in Scripture. It is a word that is used to speak of God foreordaining all things that will come to pass in world history, past, present, and future. (Isaiah 65:17-25; 2 Peter 3:10-13;

Revelation 21:1-22:5) The word also refers to God's decision, which was made in eternity past, before the world began, and before anyone was created, to decree the final destiny of individuals. God has chosen particular sinners for salvation and eternal life (Romans 8:29; Ephesians 1:4, 5, 11). He has also made an advanced decision about those who will not be saved (Romans 9:6-29; 1 Peter 2:8; Jude 1:4). Salvation and reprobation exist side by side in the doctrine of predestination.

- **Called.** The word *"call"* has many shades of meaning in the Bible. There is an external call of the gospel to salvation, and there is an internal call as well. In the external call, the gospel is preached to all people indiscriminately. Anyone can hear it, but not all will respond to the spiritual truths communicated (Matthew 22:39). In the external call of the gospel, the good news is shared, but the truth falls upon rocky soil and good soil alike. In the external call, the gospel may be resisted, and ultimately dismissed. In contrast, the internal call of the gospel is different. The internal call of the gospel is the voice of the Holy Spirit effectively applying the gospel message to the hearts of individuals with sovereign power to repentance, faith, salvation, and service (Mark 2:17; Luke 5:32; Mark 1:20; Acts 2:39). The internal call provides spiritual power for the soul that is dead in trespasses and sin, to live, hear, and believe the gospel. The internal call cannot be denied, nor does the regenerated heart want to reject the gospel.

- **Justification.** For Paul, the doctrine of justification was the heart of the gospel (Romans 1:17; 3:21-5:21; Galatians 2:15-5:1). Justification is the judicial act of God declaring sinners righteous (Romans 4:5; 3:9-24). God can declare sinners righteous because of the meritorious work of Jesus Christ, who, as the Last Adam (1 Corinthians 15:45), acted on behalf of sinners, obeyed the Law, and endured the pain and penalty of sin. Justification is possible because justice has been satisfied (Romans 3:25-26). The righteousness of Christ can be reckoned to the account of others (Romans 5:18-19). The necessary means, or instrumental cause of justification, is personal faith in the finished work of Jesus Christ as substitutionary Savior and resurrected Lord (Romans 4:23-25; 10:8-13).

♦ **Glorification.** While justification focuses attention on what God does for sinners in time, glorification anticipates what God will do for the saints in eternity. A day will one day come, when all Christians shall receive a resurrected body like that of Christ. It will not have the principle of sin, nor will it be subject to death (1 Corinthians 15:51-58; Romans 8:22-23).

Five Gospel Truths

The Five Golden Links of Romans 8:28-29 are rooted in the Five Gospel Truths of total depravity, unconditional election, definite atonement, irresistible grace, and perseverance of the saints.

♦ **Total Depravity.** This simply means that there is nothing in man that may please God. It means that the will, the mind, and the emotions have been touched by sin. It does not mean that man is as bad as he can be, but that sin has touched every facet of his soul (Romans 3:23; 8:7; Colossians 1:21; James 1:14, 15; Matthew 15:19).

♦ **Unconditional Election.** The Lord has chosen those who will be the heirs of salvation according to His good pleasure. Not according to good works, nor according to foreseen faith, nor from any power or agency in the creature, co-working with His special grace, but according to His good pleasure does God elect souls to be saved, and effectually calls them (2 Timothy 1:9; Ephesians 2:8; 1 Corinthians 2:14; Ephesians 2:5; John 5:25; Ephesians 1:19, 20).

♦ **Definite Atonement.** Particular redemption, affirms that the Lord Jesus came in the will of God the Father, to die for the elect. The death of Christ is sufficient for all, and is to be preached to all. But the *intent* of His atoning work was to save the elect. Those who limit the efficacy of the atonement often criticize those who embrace a concept of limiting the intent of the atonement. There is a branch of theology that widely proclaims Christ died for people who are not ultimately redeemed. There is a branch of theology that teaches that the death of Christ was *intended* for people who are not ultimately regenerated. There is a branch of theology that limits the efficacy of the atonement. Those Scriptures that teach that Christ came to save *His people from their sins* challenge such theology (Matthew 1:21; Hebrews 10:14; 1 Peter 1:18, 19; Isaiah 53:5, 6).

- **Irresistible Grace.** For those who are to be the heirs of salvation, there comes a time when the Holy Spirit closes the gospel net and brings the good fish to shore. There comes a time when the sheep are made the people of His pasture. There comes a time when the soul is converted to Christ in a Sovereign and gracious manner by the omnipotent God. There comes a time when the Lord makes the heart willing to come to Christ. (Romans 8:30; 11:7; Ephesians 1:10,11; 2 Thessalonians 2:13,14)

- **Perseverance of the Saints.** Those who have come to Christ by faith will continue in the faith until the very end (John 10:28, 29; Philippians 1:6; 2 Timothy 2:19; 1 John 2:19).

The Security of the Saint: Romans 8:31-39

With all of this doctrinal truth in mind, the apostle Paul can only conclude one thing: God is *"for"* the believer. The presence of suffering (Romans 8:18) does not mean that God is against the saint. Just the opposite is proven. God is *"for"* the believer and undergirds every Christian, to the point that nothing and no one shall ever divorce or separate the two. *"He that spared not His own Son, but delivered Him up for us all, how shall He not with Him also freely give us all things?"* (Romans 8:32). The answer, *"He will give us all things!"*

Special Gifts of Sovereign Grace

Some specific items may be noted in the *"all things,"* the Lord will give to those that love Him.

1. God gives an understanding of the process of how a soul is saved according to divine foreknowledge (Romans 8:29; 1 Peter 1:2); election (1 Thessalonians 1:4; 1 Peter 1:2; Romans 8:33; Colossians 3:12; Titus 1:1).

2. God gives the joy that reconciliation brings. Sinners are reconciled by God (2 Corinthians 5:1819; Colossians 1:20) and to God (Romans 5:10; 2 Corinthians 5:20).

3. God gives to the believer spiritual liberty for a redemption price has been paid for the people of His good pleasure (Colossians 1:14; 1 Peter 1:18; Romans 3:24).

4. God gives assurance of freedom from ultimate condemnation from the penalty and pollution of sin (Romans 8:1; John 5:24; 1 Corinthians 11:32; John 3:18).

5. God gives emotional relief to the heart by revealing that He has been propitiated or satisfied by the work of His Son at Calvary (1 John 2:2; Romans 3:24-26).

6. God removes all sin by the efficacious blood of His Son (1 Peter 2:24; Romans 4:25).

7. God unites the believer to Christ so that His life is shared. The believer, in the sight of God, has been crucified with Christ (Romans 6:6), buried with Him in His death (Romans 6:8; 6:4; Colossians 2:12; 1 Peter 2:24), and raised with Him to walk in the newness of life (Romans 6:4; Colossians 3:1).

8. God has provided freedom from the rules and regulations of the Mosaic Law. The believer is dead to the Law (Romans 7:4) and delivered from its dominion (Romans 7:6; Galatians 3:25; Romans 6:14; 2 Corinthians 3:11).

9. God has made the believer a member of the Royal Family (1 John 33; 2 Corinthians 6:18; Galatians 3:26). The Christian has been born again (John 3:7; 1 Peter 1:23), quickened (Ephesians 2:1; Colossians 2:13), and regenerated (Titus 3:5; John 13:1; 1 Corinthians 6:11).

10. God has given to the believer all the privileges of adult sons through the process of adoption (Romans 8:15).

11. God has given a robe of righteousness to all who believe (Romans 3:22; 1 Corinthians 11:30; 2 Corinthians 5:21; Philippians 3:9). Because of this imputed righteousness, the believer is positionally sanctified in Christ (1 Corinthians 1:30; 6:11) with a view to practical or experiential holiness (John 17:17) and ultimately the removal of the entire sin nature (Ephesians 5:27) in a final state of perfection (Hebrews 10:14).

12. God has given the legal verdict of declaring the sinner righteous in His sight. (Romans 5:1; 3:24; 8:30; 1 Corinthians 6:11; Titus 3:7).

13. God has granted forgiveness of all sin, past, present, and future (Colossians 1:14; 2:13; 3:13; Ephesians 1:7; 4:32). While the judicial or legal forgiveness before the bar of divine justice is abiding, there is still a need for family forgiveness based upon confession of sin (1 John 1:9).

14. God has given to every believer a nearer place of access to Him. In the Old Testament economy, there were many barriers between the worshipper and God. But not now (Ephesians 2:13).

15. God has granted a dramatic rescue from the powers of darkness (Colossians 1:13; 2:13-15).

16. God has given to His children a kingdom, according to promise (Colossians 1:13), with the rank of royal kings (Revelation 1:6), and all the privileges of priests.

17. God has given to the believer a sure foundation on which to build up a holy faith (1 Corinthians 3:11; Ephesians 2:20; 2 Corinthians 1:21).

18. God has given Christ to all believers, and all believers to Christ as a reward for His labors at Calvary (John 17:6, 11, 12, 20; 10:29).

19. God has cut away all the elements that hindered spiritual purity (Colossians 2:11; Philippians 3:3; Romans 2:29).

20. God has given the believer the privilege of being part of a holy priesthood (1 Peter 3:5), and beyond that, a royal priesthood (1 Peter 2:9).

21. God has given to every believer the distinction of being a peculiar, or special people (1 Peter 2:9; Titus 2:14).

22. God has given the gift of the Holy Spirit, for the expressed purpose of gaining access to Himself (Ephesians 2:18; Romans 5:2; Hebrews 4:14, 16; 10:19, 28).

23. God has given Himself to every believer, which statement means, that they are the objects of His saving power (Ephesians 1:9; Philippians 2:13); the object of His sustaining power (Hebrews 13:5; Philippians 1:6); the objects of His comfort (2 Thessalonians 2:16) and the object of His prayers (Hebrews 7:25; Romans 8:34; Hebrews 9:24).

24. God has given to the believer the privilege of being partners with Christ in life (Colossians 3:4; 1 John 5:11-12), in position (Ephesians 2:6), and in service (1 Corinthians 1:9).

25. God has given to the believer tremendous responsibilities as a minister of the New Covenant (2 Corinthians 3:6; 6:4), as an ambassador to the world (2 Corinthians 5:20), and as a living epistle, read by all (2 Corinthians 3:3).

26. God has given to the believer the opportunity to suffer with Him (2 Timothy 2:12; Philippians 1:29; 1 Peter 2:20; 4:12, 13; 1 Thessalonians 3:3; Romans 8:18; Colossians 1:24).

27. God has given to every believer a heavenly citizenship (Philippians 3:20; Ephesians 2:29; Hebrews 12:22; Luke 10:20).

28. God has made the believer a member of the body of Christ (1 Corinthians 12:13), a branch in the Vine (John 15:5), a stone in the building (Ephesians 2:19, 22), a sheep in the flock (John 10:27-29), a bride of the Bridegroom (Ephesians 5:25-27), a

priest, in a kingdom of priests (1 Peter 2:5-9), and a saint of the new covenant (Romans 1:7; 1 Peter 2:9).

29. God has given to every believer the gift of the Spirit as a down payment of all that is yet to come (Ephesians 4:30; 2 Corinthians 1:22).

30. God has given the believer all that is needed for being complete as a Christian (Colossians 2:10).

These are just some of the all things God has given to His people. And there are many other gifts of divine grace, for *"He will give us all things"* that are necessary for happiness, holiness, and ultimate glorification. Wordsworth wrote in, *See, the Conqueror Mounts in Triumph:*

> *"Thou hast raised our human nature*
> *On the clouds to God's right hand;*
> *There we sit in heavenly places,*
> *There with Thee in glory stand.*
>
> *Jesus reigns, adored by angels,*
> *Man with God is on the throne,*
> *Mighty Lord in thine ascension*
> *We by faith behold our own."*

See the Conqueror Mounts in Triumph

God is *for us*

By the gifts of divine grace, all believers can know with confidence that God is *"for us."* Christians can also stand in astonishment, because it really is an amazing thing that God would be *"for us,"* in light of what sin has done to us. Sin has turned the heart away from God. Sin has caused the tongue to blaspheme God (Romans 2:24). Sin has caused the soul to spit upon the Son of Glory (Matthew 26:67) and yet, God is still *"for us".* God is *"for us"* because in marvelous matchless grace, Christ died *"for the ungodly"* (Romans 5:6). The Bible says, that Christ gave His body *"for us"* (1 Corinthians

11:24). And He made a new covenant *"for us"* (1 Corinthians 11:25). Now, *"If God be for us, who can be against us?"* (Romans 8:31)

Three Strong Enemies of the Soul

♦ **The Devil can be against the Christian, and he is.** The Bible says, that Satan walks about as a roaring lion seeking whom he may devour (1 Peter 5:8). Satan wants to devour the saints today, as he wanted to destroy Peter, so long ago (Luke 22:31).

♦ **The World can be against the Christian, and it is.** The world is a corrupting influence upon the conscience. John Bunyan called the world Vanity Fair. In Vanity Fair there are pleasures and promises pleasing to the heart. However, pain and punishment will be, the ultimate reward for those who are persuaded to partake of the perversions of the world. *"For all that is in the world, the lust of the flesh, and the lust of the eyes, and the pride of life, is not of the Father, but is of the world, And the world passeth away, and the lust thereof; but he that doeth the will of God abideth for ever"* (1 John 2:16,17).

♦ **The Flesh can be against the Christian, and it is.** Those who are in the flesh are by nature children of wrath and enemies of God (Ephesians 2:3). Those who walk after the flesh shall die (Romans 8:13). *"Mortify therefore your members which are upon the earth; fornication, uncleanness, inordinate affection, evil concupiscence, and covetousness, which is idolatry: for which things' sake the wrath of God cometh on the children of disobedience"* (Colossians 3: 5).

Seven Things that Cannot Separate from the Love of God

Despite strong enemies of the soul, the Sovereign God will keep His own to the very end. Nothing shall separate the saint from the Savior, including the following.

♦ **Tribulation.** The reference is to outward afflictions, such as John suffered on the Isle of Patmos for preaching the gospel. *"I John, who also am your brother, and companion in tribulation, and in the kingdom and patience of Jesus Christ, was in the isle that is called Patmos,* *for the word of God, and for the testimony of Jesus Christ"* (Revelation 1:9).

◆ **Distress.** As there are outward tribulations, so there are inward concerns, which cause great consternation. Paul knew about these pressure points on the heart (Romans 8:35; 2:9; 2 Corinthians 6:4; 12:10).

◆ **Persecution.** Jesus predicted that His followers would be persecuted. *"Blessed are ye, when men shall revile you, and persecute you, and shall say all manner of evil against you falsely, for my sake"* (Matthew 5:11).

◆ **Famine.** The word in the original means *hunger,* and refers to the deprivation of food. When the children of Israel began to be in want, they discovered that God still loved them for He heard their cries and gave them manna to eat (Exodus 16:35).

◆ **Nakedness.** Perhaps a better translation would be, *in need of clothes* (2 Corinthians 11:27; Revelation 3:18). The Lord told of those who ministered to Him, because they ministered to those in need. *I was naked, and you clothed me* (Matthew 25:36).

◆ **Peril.** In 2 Corinthians much stress is laid upon many perils that Paul endured. Eight times the word is used! And yet Paul never stopped believing that God was with him, and loved him.

◆ **The Sword.** The word speaks of a form of judicial punishment. Many Christians were legally killed for preaching about Christ. Rome felt threatened by the message of the Messiah, so they executed the messengers through various forms, including beheading by the sword and crucifixion. The philosopher Cicero declared that crucifixion was the most cruel, and hideous, of punishments. During the dark days of religious destruction, the love of God was still present. *"Nay, in all these things we are more than conquerors through Him that loved us"* (Romans 8:37).

The Triumph of the Tested

The triumph of the saints involves strategic conquests over specific entities.

- **Death**. Physical death brings no separation between God and the believer. Indeed, death is the entrance into the splendors of heaven.

- **Life**. The distractions of life cannot diminish the fellowship between the believer and God (Psalms 23:16; 63:18; 73:23; 116:1; Romans 14:8, 9).

- **Angels**. While the elect angels are superior to man, in his present condition, God does not love them more.

- **Principalities and powers**. In Jewish writings, *principalities* and *powers* are a reference to angels (study 1 Corinthians 15:24; Ephesians 1:21; 3:10; 6:12; Colossians 1:16; 2:10, 15; 1 Peter 3:22). The Bible teaches that even angels, good or bad, real or unreal as they exist in the imaginations of men, cannot separate us from the love of God in Christ Jesus.

- **Things present and things to come.** The present with all of its problems, and the future with all of its concerns, can do nothing to disunite the Christian from the deep and abiding love that God, in Christ, enjoys with the believer.

- **Neither height nor depth.** If time cannot divide the saint from the Savior, and from the love of God, neither can space. Jesus took His disciples to great spiritual heights, in the Mount of Transfiguration (Matthew17: 2), and when Jonah was still in the belly of the whale, God had mercy upon him (Jon. 2:10).

A Summary of the Section

In Romans 8:31, 39 the believer finds great assurance in the fact that nothing in heaven or earth shall separate the child of God from his heavenly Father. In time of persecution or personal adversity, people are prone to question, and to doubt their salvation. Some of the doubt is natural to the fallen nature. Some of the doubt is because of false teaching that says a child of God can fall from grace after salvation, and be ultimately lost. Some of the doubt comes from satanic suggestions that God will not be found faithful, for He does not mean what He says (Genesis 3:15). Whatever the source of temptation, to doubt the relationship with God, the Christian may turn to the scriptures, and find Divine comfort, and an ultimate commentary, on the matter. Nothing shall separate the saint, *"from the love of God, which is in Christ Jesus our Lord"* (Romans 8:39). By faith, this gospel truth must be believed. Faith is to be exercised, as the promises of God are claimed. God has promised that He will never sever the relationship with those whom He has elected and Christ has died. The Word of God has never failed before, and it shall not fail in the future.

A Word of Warning

Believing in the final security of the saint does not mean there is a license to sin. Those who believe that teaching the security of the believer, encourages sin, fail to take into consideration that the Christian is given at the moment of salvation a new heart, a new will, and a new mind (2 Corinthians 5:17). There is also failure to consider the personal ministry of the Holy Spirit.

Those who teach that the Christian can lose salvation, are in grave danger of denying the plain teaching of Scripture, which states categorically that *nothing* shall separate the believer from the love of God. The Sovereign Ruler of the universe shall not be frustrated in His purposes (Jeremiah 32:27; Revelation 19:6). Those whom God has eternally loved, those whom God has predestined, those whom God has called, and justified, will be glorified. So certain is this fact that it is put in the past tense (Romans 8:30). The souls, for whom Christ has died, shall be saved. From his prison cell in Rome, Paul found much comfort in these truths. May they continue to be a source of comfort for all of God's children.

> *"Let me no more my comfort draw*
> *from my frail grasp of Thee;*

*Let me henceforth rejoice with awe
in Thy strong grasp of me."*

9

Romans 9

Paul's Pastoral Heart: Romans 9:1-5

The life of Paul, as presented in Scripture, suggests that he was a very emotional personality. There is pathos, there is energy to the apostle that surges through the Divine narrative, as the record of his life is revealed. The emotional intensity that characterized the man also characterized his writings. At times, Paul tumbled out one thought after another, in an eager attempt to say something majestic (Ephesians 2:1-19). He was not opposed to interrupting himself or simply switching to another topic, which is what he did in Romans 9, 10, and 11. In this section of Scripture, there is no immediate connection to the narrative of Romans 8, and the preceding verses. What happened was that a new thought came to Paul as he meditated on all that God will do for His own. *"But was not Israel considered God's own people? Does God have nothing for Israel? What shall happen to his brethren according to the flesh? Have they failed God to the point that they are no longer part of His eternal plan?"*

In Romans 9, 10, and 11, Paul argues that Israel did indeed fail God. Israel failed to enjoy all of the privileges associated with the Person, and work, of Jesus Christ. The reason for their spiritual failure was pride, and self-sufficiency. Israel had neglected to read the Scriptures properly, or interpret them accurately. As a result, Israel began to trust in their own good works, by the deeds of the Law. They were proud of their own fleshly heritage to the point there was no repentance of sin, and there was no worshipping of the Lord in sincerity. In short, they failed God. However, Israel's failure is not to be considered *total* for souls do come to faith. Many Jews are converted to Christ. Nor is Israel's failure *final*. All Israel shall yet be saved in the glorious future to come.

Special Note. Keeping in mind Paul's elliptical style of writing, his burden for national Israel, and his ministry to the Gentiles, the main challenge for biblical commentators is to determine what Paul means when he teaches that all Israel shall be saved. Is all Israel a reference to a particular generation of nationalistic Jews, or does all Israel refer to the Church as a whole, Jew and Gentile?

In developing the future of Israel whom Paul calls, *"my brethren, my kinsmen according to the flesh,"* (Romans 9:3) the apostle expresses the deep anguish of his heart, testified to by the *"witness in the Holy Ghost"* (Romans 9:1). Here is an amazing thing really for the people to whom Paul agonizes over, are the very ones who sought to kill him (Acts 21:31). Despite repeated attempts on his life, Paul writes, that his heart is so burdened for the Israelites, that he was even willing to be cut off from Christ Himself, if such action would lead to the conversion of others (Romans 9:3).

With these words, Paul reveals the pastoral heart that he possessed and which others have possessed before him. Moses had such as heart. When the Lord was angry with the Israelites for their idolatry, only the prayer life of Moses stood between himself and his brethren, and the nation was spared (Exodus 32:9-14).

A pastoral heart, in spiritual leaders, that does not want to see others perish, reflects the heart of the Great Shepherd Himself, who one day had a need to go through Samaria. There was a lost sheep that had wondered astray and needed to be rescued from sin, and shame. There was a woman who would draw water from the well at noontime, and Jesus had to meet her, and offer her living water so that she would never thirst again (John 4:1-26).

In the early days of America's history, there was a great missionary to the Indians, by the name of David Brainerd (1718-1747). Well-educated, and personable, David could have accepted a comfortable church position as pastor in a large town. However, with reckless abandonment he gave his health, and therefore his life, preaching in the wilderness to the Indians. *"I dream of lost souls, he wrote. I care not what sufferings I undergo as long as I see souls saved."* Brainerd did suffer. He contracted tuberculosis, and perished in the prime of his productive life. Faithful pastors, and concerned Christians, can understand what Paul meant when he wrote, *"For I could wish that myself were accursed from Christ for my brethren, my kinsmen according to the flesh"* (Romans 9:3). In the words of Richard Baxter, Paul had *"tears in his voice"* when he uttered these words.

Eight Privileges of a Chosen People

The agony of Paul's soul was intense, because the apostle understood how great were the privileges his brethren had, historically. He mentions eight great particular privileges, associated with national Israel. (Romans 9:4-5)

- **Israel had the adoption of God.** There was a time when the Jews were not the sons of God. But then one day God laid His mighty hand upon Abraham. God sovereignly chose a devil worshipper from Ur of the Chaldees to save in order to bring forth a people of His delight. The Lord adopted national Israel as a son. (Exodus 4:22, 23)

- **Israel had the glory**. There was the Shekinah (*dwelling*)—a visible manifestation of the presence of God. Although the word is not found in the Bible, it occurs frequently in extra biblical Jewish writings. It refers to the times when God manifested Himself openly to Israel. (Mt. Sinai Exodus 24:9-18), in the Holy of Holies of the Tabernacle, and in Solomon's Temple. The Shekinah was a resplendent cloud that stayed above the altar in the place of worship and gave light to the room. When the Babylonians destroyed the Temple in 586 BC, the Shekinah glory deceased. There was no Shekinah, in the Second Temple reconstructed later under Zerubbabel (c. 516 BC) and Herod, governor of Judea (374 BC). In addition to the Shekinah glory, Israel was led by the glory of a cloud by day and a pillar of fire by night during their wilderness journeys (Exodus 12:20-22; 16:10). What a miracle that was. They had The Glory Cloud to give protection by day from the burning sun and warmth at night from the frigid air. As long as Israel followed The Glory Cloud, they were safe and secure in the Lord. If, at night, they moved without the pillar of fire, they would walk in darkness. Individuals always walk in darkness when they do not go with God.

- **Israel had the covenants**. There was the Abrahamic Covenant, whereby God promised to give Abraham a seed, a name, and a land (Genesis 12, 13). There was the Davidic Covenant whereby God promised a seed to sit upon the throne forever (2 Sam. 7). There was the New Covenant (Jeremiah 31), which was to undergird, in righteousness, all the covenants including the Mosaic Covenant of works (Exodus 20). Some Bible students like to speak of these covenants, as being unconditional, in the sense that God made certain promises He would keep, regardless of the behavior of the Israelites. However, it can be pointed out that even to Abraham, God says, that His blessings were bestowed *because of* Abraham's obedience and unswerving faith in the promises of God and in the God of promise. *"And [God] said, By myself have I sworn, saith the Lord, for because thou hast done this thing, and hast not withheld thy son, thine only son: That in blessing I will bless thee, and in multiplying I will multiply thy seed as the stars of the heaven, and as the sand which is upon the seashore; and thy seed shall possess the gate of his enemies; and in thy seed shall all the nations of the earth be blessed; because thou hast obeyed my voice"* (Genesis 22:16-18). Covenants are intrinsically conditional. God made certain promises to Abraham, and to his descendants, and kept them. The name of Abraham did become great. The seed of Abraham prospered and the Land of Promise was taken (Note especially Joshua 21:43-45; 24:14). In turn, Abraham kept the faith. He wavered not at the promises of God, but his descendants did. Time after time they became faithless, despite the fact they had the covenants.

- **Israel had the Law.** To have the Law of the Lord, written by the finger of God, was a great blessing indeed (Exodus 31:18; Psalms 119 [All]). During the days of Paul, the nation looked upon the Law as its most holy possession. Individuals would memorize the entire Torah.

- **Israel had the service of God.** The Tabernacle in the desert, and the Temple in the land, provided a platform for spiritual service. Israel had a glorious priesthood, to structure the worship, and to process the offerings that were given to God. There was much beauty and pageantry in the holy ceremonies and services that were conducted on a daily basis. Special high, and holy days, enhanced the glory associated with the services of the Lord, especially when the High Priestly garments were worn.

- **Israel had the promises.** In particular, there were the Messianic Promises of a Priest to come, a Prophet to come, and a King, to come (Genesis 3:15; Num. 24:15-19; Deuteronomy 18:15-22). The Prophet, Priest, and King would come in One humble Servant of the Lord (Isaiah 53). A Child would be born, a Son would be given, and the government would be placed upon His shoulders (Isaiah 9:6). There were great and glorious promises that Israel had concerning the Messiah who would suffer in a vicarious (Isaiah 53:49), and victorious manner (Isaiah 53:10-12).

- **Israel had the fathers.** Most Americans are proud to honor George Washington as the Father of this Country. Other Founding Fathers are held in high esteem: Thomas Jefferson, Benjamin Franklin, James Madison, James Monroe, and Paul Revere. The list is long and lustrous. But Israel had *the* fathers of the faith: Abraham, Isaac, Jacob, Moses, Noah, and David. What a privileged people they were.

- **Israel had the Messiah.** Best of all, Israel had Christ the Messiah, who is God, blessed. Amen. And yet, despite all of their spiritual advantages and blessings, Israel took the Lord of Glory and crucified Him. Israel killed the Messiah King. Israel despised the Son of the Living God. Israel did not believe that, in Christ, all of the prophecies were fulfilled.

Scripture Interpreting Scripture: Romans 9:6-13

The historical fact, of Israel killing the Lord of Glory, raises a theological inquiry. *"How did it happen that Israel did not recognize her Messiah?"* Moreover, *"What shall become of the nation?"* These unspoken questions, which Paul anticipates, are not easy to answer. The best Paul can do is to turn to various Old Testament passages to show several reasons why Israel rejected the Messiah—despite the promises, and general expressions of love by God, in so many ways.

- The people of Israel failed as a nation to see their need for a *personal* Savior. They held an erroneous belief that the act of circumcision, in association with keeping the Law, and being a physical descendant of Abraham was enough to secure salvation (Romans 9:6-29).

- The lack of spiritual discernment led the Jews to pursue righteousness by works rather than by faith. This was united with an innate sense of self-righteousness to produce a hardness of heart toward the Gift of Heaven (John 6:31-35; Romans 9:30-33).

- The Jews had a zeal for God, but it was not based on knowledge (Romans 10:2, 3). Israel failed to discern that there is a *spiritual*, as well as a *physical* seed of Israel, and the true Israel of God is to be found in the *spiritual* seed.

To prove that there are two seeds of Abraham the apostle cites four Old Testament passages and comments upon them: Romans 9:7; Genesis 21:2; Romans 9:9; Genesis 13:10, 14; Romans 9:12; Genesis 25:23; Romans 9:13; Malachi 1:2.

The Two Seeds of Israel

In Romans 9:7, the apostle begins, by acknowledging that there is a *physical* seed of Israel consisting of all the direct descendants of Abraham, Isaac, and Jacob. Also to be numbered in the *physical* seed of Israel, are Gentiles, who have been proselytized to the Law of Moses. Nevertheless, *They are not all Israel, which are of Israel.* (Romans 9:6)

In the sight of the Lord, there is a *spiritual* seed to consider. Attention is focused upon the promise given by God to Abraham, that he would have a son. *"Nevertheless, because they are the seed of Abraham, are they all children: but, in Isaac, shall thy seed be called."* (Romans 9:7) Isaac would be a child of promise. Isaac would be a child of faith. Isaac would be the prototype of the *spiritual* seed, through which the

Messiah would ultimately come. It is the *spiritual* seed of Israel that Paul wants to emphasize, by noting the distinguishing grace of the Sovereign God between one part of Israel, and another. The *spiritual* seed of Israel includes all Jews, and all proselytized Gentiles, such as Rehab, and Ruth (Hebrews 11:31; Ruth 1:16), who have the *faith* of Abraham, Isaac, and Jacob.

Hostility to the Doctrine of Election

By making this dramatic distinction between the *physical* seed of Abraham, and the *spiritual* seed, Paul knows that this facet of the truth will not be well received by the Jews. The doctrine of election, the doctrine of distinguishing grace, is a doctrine that is neither wanted, nor appreciated by the natural man, despite the fact that the doctrine is designed to manifest the free mercy of God and reveal His glory, while humbling those who are the objects of His grace.

Even when Jesus preached the doctrine of distinguishing grace, hostility was shown (Luke 4:25-29). The doctrine of election strikes at the root of man's self-righteousness. In his natural religious arrogance, man cannot help but believe, that there is something about himself that is so wonderful, God must move to love and receive him. Had the Jews read the Scriptures more carefully they would have realized that this is not true. The prophet said *"All we like sheep have gone astray; we have turned every one to his own way"* (Isaiah 53:6). *"The Bible says there is none righteous, no not one"* (Romans 3:10; Psalms 14:13 with Psalms 53:13). The only hope for lost souls to be saved is for the Good Shepherd to come and rescue whom He wills.

The Basis of Divine Election

In eternity past, in matchless sovereign grace, God did decide to save some members of the fallen race of Adam, but not all. So God made a choice between Ishmael and Isaac (Romans 9:7, 8), and between Esau and Jacob (Romans 9:1013). That choice was not based upon foreseen faith, nor upon good works, but upon God's own good pleasure. *"For the children being not yet born, neither having done any good or evil that the purpose of God according to election might stand, not of works, but of his that calleth"* (Romans 9:11).

Had God based His election upon the goodness of a person, then He probably would have chosen Esau over Jacob, for in many ways, Esau was a better man. It was Jacob, who cheated Esau of the blessing. It was Jacob, who was always scheming and plotting to get ahead in life, at the expense of others. God did not choose Jacob because he was basically a good or better person than Esau. God chose Jacob according to His own sovereign will. God never chooses anyone on the basis of some personal goodness.

Nor does God base His election upon foreseen faith. If God basis His election upon the foreseen faith of a person, then He does not chose anyone according to *grace,* but according to *works,* for faith is a good work. Faith is something that pleases God. If man has innate faith or the ability to believe in God, then God is not sovereign in choosing whom He wills after all, for God is under a moral *obligation* to save and to show mercy to all who perform the good work of faith—even when it is expressed *in the flesh.* But that is not possible. The Scriptures teach, those who are in the flesh, *cannot please God* (Romans 8:8). The scriptures teach that God operates according to His own good pleasure (Ephesians 1:5; 1:9). God does whatsoever He wills (Ephesians 1:11). And faith? That too is a gift of divine grace (Ephesians 2:8, 9). The ultimate basis of election is not the goodness of any person, nor foreseen faith, but divine grace.

> *"Marvelous grace of our loving Lord,*
> *Grace that exceeds our sin and our guilt,*
> *Yonder on Calvary's mount outpoured,*
> *There where the blood of the Lamb was spilt.*
>
> *Grace, grace, God's grace,*
> *Grace that will pardon and cleanse within;*
> *Grace, grace, God's grace,*
> *Grace that is greater than all our sin."*
> —Julia H. Johnson

Is There Unrighteousness with God? Romans 9:14-33

While trying to understand, and convey, the meaning of the message of Romans 9, Dr. Donald Gray Barnhouse asked the Lord to give him a human illustration that would cover the great revelation of divine election. What the Lord provided was a wonderful reminder that God's *word*, on any given matter, is sufficient even when there is not clear understanding of what the words mean. *"Let us imagine,"* said Dr. Barnhouse, *"a small boy has a pet dog which he loves very dearly. He plays with that dog every day and the dog sleeps beside him at night. One day the boy opens the door of the family garage just in time to see his father kill the dog. The fatal shot rings out and the boy screams and rushes toward the dog. The father catches the boy who kicks and screams against him. 'You killed my dog! You killed my dog! I hate you! I hate you!' The father carries the boy into the house and says, 'My son, I will tell you why I had to kill him.' But the boy runs away from his father, screaming, 'I hate you! I hate you! You killed my dog!'"*

In the years to come, when the child grew up, he began to understand something about the nature of disease. He was given a newspaper clipping that showed that there had been an epidemic of rabies in his neighborhood. A mad dog bit several other dogs in the neighborhood, and so it was necessary for local dog owners to destroy their pets. *"From his maturity the boy can look back on his childhood, and see how warped were his opinions of his father. He had carried hatred of his father through the years because his father had crossed his childish will when he was four or five years old. Yet now, he sees the evidence that his father was acting in wisdom and love, and that his pet dog might have bitten him and caused his own death."*

Many people are theologically like that little boy. They hear the doctrine of election and are offended with God. In emotional anger God is charged with being unkind and unrighteousness. An explanation is demanded for murder and rape, tornadoes and war, floods and famine. When no immediate rational explanation is given, frustration is directed against the Lord. *"Where is God?"* Hurting hearts ask. *"Surely God must be unrighteous to allow bad things to happen to good people!"* One atheist was even so bold as to tell a Christian, *"Your God is my devil."* Ugly remarks are made because men are children before Almighty God. Men do not understand sin, death, disease, election, and divine sovereignty. Instead of bowing before the Creator in humility, in infantile ignorance, God is accused of being unrighteous—until there is growth in grace and knowledge of spiritual things. *"Is there unrighteousness with God?"* Not when we understand Him.

The Strategic Point of Conflict

While individuals rage and charge God with unrighteousness, while answers are demanded, the Lord is not intimidated. Nor is God pressured into answering life's ultimate questions too readily. In the area of salvation, God does not explain in His Word why He selects one person over another. Perhaps one day He will.

For now, God calls upon souls to submit to the principle of His right to rule in the universe the way that He sees fit. Submission to the sovereignty of God is needed because it is the very starting point of spirituality, and a right relationship with the Lord. It was because Adam did not submit to the sovereignty of God that all of humanity has been affected by The Fall.

As the story is told in Genesis 3:17, the Lord told Adam not to eat of the fruit of the Tree of Knowledge of Good and Evil. Encouraged by Satan, to violate the known will of the Lord, Adam rose up in rebellion against God, and partook of the forbidden fruit. In this manner, a sin nature was *acquired*, so that Adam, and his posterity, has become responsible for the just judgment that was rendered. Had Adam submitted to the righteousness of God, to organize, and control, His universe as He saw fit, there would have been no Fall.

The strategic battleground for the sons of Adam is the sovereignty of God. The most foundational truth of the Christian faith is that God exists (Hebrews 11:6), and He rules supreme according to the good pleasure of His will. Until this point is resolved, nothing else really matters. Jesus said, *"And why call ye me Lord, Lord, and do not the things which I say"* (Luke 6:46).

A Fundamental Lesson of Faith

The sovereignty of God is taught to all of God's children, for therein lay their comfort, security, humility, and submission to the Savior. Absolute divine sovereignty was taught to Moses. *"For he saith to*

Moses, I will have mercy on whom I will have mercy, and I will have compassion on whom I will have compassion" (Romans 9:15). Moses had no power to persuade people to follow him. When he tried in his own power to lead, he was a failure (Genesis 2:11-14; Acts 7:22-29). Moses had to learn that only God can change hearts according to His omnipotent power. Only God can deliver His people from the bondage of slavery. Only God can show mercy upon the many. And God said, *"I will. I will have mercy. I will have mercy upon whom I will have mercy. I will have compassion. I will have compassion on whom I will have compassion. So then, it is **not** of him that willeth, nor of him that runneth, but of God that showeth mercy."* (Romans 9:16; John 1:13) Tragically, much of the modern evangelical community does believe that it **is** of *him that willeth*, especially in the area of salvation. But the Word of the Lord is plain. Salvation is of the Lord. All who are born again are the objects of the God that showeth mercy to whomsoever He wills (Romans 9:16).

The Plight of Pharaoh

To press home the absolute sovereignty of God, Paul brings to the forefront the plight of Pharaoh, the mighty monarch of the Exodus Generation. Pharaoh thought that he was the ruler of millions and the ultimate master of the multitudes. Pharaoh thought he could treat his subjects in any manner that he pleased. Proud Pharaoh thought he held life, and death, in his hands. If he wanted to practice ethnic cleansing, he would do just that. The royal order was given (Exodus 1:8-22). The Hebrew male children were to be murdered, but one baby, in particular, God said in His secret counsel (Deuteronomy 29:29), *"Touch him not,"* and Moses was spared. Time passed and truth crystallized: Pharaoh's free will was subject to the Sovereign will of God.

In fact, as the Plan of God unfolded, Pharaoh was nothing more than a vessel, fitted to destruction! (Romans 9:22). *"For the scripture saith unto Pharaoh, Even for this same purpose have I raised thee up, that I might show my power in thee, and that my name might be declared throughout all the earth. Therefore hath he mercy on whom he will have mercy and whom he will he hardeneth"* (Romans 9:17, 18).

Opposition to Absolute Authority

Now if it is true, that salvation is of the Lord, if it is true, that God wills who is to be shown mercy and who is not, *"Thou sayest then unto me, Why doth he yet find fault? For who hath resisted his will?"* (Romans 9:19) This is a natural question, and it is an old question. It was asked 2,000 years ago and it is still being raised today. How is the Christian to respond? The answer is this Christian: stay close to the Scripture.

The Sovereign needs no Human Security

The temptation comes to Christians to try and protect the character of God. This is usually done by making God out to be less sovereign than He is. But God needs no human protection. God takes full responsibility for His universe and all that happens in it including sin, sorrow, and suffering. *"That they may know from the rising of the sun, and from the west, that there is none beside me. I am the Lord, and there is none else. I form the light, and create darkness: I make peace, and create evil: I the Lord do all these things* (Isaiah 45:6, 7). The greatest evil of all was Deicide, in the killing of Christ, and yet even that was *foreordained before the foundation of the world"* (1 Peter 1:18-20).

Under the Royal Reign

Despite the sovereignty of God, the Lord still holds individuals responsible for their attitude and actions—which is what prompted the question of Romans 9:19. *"Why doth He yet find fault? For who hath resisted his will?"* To fallen humanity, there is a sense of frustration, to be told that God is sovereign, and yet individuals are still held accountable for what they say, and do. It does not seem fair, until it is remembered, that there is a parallel in human affairs. Consider the evidence. A man and a woman meet, fall in love, and desire to get married. Included in their marriage plans are children. Once the children are born, and reach a certain level of maturity, what happens? They are often assigned household chores, and then they are held accountable for their job performance.

A resourceful child might think about this someday and decide to protest, and ask some interesting questions. *"Why do you hold me accountable for these things? I never asked to be a member of this family. I never asked to be born. You could have taken steps to prevent my birth. How can this be fair?"* While the questions deserve attention, they will not change reality. Once the decision was made to create a child, in love by a married couple, then all the dynamics involved in that decision were engaged, including teaching the offspring to accept responsibility.

In a similar way, once God decided to create the universe the way He did, He has the right to hold His creation to whatever level of accountability He chooses. Discussion ends for, *"Shall the thing formed say to him that formed it, Why hast thou made me thus? Hath not the potter power over the clay, of the same lump to make one vessel unto honor, and another unto dishonor?"* (Romans 9:20b-21)

The Greatness of Divine Glory

Though God does make vessels fitted for destruction, He is also pleased to make many vessels of mercy in order to make known His glory. The greatness of the glory of God is revealed in part against the black backdrop of sin. We would never know anything about grace if it were not for sin and the agony of the Savior. We would never know anything about mercy and infinite love apart from sin. The angels do not know about mercy and grace, which is one reason why they are curious about the things associated with salvation (1 Peter 1:12).

Those who are the heirs of salvation are a privileged people. What a blessing it is to understand something about the, *"riches of his glory on the vessels of mercy, which he had afore prepared unto glory"* (Romans 9:23). What a privilege it is for Gentiles in particular to be united with the spiritual remnant of elect Jews (Romans 9:27-29) in order to discover a righteousness that was never sought. Only sovereign grace has made it possible for the Gentiles to be converted. Only sovereign grace has made it possible for a remnant of Jews to remain alive in order to be saved. Only sovereign grace has kept stumbling souls from the second death. (Revelation 20:6) Only sovereign grace has devised a system of salvation so that, *"whosoever believeth on him* [Christ] *shall not be ashamed"* (Romans 9:33). Believe on Christ and you will never be ashamed. Believe on Christ and you will know you are numbered among the elect (1 Thessalonians 1:4).

10

Romans 10

Religious Zeal is not Salvation: Romans 10:1-4

Once more, the apostle states that his deepest desire for Israel is that the nation might be saved (Romans 10:1). With all of their spiritual privileges, and opportunities, the people of Palestine should have come to faith. But instead, they went *"about to establish their own righteousness"* (Romans 10:3). They did this with zeal, but it was a zeal that could not save. Paul knew all about such religious enthusiasm, for he was once more passionate than all others. The apostle could boast, that he was *"Circumcised the eighth day, of the stock of Israel, of the tribe of Benjamin, a Hebrew of the Hebrews; as touching the Law, a Pharisee; Concerning zeal, persecuting the church; touching the righteousness which is in the Law, blameless"* (Philippians 3:5, 6). But it mattered nothing at all in the sight of God *"for by the works of the Law shall no flesh be justified"* (Galatians 2:16). God is not impressed with what man tries to accomplish religiously in the flesh. The Lord has shown the world the way of salvation in the person of His own dear Son, Jesus Christ. Knowledge of Christ alone will save. Religious zeal can never be substituted for submission to the Savior.

It is popular for people to say that, *"It really does not matter what a person believes, as long as they believe something, and they are sincere."* Or, *if we just do the best we can in life, then everything will work out all right.* None of that is correct. Saving truth is always according to knowledge, concerning Christ. Jesus said, *"I am the way, the truth, and the life: no man cometh unto the Father but by me"* (John 14:6). Hearing these words, the nation of Israel still turned away from Christ in an act of religious rebellion to establish their own righteousness. But national Israel is not alone in rejecting the rule of righteousness by Christ. All over the world, individuals turn away from the Lord, in order to establish their own righteousness, through church membership, baptism, attendance at the Lord's Supper, and being a good citizen—and God rejects it all.

If zeal alone could merit the approval of God and bring salvation to the soul then every Mormon, every Jehovah Witness, and every other cult member would be saved. Like Israel of old these religious organizations try to establish their own righteousness with fervor and determination. And, like Israel of old, they do it without knowledge. The Bible is plain. Only Christ saves. There is salvation in no one and in nothing else, *"for there is none other name under heaven given among men, whereby we must be saved"* (Acts 4:12). Salvation is to be found in Christ alone *"for Christ is the end of the Law for righteousness to every one that believeth"* (Romans 10:4). The apostle means three things by these words.

First, Christ is the *goal* of the Law, in the sense that all of the moral obligations of the Law are fulfilled in Him. Certainly Jesus did not come to violate the Law, but to fulfill it, which He did perfectly (Matthew 5:17; John 8:46).

Second, Christ is the end of the Law's *antitypes*. In the Old Testament, many sacrifices and offerings were established to teach some spiritual facet of the coming Messiah. In particular, there was the Burnt Offering, the Meat Offering, the Peace Offering, the Sin Offering, and the Trespass Offering (Study book of Leviticus). In Christ, all of the types find fulfillment.

This then, is the gospel for the salvation of the sinner. Jesus was sacrificed, according to the Scriptures. The Lord died a substitutionary death. Christ was buried, and God raised Him from the dead. There remaineth now no more sacrifice for sin (Hebrews 10:1-8). Christ is the end of the Law in this matter so that the saint can say,

> *"No blood, no altar now,*
> *The sacrifice is o'er;*
> *No flame, no smoke ascends on high,*
> *The lamb is slain no more."*

As Christ is the goal of the Law, and the end of all antitypes, so in Him the Law terminates. The Law holds no binding authority over the believer, as a rule of life, ceremonially, or socially. Christ has terminated it. Now the believer fulfills the righteousness of the Law, by walking in the sphere of the Spirit, in the newness of life. What was once written on stones is written in the heart (Hebrews 10:16).

Two Types of Righteousness: Romans 10:5-13

Having established the fact that *Christ is the end of the Law for righteousness to everyone that believeth* (Romans 10:4), the apostle presses his point by drawing a contrast between *"Legal Righteousness and Gospel Grace. Moses,"* said Paul, *"describeth the righteousness which is of the Law, That the man which doeth those things shall live by them"* (Romans 10:5). One passage that Paul may have had in mind, by referring to Moses, was Deuteronomy 30:10-16. In that passage, the commandments and statutes of the Lord are set forth, with the injunction to love God, walk in His ways, keep His Law, and live. But therein lies the problem. Who can ever do all that the Law demands? Who can live? Many have sincerely tried to obey the Law. Many have tried to do good in order to earn, or merit, eternal life. Many had a zeal for God, through Legal Righteousness, but there was no one who could abide by the Law perfectly.

In the gospel of Luke, the story is told that, one day, a lawyer came to Jesus. He had a question. *"Master, what shall I do to inherit eternal life?"* (Luke 10:25) Like most men, the lawyer thought that *he* had to do something himself, in order to merit the mercy of God. Like most religious men, the lawyer was under the illusion that he could do something to please God, if only he knew what to do. The Lord engaged the lawyer on this very point. Since he wanted to do something magnificent Jesus asked, *"What is written in the Law? How readest thou?"* (Luke 10:26) And the Lawyer answered, *"Thou shalt love the Lord thy God with all thy heart, and with all thy soul, and with all thy strength, and with all thy mind; and thy neighbor as thyself"* (Luke 10:27).

When he was finished Jesus said unto him, *"Thou hast answered right: this do, and thou shalt live"* (Luke 10:28). In other words, *"You want eternal life? You want to do some magnificent work? Than all you have to do is to keep on doing what the Scriptures tell you to do, love God perfectly!"* Now, can anyone really do that?

Of course not! And since no one can love God perfectly then no one should ever hope to have a pure *Legal Righteousness* that is acceptable to God. What then, is to be done? If Legal Righteousness cannot be obtained, is there another righteousness that can be found? The answer is, *"Yes! There is a Righteousness of Faith."*

The True Word of Faith

What characterizes the Righteousness of Faith? Good works of another nature? No. *"Say not in thine heart, Who shall ascend into heaven? (That is, to bring Christ down from above) Or, Who shall descend into the deep? (That is, to bring up Christ again from the dead.)"* (Romans 10:6, 7)

The Righteousness of Faith is not found by going forth to personally bring Christ from heaven to earth, or by bringing Him back from the dead, that would be works. But what saith the Righteousness of faith? (Romans 10:8) *"The word is nigh thee, even in thy mouth and in thy heart: that is, the word of faith, which we preach."* What is the word of faith? It is the gospel that is proclaimed! And this is the gospel, *"That if thou shalt confess with thy mouth the Lord Jesus, and shalt believe in thine heart that God hath raised him from the dead, thou shalt be saved"* (Romans 10:9).

The word *confess* is a very important word. To confess Christ, does not necessarily mean to walk down an isle during a modern religious service, and tell others you have believed in Jesus. Confession may include this novel innovation, if such activity is discerned to be the will of the Lord. However, in the first century, to confess Christ meant a willingness to honor Jesus before a watching world, which hated Him.

Both Judaism, and Rome, felt threatened by the Lord, and His followers. For the Jews, if Christ was the Messiah, then the Jewish leaders had committed a horrible act in delivering their King to be crucified. Moreover, if the Law really did end in Christ, as the new theology taught, then the sacrificial system should cease. But a sudden termination of the sacrifices and offerings would disrupt the economy of the Temple, and that could not be allowed to happen.

The Roman concerns were far different than the Jewish interests. It was widely believed that the ultimate bonding of the empire relied upon a social recognition, that Caesar was master or lord. To deny Caesar was lord was to unleash the forces of lawlessness, and anarchy, as individuals struggled with whom would be master of the multitudes. Therefore, patriotism demanded that honor be paid to Caesar in a special way. This, the Christians refused to do. They would confess no one to be their Lord or Master except Jesus. To confess Christ was to publicly declare allegiance to Him in a hostile world. Confession of Christ was not something that was done in the safety of a religious ceremony. Rather, it was done in the market places of the masses on a daily basis.

The Reward for Confessing Christ

Paul assures the Roman Christians that confessing Christ, and believing that God raised Him from the dead, brings salvation. *"Thou shalt be saved"* (Romans 10:9). Salvation, what a lovely word that is though it is no longer valued very highly. Time has passed. We are living in a generation that no longer asks, *"What must I do to be saved?"* But, *"What must I do to be happy?"* While it is happiness that men seek after, it is salvation that they need. Now, those who do seek for salvation, those who do confess Christ openly, will never be ashamed, for whether Jew or Gentile, the same Lord will rule over both. Whosoever comes to Christ will be saved (Romans 10:11-13).

The only issue remaining for individuals to determine is whether or not they will call upon Christ, or try to be saved according to Legal Righteousness. The choice is real. Either a system of salvation by works, resulting in Legal Righteousness will be pursued, or the Righteousness of Faith will be followed after. In deciding between the two, it must be said, once more, that Legal Righteousness, based upon the Law, will never be obtained, and the Law itself is weak and inadequate to help.

"Run and live! The Law commands

> *But gives me neither legs nor hands.*
> *Yet better means the Gospel brings,*
> *It bids me fly and gives me wings."*

Come to Christ by the Faith of Righteousness. Believe on the Lord Jesus for salvation for, *"If ever man was God, or God was man, Jesus Christ was both"* (Lord George Byron). As the God-Man, Christ can help as no one else. Great moral teachers cannot save. Confucius confessed, *"How dare I lay claim to holiness or love; a man of endless cravings who never tires of teaching, I might be called, but nothing more."* Great religious leaders cannot help. The grave of Mohammed can still be visited today. But the grave of Christ is empty. He is a risen Savior. Call upon Him, and you will never be ashamed in time or in eternity for you will stand clothed in His perfect righteousness—by faith. To call upon Christ means to believe. To call upon Christ means that you say, *"Lord, help me. Lord, save me from the penalty, the power and the pollution of sin. I do believe that thou art the Christ, the Son of the Living God. I do believe that God has raised you from the dead. I do believe that you and you alone are Lord. Amen."*

A Reasonable Inquiry: Romans 10:14-21

Having made a dramatic distinction between the Legal Righteousness of the Law, that cannot save, and the Righteousness of Faith, that produces salvation, the apostle continues his reasonable inquiry regarding the way of redemption. Several rhetorical questions are raised, resulting in specific conclusions that may be summarized.

- Every sinner must *call* upon the Lord Jesus Christ, and recognize Him as Lord, in order to be saved.

- No one can call upon Christ unless they *believe* in Him.

- Belief in Christ is impossible without *hearing* about Him.

- Hearing about Christ cannot take place, unless the message of the gospel is *preached*.

- The message, and the messenger, must be divinely *sent* if sinners are to be saved.

Concerning the matter of the messenger being sent, Jerome (c. AD 345-419), one of the great Bible teachers of the early church, observed that there are several classes of ministers. First, there are individuals who have been sent directly from God, such as the prophets, and the apostles. Second, there are individuals sent by God, but through men. The church has commissioned these individuals, because the local assembly believes that God has honored their ministry in a special way. Barnabas might fall into this category, as well as Timothy. Then third, there are those who are sent by men, but not by God. This is the professional minister who sees the ministry as a career choice, and not as a divine calling. To this fourfold group, a fifth classification could be made, according to 2 Corinthians 11:14-15. There are those who are sent by Satan. They are preachers of righteousness, but they are ultimately servants of the Wicked One.

Despite false ministers, those who have been sent are happy to proclaim the gospel. They set forth the fundamental character of the gospel, as well as its terms, knowing that it will have different effects on different people. Someone has said that the gospel of the sovereign grace of God *"makes sinners mad; it makes the saints glad; and it makes pretenders bad."* How true that is. The gospel reveals sin, and that makes sinners mad. The gospel brings assurance of salvation, and that makes the saints glad. And the gospel make pretenders bad, by stressing free grace and not free will.

How to Increase Faith

Those who hear the gospel preached are under a divine injunction to respond in a positive manner, by faith. It is faith that saves the soul. But how does one get such saving faith? The divine answer is, by hearing the word of God. *"Faith cometh by hearing, and hearing by the word of God"* (Romans 10:17). Mr. Spurgeon liked to say, *"Faith cannot be washed into us by immersion. It cannot be sprinkled upon us at a christening. It is not to be poured into us from a chalice. It is not generated in us by a consecrated piece of bread. Faith cometh by hearing, and hearing by the word of God."* As the Bible is read, Faith leads the soul to the Garden of Eden, to experience once more the Fall. As the gospel is heard, Faith leads the soul to the Garden of Gethsemane, where Christ prayed with blood, and sweat, and tears. Faith takes the soul by the hand and leads it to Calvary and says, *"Here is your Lord and your God. Believe."* By faith, the soul is able to say, *"I believe."*

> *"Before the Cross in awe I stood,*
> *Beholding brow and pierced hand;*
> *For me it was He bled and died,*
> *No other price for sin beside*
> *Could pay the price for me.*
>
> *His precious blood, there flowing red,*
> *Was love's best gift, most freely shed;*
> *No one but He the price could pay,*
> *Or save from death and point the way*
> *For sinners, you and me.*
>
> *And as I gaze, I seem to hear*
> *Him gently say, My son, draw near;*
> *New life I give and power withal,*
> *Free unto all who on Me call,*
> *Now and eternally."*
> —Ernest O. Sellers

We are to believe the gospel. Many years ago, the English preacher, John Henry Jowett (1863-1923), was invited to speak at Spurgeon's Tabernacle. He made an appealing statement, while talking about the woman with the issue of blood (Matthew 9:20, 22), and how she pressed forward so that she might touch the garment of Jesus and be healed.

As he finished his sermon, the minister exhorted the audience, *"Touch Him! Touch Him! And you shall be saved."* And then, anticipating that someone might say, *"But I don't know how to touch Him,"* the minister cried, *"And if you do not know how to touch Him, tell Him you don't know how, and that will touch Him."*

God is not disinterested in us. He is ready to move, when we call upon His name. Dr. T. T. Shields was a great pastor in Canada, for many years, he ministered at the Jarvis Street Baptist Church. He tells the true story of something he witnessed one day. The setting took place in northern Ontario where fences were built around the fields. Dr. Shields was looking out the window of his farmhouse, when he noticed a group of children, coming down the road from school one day. In the midst of the young people, was a cripple boy on crutches. For some reason the others suddenly turned upon the cripple boy. His crutches were taken away, and he was leaned up against the fence. Then the cruel children started to pelt him with rocks. The child was wounded and frightened. He looked across the fields, and there was his papa plowing the ground. *"Father!"* he cried. *"Father, help me!"* His father looked up, heard the child's cry, and came racing to the rescue. He jumped the fence, scattered the son's enemies, picked the child up, kissed him, and took him home. That is what it means to be saved. The Father will come to all, that call upon the name of the Lord. They will be saved.

No Excuse for Israel

Because God will save all that call upon Christ, Israel is without excuse. *"Have they not heard?"* Yes, Israel has heard the gospel. *Verily, their sound went into all the earth, and their words unto the ends of the world* (Psalms 19:4; Matthew 24:14; Mark 16:15; Romans 1:8; Colossians 1:6, 23). *"Did not Israel know?"* Yes, Israel knew the gospel according to Moses and the prophets. *"First, Moses saith, I will provoke you to jealousy by them that are no people, and by a foolish nation I will anger you"* (Romans 10:19; Deuteronomy 32:21). And Isaiah boldly said, *"I was found of them that sought me not; I was made manifest unto them that asked not after me"* (Romans 10:11; Isaiah 65:1). So Israel knew, that God would one day exalt the Gentiles, and entrust to them the gospel, so that the entire world, including Israel, would be without excuse. Israel knew the gospel, Israel heard the gospel, but Israel rejected all the incessant expressions of unwearying mercy that were extended. *"But to Israel he saith, All day long I have stretched forth my hands unto a disobedient and gainsaying [contrary] people"* (Romans 10:21; Isaiah 65:2). It is difficult to stretch out one's hands, for even a few minutes, let alone a whole day. Yet God says that He has stretched out His hands for a long,

long while. Though Israel rejected the outstretched hands of God, we must not.

At Calvary, God stretched out His hands once more in the person of His Son, in order to express the extent of His great love and mercy. Believe on Christ and receive Him as Lord and Savior. There will be no excuse for not doing that in the day of divine judgment.

11

Romans 11

A Remnant of Grace: Romans 11:1-10

As the apostle continues his line of reasoning in Romans 11, he asks a rhetorical question that demands a negative answer. *Hath God cast away His people?* The proper response is an emphatic, *"No! God has not cast away His people."* Paul is a personal testimony, that racial Jews can become spiritual Jews, by having the same faith as Abraham, Isaac, and Jacob. *"For I also am an Israelite of the seed of Abraham, of the tribe of Benjamin"* (Romans 11:1). As a regenerate Jew, Paul is not alone. He is just one, of an elect remnant of grace that includes Simeon (Luke 2:25-35), Anna (Luke 2:36-40), Nicodemus (John 3:121), Joseph of Arimathea (Matthew 27:57-60), and many more. Racial Jews, in every generation, are being and shall be saved, until the end of time. *"God hath not cast away His people which He foreknew"* (Romans 11:2).

The repetition of the words, *His people,* is important to note, because the scripture is very careful to define what is meant by *His people.* The *people* of God are those whom He foreknows (Romans 11:2; 8:28-30; John 8:27, 28), that is *"on whom, from the foundation of the world, He had set His love. He had made them the object of His special delight, a delight beginning in eternity, continuing in connection with their conception and birth, and never leaving them"* (*Romans,* William Hendriksen). Because God has foreknown Israel, souls shall be saved.

A Parallel from the Past

Additional proof for a present keeping of a spiritual elect of national Israel, is found in the historical preservation of just such a group. The apostle argues that a parallel to the situation in the first century could be found in the time of Elijah. Having defeated the prophets of Baal, on Mount Carmel, Elijah entered into a period of personal depression when word reached him that Jezebel sought his life. Suddenly, filled with fear Elijah cried out to God saying, *I am alone and they seek my life* (Romans 11:3b; 1 Kings 19:10, 14, 18). But Elijah was not alone, for, *"what saith the answer of God unto him? I have reserved to myself seven thousand men, who have not bowed the knee to the image of Baal."* The point becomes crystal clear. *"Even so then at this present time also there is a remnant according to the election of grace"* (Romans 11:5). Within the nation of Israel, in the first century, there was still, *the election of grace.* God had preserved faithful followers before in Israel, He would do so again.

What does all of this mean? It means that while national Israel has never obtained that for which she has sought, an election based upon the righteousness of good works, there is a spiritual election, according to the righteousness of grace (Romans 11:57). The remnant, which has been elected, according to the righteousness of grace, has been allowed to see the glorious gospel of Christ, while the rest of the Jews have been blinded to gospel truth. Who has blinded Israel? God Himself has administered this judicial judgment (Romans 11:8; Isaiah 29:10, 13; Deuteronomy 29:3, 4; Isaiah 6:9; Matthew 13:13; John 12:40; Acts 28:26, 27).

An Imprecatory Prayer

David, who prayed that God would destroy his own enemies, anticipated the presence of a divine judgment upon national Israel, in a Messianic sense (Romans 11:9, 10; Psalms 69). The point is established: when national Israel rejected God's way of salvation by grace, and entered into a system of salvation by works (Romans 11:7a) God rejected national Israel, but not totally. With tender mercy, the Lord set His affection upon some and drew those individuals to Himself as a remnant of grace. The rest were blinded by God (Romans 11:7b), so that individuals might realize that *"When men are saved they are saved by the sovereign grace of God, and when they perish, it is by the appointment of God, Jude 4, through their own fault"* (*Romans*, Robert Haldane).

The Legalism of the Lawless

One great lesson to be discerned afresh from this portion of the Divine narrative is that God will never accept any righteousness that is based upon works, not even from national Israel. The legalism of the lawless is an abomination to the Lord, when it is offered to Him as a basis of spiritual fellowship. Legalism is inadequate for intimacy with the Holy God, and insufficient to satisfy Divine justice. God rejects all forms of human good and bids sinners look to His Son as the only sufficient Savior of the soul that salvation might be according to grace. David Brown comments, *"The general position here laid down* (Romans 11:6) *is fundamental, and of unspeakable importance. It may be thus expressed: There are but two possible sources of salvation—men's works and God's grace; and these are so essentially distinct and opposite, that salvation cannot be of any combination or mixture of both; it must be wholly either of the one or the other"* (Ephesians 2:8, 9).

Murder on the Altar of Religious Mystery

Many seeking souls have been slaughtered upon the altar of religious good works, in more recent years, by embracing a diversity of doctrinal beliefs that interests and entertains, stimulates and stir up conversation, but cannot save. Many seeking souls have been made a martyr to religious error found in existentialism, communism, evolutionism, and certain forms of biblical criticism. If the end result of any intellectual insight (Form Criticism, Textual Criticism, Redaction Criticism, Demythologization) is to reduce the Bible to rubbish, and substitute human reasoning in its place, then it too will be found unacceptable to God.

Special note

Form Criticism. This method of biblical interpretation, seeks to go beyond the written Gospels and their literary sources, to the oral stage of Gospel tradition, in order to examine the various forms or types of stories, utterances, and legends represented in the oral tradition. The major division in the classification of Form Criticism in the Gospel material is between the narratives and the sayings. The narratives have been subdivided into pronouncement stories (Mark 2:1-12; 2:27), miracles stories, and stories about Christ (His birth, baptism, temptation etc). The sayings have been subdivided in wisdom sayings, prophetic sayings, commandment sayings, and the parables. The basic assumption of Form Criticism is that the oral tradition influenced what was finally written—without much regard for the truth.

Textual Criticism. Not having the original biblical documents, or autographs, the question has arisen, as to the reliability of the extant copies in regards to the number of manuscripts (MSS). Textual criticism, seeks to examine the textual transmission, and the content of the material preserved, taking into consideration the time interval between the original, and extant copy. Under girding textual criticism, is a fundamental assumption that there are many errors, both deliberate and unintentional, in the manuscripts which have corrupted, the extant texts of each book of the Bible, making it obligatory to ascertain and correct these corruptions, in order to reestablish the true wording of the original autograph, or manuscript of the author.

Redaction Criticism. Primarily concerned with the Old Testament, it is believed that a good deal of editorial activity took place, especially during the post exilic period. The purpose of Redaction Criticism is to investigate the Redactors (one who edits, revises, or molds, the literary sources) and the work they did.

Demythologization. As a former professor of New Testament studies at universities in Germany, Rudolf Bultmann (18841976) has influenced the modern Church through his theological method of *demythologizing* the New Testament. Bultmann sought to emancipate Christ from the need for historical validity. He believed this could be done by presenting Christ, not as a mythical figure, but as a real Man, like other men. He was a Great Man, to be sure, for He predicted the imminent end of the world, and the destruction of the rule of God, according to sacrifices and ceremonies. Jesus also protested against legalism, and a cultic worship of God, which is all very good. However, everything beyond what Jesus said is uncertain and legendary. Therefore, the Church must rid itself of the *myths* surrounding Christ. The basic problem with the thinking of Bultmann and his followers is that they dare to take the Scriptures apart verse by verse and decide what is *myth* and what is not. The Scriptures are not *God breathed* as they claim for themselves (2 Timothy 3:16), but a collection of fanciful stories about the Savior. For conservative Christians, such scholarship is unacceptable and needs to be challenged.

No Final Fall: Romans 11:11-12

The first words of Romans 11:11, *I say then*, are the same ones used in Romans 11:1. The apostle uses this language to introduce a new section, showing that the stumbling of Israel, *as a nation*, is not a final fall. In fact, the present remnant of a spiritual Israel, serves as an earnest or down payment that the best is yet to come. So strongly does Paul feel about this topic, that he uses a strong expression, to stop any thinking that the stumbling of Israel has resulted in a fatal future. *"God forbid,"* he says that such a concept should be considered. What then is the purpose of Israel's stumbling? It is this: *"through their fall salvation is come unto the Gentiles, to provoke them to jealousy"* (Romans 11:11).

Two grand objectives are achieved through the fall of national Israel from the place of prominence in the visible plan of God.

(1) There is a greater manifestation of Gentile salvation, and,

(2) The Jewish nation is stirred up to jealousy, as they see spiritual and material blessings, being poured out upon the Gentiles—according to grace. (Note a historical case of jealousy in Esau, (Genesis 28:69) Being stirred up, Paul believes the Jews will want to share in the grace of God.

Matthew Henry hears the Jews asking themselves, *"Shall the despised Gentiles run away with all the comforts and privileges of the gospel, and shall not we repent of our refusal, and now at last put in for a share? Shall not we believe and obey, and be pardoned and saved, as well as the Gentiles?"*

Rejection Brings Spiritual Resurrection: Romans 11:13-24

Lest the Gentiles be puffed up with their own spiritual pride at the unexpected blessings of God, Paul has something to say to them as an apostle and as a pastor (Romans 11:13). First, Paul wants everyone to know that it is still his intense desire to provoke his kinsmen according to the flesh to jealousy that some of them might be saved (Romans 11:14). Paul feels he can do this best by continuing to preach the gospel to the Gentiles (Study Acts 18:6; 22:21; Romans 1:5; 15:15, 16; Galatians 2:2, 8; Ephesians 3:1, 8; 1 Timothy 2:7; 2 Timothy 4:17). So while he ministers to the Gentiles Paul hopes that some Jews might be saved. This hope was not without merit for it was grounded in God's promise that a remnant of Israel would be saved. Second, Paul wants the Gentiles to understand that if national Israel is cast away in order that the world of the Gentiles might come to faith, that casting aside will not be final or fatal. Indeed, the receiving of the Jews back into the Redemptive Plan of God based upon conversion is nothing but *life from the dead* for them (Romans 11:15; Isaiah 26:16-19).

Some Jews shall be Saved

Two illustrations are used to further encourage the belief that Jews will be saved and received into the Church.

- **First Fruits.** The apostle argues that, *"if the first fruit be holy, the lump is also holy"* (Romans 11:16). The historical reference is to the Jewish practice at harvest time of offering a sheaf (or cake) to the Lord on the second day of the Feast of Unleavened Bread. (Leviticus 23:10, 11; Num. 15:19, 21) This token offering acknowledged that the Lord was the ultimate owner of all the land's resources. The first fruits in particular belonged to Him but so did the rest of the ingathering. It was *holy* [i.e., consecrated] to Him. Turning to the New Testament the image of something being a *first-fruits* is found several times by way of illustration.

- The Holy Spirit is said to be the *First fruits* or the first installment of a glory yet to come (Romans 8:23).

- Jesus Christ, by His resurrection from the dead, has become the *First fruits* of all those who have died in the Lord. The *first fruits* in Israel anticipated the harvest to follow. So the resurrection of

Christ anticipates a general resurrection (1 Corinthians 15:20; John 5:28).

- ❖ Individual believers who have come to faith in a specific geographical location are called *first fruits* (Romans 16:5).

- ❖ All believers who are born again by the Word of God are called *first fruits* because they are the first part in the redemption plan of God that will include a restoration of creation to its pristine glory (James 1:18; Romans 8:19, 20).

- ❖ Those souls, which suffered for Christ, during the days of the great tribulation of the first century, are called, *the first fruits unto God and unto the Lamb* (Revelation 14:4).

Returning to Romans 11:16, Paul's point, is that if the *first fruit* be holy (the separation unto God of Abraham, Isaac, and Jacob), the lump (the covenantal promises) sanctified the rest of the produce and so some souls will be saved. But only some will come to faith. *"Though he [Paul] was such a powerful preacher, [though he] spoke and wrote with such evidence and demonstration of the Spirit, yet of the many he dealt with he could but save some"* (Matthew Henry).

- ◆ **A Holy Root.** Not only is the lump holy, which produced the *first fruit*, but next, the apostle argues, *"if the root be holy, so are the branches"* (Romans 11:16b). The root, to which Paul refers, is the covenantal promise made to Abraham, of a spiritual seed. Matthew Henry notes that it is *"Not the root of communication, so Christ only is the root, but the root of administration, He being the first with whom the covenant was so solemnly made"* (Genesis 12:17). The branches are the descendants of Abraham, Isaac, and Jacob (Romans 11:28). Though some of the natural branches are broken off, some spiritual branches shall yet be grafted into their own olive tree (Romans 11:24).

When shall Israel be Saved?

There are two questions that now need to be considered.

First Question. *"When shall the natural branches [of individual Jews] be grafted in again, to enjoy the root, and fatness of the olive tree?"* (Romans 11:17b)

Answer. Immediately. At the present hour! Right now! From the moment of apostolic writing to the present hour.

Second Question. *"How is that response established? How can someone be certain, that even now Jews will come to faith?"*

Answer. When Paul wrote to the Romans, God had already rejected Israel, as a spiritually special nation. The reply of Christ to the disciples in Acts 1:6-9 was practically an admission that national Israel, was in some sense, no longer part of the covenant.

Though an exact moment of Israel's Divine Rejection may not be pinpointed, the Divine Repulse was certainly anticipated during the earthly ministry of Christ (Matthew 21:43). Following the resurrection, the Lord told His disciples to preach the gospel to all the nations of the earth (Matthew 28:19-20). The Divine Rejection of Israel probably took place the day Christ was killed (Luke 19:41-44). Everything was different on the other side of Calvary. The significant thing is that when Paul wrote *The Epistle to the Romans* (c. AD 56-58), he was dealing with a present situation.

In the Divine Economy, God had already officially cut off Israel, as a nation, to be entrusted with the gospel. Proclamation of the kingdom of heaven had been given to the Gentiles, who were responding en mass to Christ, thereby provoking the Jews to jealousy. However, if the Gentiles did not continue to persevere in the goodness of God, if the Gentiles started to boast, God would not spare them either. They too would be cut off (Romans 11:21). Furthermore, if Israel stopped abiding in unbelief, they would be grafted back in to the root of righteousness they had recently been cut off from, *"for God is able to graft them in"* (Romans 11:23).

The Future is Now

This regrafting of the natural branches, this saving of some, this hope for the holy lump [lit., a mingling—of flour and water, etc.], in regard to Jewish converts, is not only a continuing future hope but a **present** reality. When the apostle mentions 'their rejection', and 'their acceptance', he is not referring to what is going to happen in connection with The Great Consummation. We should not forget the context. The immediately preceding context is: I take pride in my ministry, in the hope that I may show how to arouse my own people to envy, and save some of them. The immediately following context is: *"Moreover, if some of the branches have been lopped off, and you, though being a wild olive shoot, have been grafted in among them and have come to share the nourishing sap from the olive root, do not gloat over this at the expense of those branches"* (*Romans*, William Hendriksen).

It is not some terminal generation, two thousand years plus, into the future that Paul has in mind to be saved, but his own kinsmen, and some of them through his own ministry! Therefore, Gentiles are not to boast, for, *"If thou boast, thou bearest not the root, but the root thee"* (Romans 11:18). The Gentiles are not to be arrogant or high minded, but they are to fear (Romans 11:20), and for a good reason: *"if God spared not the natural branches"* [racial Israel] He will not hesitate to disregard the wild branches which have been grafted in (Romans 11:21*). Behold* therefore *the goodness and severity of God* (Romans 11:22).

Does National Israel have an Ethnic Future? Romans 11:25-32

To summarize the situation, in context Paul has been speaking about the rejection of ethnic Israel. He has said that Israel's repulse is neither total, nor final, for certain promises were made to the fathers that shall still be honored. Some Jews shall yet be saved. The evidence that God will honor His word, of a spiritual seed to the patriarchs is reflected in the apostle's own salvation and the fact that if any Jew would stop abiding in unbelief they would be grafted back into the olive tree as a natural branch (Romans 11:23). While God is dealing with Israel, the Gentiles must not boast of their new spiritual privileges, for if they *"were cut out of the olive tree which is wild by nature, and wert grafted contrary to nature into a good olive tree: how much more shall these [individual Jews], which be the natural branches, be grafted into their own olive tree"* (Romans 11:24).

In the discussion of these things, there is a great mystery that Paul does not want the Gentiles to be ignorant of. The mystery is that *"blindness in part is happened to Israel, until the fullness of the Gentiles be come in"* (Romans 11:25).

The term *mystery* (Gk. *musterion*) does not refer to something that cannot be comprehended or understood, but something that has been kept secret, either in whole, or for the most part, in order to be presently revealed (Romans 16:25; 1 Corinthians 2:7-10; Ephesians 1:9, 10; 3:36, 9, 10). Paul wants the Church of Rome to openly know that the present spiritual state of Israel is not their final condition. Their blindness is only *in part*. It will not last forever nor is it complete. They will be grafted into the Redemptive Plan of God because the Lord will bring about a restoration of His people to favor based upon regeneration.

Hearts that cannot Feel

Until the day of Divine restoration *"blindness* [lit. hardness] *in part has happened to Israel until the fullness of the Gentiles be come in"* (Romans 11:25). The word for hardness speaks of callousness or dullness. The Jews are under a Divine judicial hardening of the heart until all the Gentiles who have been ordained to eternal life come to faith in Christ. As soon as that full Gentile complement (*pleroma*) has come in, God will change His dealings once more with the Jews *"and so all Israel shall be saved"* (Romans 11:26).

The Saving of *all Israel*

But what does Paul mean when he speaks of *all Israel? "Some interpreters understand the expression to refer to the true spiritual Israel,* [study Acts 10:34, 35] *while others seem to interpret this as a reference to the people taken as a race. Remembering Roman 9:68, where Paul stresses the spiritual nature of the true Israel, some interpreters see the words here as referring to the true and eternal seed of Abraham, which includes, of course, both Jews and Gentiles (Galatians 6:10). Calvin also interprets the expression to refer to spiritual Israel. Bruce reminds us that 'all Israel' is a recurring expression in the*

Jewish literature, where it surely does not mean 'every Jew with no exception' but rather 'Israel as a whole.' Therefore, 'all Israel, has a portion in the age to come,' says the Mishnah. Tractate, Sanhedrin (10.1). Other commentators say that these words should not be all embracing, because the phrase has the same meaning in relation to the Jews as do the terms 'fullness of the Gentiles' in relationship to the Gentiles, that is, 'all' means 'all those who will turn in faith to Christ.' Davidson and Martin point out that interpreting the expression as a reference to universal salvation conferred upon all men in view of their physical birth irrespective of their belief would contradict all else that Paul has taught (see Romans 2:28,29). However, some interpreters do insist upon the meaning of the ultimate ingathering of Israel as a nation in contrast to the present 'remnant.' These interpreters note three confirmations of this interpretation, two from the prophets and a third from the Abrahamic covenant itself" (New Commentary on the Whole Bible, Jamieson, Fausset, Brown).

The Diversity of the Divines

The diversity of scholarly opinion in understanding this section by godly commentators should lead all Bible students to guard against two extremes. The first extreme is to build a system of theology in which national Israel and *not* the Church is the focal point of interest and love (Ephesians 5:23-27). The other extreme is to reject the possibility that national Israel may yet have a new role in its own redemptive history. What is certain is that all of the elect of all the ages shall be saved for the Divine Deliverer has come according to promise to *turn away ungodliness from Jacob* (Romans 11:26). What is also certain is that Israel did not recognize her King when He came.

The story is told of the good monarch King George V, of England (1865-1936), who one day decided to visit a children's hospital. The young people were told of his coming but not all understood just what it meant, or even what the king looked like. About 4:00 p.m. a rather plain looking gentleman made his way through the wards, talking to the patients and then he left. When the visitor was gone, and no one else came, after a while, one little boy dared to ask the nurse when the king was coming. *But the king did come,* was the reply. *Don't you remember the nice gentleman who patted you on the head, and spoke kindly to you, and everyone else on the ward?* The little boy's eyes grew big, as he remembered the man. *That was the king?* he exclaimed. *But he didn't have his crown on!* When Jesus came as the Suffering Messiah to Israel, He didn't have His royal crown on in a visible manner and so the nation did not recognize her King. As a result, with wicked hands they took and killed their Sovereign.

> *"Hath He diadem as monarch*
> *that His brow adorned?*
> *Yea, a crown in very surety,*
> *but of thorns."*

Enemies of the Cross

Having killed Christ, having been placed under judicial discipline by God, Israel in general, and the Israelites in particular, became the enemies of Christ, and enemies of the gospel message (Romans 11:28a; Philippians 3:18). Nevertheless, Israel is still *beloved for the fathers'* [i.e., patriarchs'] sakes. *"For the gifts and calling of God are without repentance* (Romans 11:28b, 29). The gifts of God are irrevocable. The gifts of God are not to be recalled or to be altered. *Paul reminds us that the Jews are God's enemies because they have rejected the gospel, but from the standpoint of election they are His beloved. In their activities of that time the Jews were aligned against Christ and therefore characterized by disobedience to God and to God's purpose. Paul indicates that this situation existed so that the Father could have mercy on both Jew and Gentile alike. The idea of their obtaining 'mercy' is an entirely new idea [a mystery]. The apostle has hitherto emphasized the unbelief of the Jew and the making way for the faith of the Gentiles—the exclusion of the one occasioning the reception of the other. Then, opening a more cheerful prospect, Paul speaks of the mercy shown to the Gentiles as a means of Israel's recovery. It means that it will be the instrumentality of believing Gentiles that Israel will at length turn to the One whom they have pierced.* (Zecharius 12:10) *'For God hath concluded them all in unbelief [disobedience], that he might have mercy upon all"* (Romans 11:32) (*New Commentary on the Whole Bible*, Jamieson, Fausset, Brown).

The Mercy that Men Need

Mercy is what both Jews and Gentiles need. Mercy is what all men need, and mercy is what individuals can receive through Jesus Christ the Lord. In the city of Verden, Germany there is a large church built many centuries ago. On one part of the stone facade of the building there is a lamb carved because of a true event. There was an accident while the Church was being constructed.

A workman fell from a great height. He would have hit the ground, and been seriously hurt, or even killed, if he had not fallen providentially onto a sheep below. The lamb was crushed by the fall, and died, but the workman survived. He lived to tell the story, and then he did something else. He carved a lamb on the building to immortalize the sacrifice that was made on his behalf. Jesus Christ is the Lamb of God that was sacrificed for poor sinners. His redemptive work at Calvary is to be immortalized by every Christian who has fallen upon Him for mercy and grace. Come to Christ. *"Believe on the Lord Jesus Christ and thou shalt be saved"* (Acts 16:31). Salvation is a great act of Divine mercy.

In Praise of Divine Wisdom: Romans 11:33-36

Having argued for a present and future engrafting of ethnic Israel, back into the Olive Tree of Righteousness, according to God's immutability (Romans 11:29), Paul breaks forth in praise of Divine wisdom and glory. He can do no less. Indeed all such contemplation of the outworking of the Plan of Redemption, elicits a wonder at the Lord's infinite mercy and grace. It has been said that grace is for the guilty, and mercy is for the miserable. But those who are guilty, are also miserable. Sin makes men miserable. Mercy makes men hopeful. Though all have been placed in unbelief and helpless bondage (Romans 11:32), though all are full of guilt and shame, there is yet hope in God. The Lord God Omnipotent will yet come, and deliver souls from the pits of human depravity *"as it is written, There shall come out of Zion the Deliverer, and shall turn away ungodliness from Jacob"* (Romans 11:26). The Lord of Glory will give new hearts, and minds, and wills to worship Him. The Lord will yet have mercy upon those *"who have fulfilled the lusts of the flesh and of the mind; and were by nature the children of wrath"* (Ephesians 2:3).

Why God is willing to show such mercy to desperate, depraved, despicable sinners is something that is unsearchable! His ways are beyond tracing out. No one can trace the mindset or the methods by which God carries His plans into effect. All that individuals can do is to kneel in gratitude and wonderment before infinite wisdom as it accomplishes the ends intended—the salvation of souls. *"For who hath known the mind of the Lord? Or who hath been His counselor?* (Job 15:8; Jeremiah 23:18; Isaiah 40:13, 14) *Or who hath first given to him, and it shall be recompensed unto Him again?* (Job 35:7; 41:11) *For of Him, and through Him, and to Him, are all things: to whom be glory for ever. Amen."*

Commenting on this final thought William R. Newell exclaimed, *"What a prospect for a redeemed sinner! In the ages to come—ages of worship without end, in which glory will be ascribed to God, and that with ever increasing delight! And the word of eager, glad heart consent ends it all: Amen"* (Romans, Verse by Verse). In like manner, Dr. Donald Grey Barnhouse notes, *"No wonder Paul, the theologian and philosopher, sings. He insists in looking at God's wisdom through the eyes of a sinner redeemed. For he has a part in this great cosmic drama of grace. He is a participant in this display of God's wisdom. The unknown cosmic intelligences are merely observers of it."*

> *"Marvelous, infinite, matchless grace,*
> *Freely bestowed on all who believe;*
> *You that are longing to see His face,*
> *Will you this moment His grace receive?*
>
> *Grace, grace, God's grace,*
> *Grace that will pardon and cleanse within;*
> *Grace, grace, God's grace,*
> *Grace that is greater than all our sin."*
> —Julia H. Johnston

12

Romans 12

*"Faith deals with the invisible,
But God hates that love which is invisible."*
—Thomas Watson

*"Affection without action is like Rachel,
beautiful but barren."*

From Principle to Practices: Romans 12:1-2

It has been said that all doctrine should be practical and all practice should be doctrinal. The Apostle Paul would agree. It is a distinction, in Paul's style of writing, to move from a doctrinal section to a practical section. This dramatic division can be noted in *The Epistle to the Ephesians*. Chapters 1-3 are full of glorious doctrinal truths. Then in Ephesians 4:1, we read, *"I therefore, the prisoner of the Lord, beseech you that you walk worthy of the vocation wherewith ye are called."* In like manner, in *The Epistle to the Romans,* Paul has been setting forth the great doctrine of justification by grace through faith. Now, he speaks to the hearers to move from the doctrine, to Christian duty. He wants the saints to go from revelation, to responsibility, or from the things that are to be believed, to the things that are to be done.

The Mercies of Divine Majesty

In moving the believers from principle to practice, Paul does not demand, but pleads. *I beseech you,* he says. Though he is an apostle of the Lord Jesus Christ with ultimate spiritual authority over all the churches, yet the apostle condescends to beseech the brethren to do some specific things because of the mercies of God. The mercies of God are the mercies that Paul has been explaining in Romans 1-11.

- There is the mercy of justification, whereby guilty sinners are declared righteous in the sight of God, through faith, in the redemptive work of Christ at Calvary.

- There is the mercy of salvation whereby the heart is opened to the gospel so that the Savior is seen in all of His splendor and glory and the heart cries out, My Lord and my God!

- There is the mercy of sanctification or the process of being conformed into the image of Christ through the manifestation of the flesh.

- There is the mercy of glorification. One day sin shall cease. One day the soul shall be set free from the body of sin and then will come the resurrection day in a new heaven and new earth.

In addition to the general mercies of God, there are specific mercies.

- God has set His eternal love upon select individuals.

- God has given the gift of faith in order to believe.

- God has caused the soul to hear the voice of the Savior.

- God has ordained that every Christian shall be conformed into the image of Christ.

These are just some of the mercies of God designed to make the Christian want to respond in a definite way and present the body as a living sacrifice. The word *present* is a positive word. Paul does not use the word *yield* for that would suggest hesitancy on the part of the worshipper. The force of thought here is a direct volitional act in which the body is dedicated to the Lord.

A Living Sacrifice

It is an amazing concept that the body presented to the Lord is even wanted by Him. The world, the flesh, and the devil have used some bodies for unholy purposes and pleasures. Some bodies are old and limited in strength and vitality. Some bodies are diseased or crippled, and yet, God invites individuals to give them to His service. From a human perspective, the reason, in part, is this:

> *"Christ has no hands but our hands*
> *To do His work today;*
> *He has no feet but our feet*
> *To lead men in His way;*
>
> *He has no tongue but our tongues*
> *To tell men how to die;*
> *He has no help but our help*
> *to bring them to His side."*
> —Annie Johnson Flint

There is another sense to the Christians' concept of presenting their bodies to the Lord; the word *bodies,* as used in Romans 12:1 refers to the body as it relates to this world. The understanding is that God wants believers to be separated from sin and for good reason. A willful pursuit of sin in the flesh leads to eternal judgment. The Christian is to flee fornication and all manner of evil (1 Corinthians 6:18; 10:8). The Christian is to die to sin and live unto God (Galatians 5:19; Ephesians 5:3; Colossians 3:5; 1 Thessalonians 4:3; Jude 1:7). The Christian is to be a *living sacrifice* unto the Lord.

The concept of a *living sacrifice* stands in contrast to all the Old Testament dead sacrifices. No animal ever went in a willing manner to death, but they had to die. Unlike that, the Christian is to be alive unto God with the assurance that the presentation if done properly will be holy and acceptable in His sight. Not only that, but an initial, dramatic, and definite presentation of the body to God for His service is very reasonable. It is reasonable because it is *un*reasonable to pursue a path that will result in ultimate and eternal damnation.

Conformed into the Image of Christ

In addition to presenting the body for the service of the Savior, the apostolic injunction continues, *"And be not conformed to this world"* (Romans 12:2). The word for *conformed* means, *to be pressed into a mold.* Though the world wants to make every Christian a copy of the first

Adam, fallen and depraved, the apostolic counsel is not to allow that to happen. Rather, *"be ye transformed by the renewing of your mind"* (Romans 12:2). The antidote to sin, the solution to worldliness is a transformed mind. The mind is transformed spiritually in several ways: through reading the Word of God (Psalms 119), by the power of the Holy Spirit (1 Thessalonians 5:23), by an act of the renewed will (1 Peter 3:15), and by the knowledge of the truth (John 17:17).

The Will of God

By a voluntary presentation of one's body to Christ, by not being pressed into the mold of this world, by being transformed through the Word, the will of God is found to be *good, and acceptable, and perfect* (Romans 12:2). Concerning the will of God, a distinction can be made between the decretive will of the Lord, and His preceptive will. God's *decretive* will, determines whatsoever comes to pass (Psalms 115:31; Daniel 4:17, 25, 32, 35; Acts 2:23; Ephesians 1:5, 9, 11). The decretive will includes every raindrop that falls, every sparrow that dies, every hair on the head, and even every sin that is committed. Nothing happens in God's universe outside of the divine decree (Genesis 6:18; 7:15-24; Matthew 10:29; Acts 2:22, 23).

In contrast, God's *preceptive* will, is His will by precept or command. It is His moral will. It is the will of God, in the things which pleases Him. For example, God commands all men everywhere to repent (Acts 17:30). That is His preceptive will; repentance pleases the Lord. However, we know that not all men will repent. Therefore, the preceptive will, the moral will of God, will not always be fulfilled. But the decretive will of God will always be honored (Romans 9:19), though it be inscrutable. While no person can fully understand the decretive will of God, any more than the nature of God may be fully comprehended (Job 9:10; Romans 11:33), there is a holy obligation, to submit to the Lord, in reverent obedience, knowing that He does all things well for His will is good, acceptable, and in the end, perfect (Isaiah 45:12, 13; Romans 9:16-23; 12:2).

An Ethical Outworking of Righteousness: Romans 12:3-8

Having pleaded with the saints, to present their bodies to the Lord for spiritual service, the apostle explains why this should happen.

There should be an ethical outworking, of the righteousness of God because of the grace that has been bestowed. Because God has been good, it is only right for the redeemed to act in a gracious manner, with all due humility.

It has been said, that humility is not thinking how lowly one is, humility is not thinking of self at all. According to the Bible, humility is not thinking of one's self more highly than one ought to think (Romans 12:3). Humility is having a sober, and realistic, evaluation of one's gifts and abilities, with a willingness to serve in the sphere that the Sovereign has ordained. Biblical humility, allows for individuals to think well of themselves, in the sense that a person can know if he, or she, is intelligent, capable, well organized, personable, attractive, a good singer, etc. There is nothing wrong with being aware of one's talents, and abilities. But there are limits to just how highly a person is to admire, or love themselves, and not go beyond what natural grace, and Divine gifts, allow. Remembering that God *"hath dealt to every man the measure of faith"* will help to restrain the natural arrogance of the heart. This should not be all that difficult for ultimately there is nothing in life that a person has not been graciously given by the Lord. There is no such thing as a self-made man or woman. God has given all things in life—wisdom, health, opportunity, time, education, and resources—without which, no one would be a success, by any standard.

In the Church, the Christian is to restrain from exalting one's self, or debasing one's spiritual gift either. We are not to ignore the fact, that God has given to each person, a spiritual gift that is to be used. There is such a thing as feigned humility. It is possible to hold the grace, and gifts of God, in contempt, by refusing to function in the Church Body as God intended. The apostolic exhortation comes to show true humility, in a spirit of essential unity.

Diversity and Unity

The unity of the body of Christ is self-evident, in the fact that, *"as we have many members in one body, and all members have not the same office; So we, being many, are one body in Christ, and every one members one of another"* (Romans 12:4, 5). Only God is truly independent. Only God is self-sufficient. All else in creation is dependent, and interdependent. The Church is no exception. The Church comes together from diverse sources, denominational distinctives, and doctrinal differences, to form one spiritual body in Christ.

The Spiritual Gifts of Grace

The vital unity of Christians with one another is possible because of the gift of the Holy Spirit (John 15:26), and beyond that, the gifts the Holy Spirit brings to bestow, in order for Christian service to take place (1 Corinthians 12:1-12).

- It is God the Holy Spirit who determines what every person will do within the body of Christ (1 Corinthians 12:12-14).

- Every person has at least one spiritual gift (1 Corinthians 10:17; 12:8-10).

- While the spiritual gifts are different in importance, all are necessary.

- In Romans 12, a natural distinction can be made between Utterance Gifts, and Non-utterance Gifts. The Utterance Gifts are: prophecy, teaching, and exhortation. The Non-utterance Gifts are: ministry, giving, and ruling.

- Some spiritual gifts are temporary, while others are permanent. For example, there is no discernible evidence that the gift of prophecy exits today like it did in the life of Agabus, who is clearly said to be a prophet. Agabus said that there would be a famine, and there was a famine. He said that Paul would be arrested if he went to Jerusalem, and Paul was arrested (Acts 11:28; 21:10, 11). A true prophet of God is one who is able to tell with authority, what will come to pass, and it always comes to pass, according to the objective rule of faith. Modern day prophets, so called, are notorious for their false predictions. During the Old Testament economy they would have been put to death (Deuteronomy 18:20-22). Certainly today's untrue prophets, are at least worthy of censure, for the mischief they bring into the Church (Romans 16:17), not only by erroneous predictions but also by inaccurate teaching. They do not *"prophecy according to the proportion of faith"* in that there is no objective rule of faith. It is a foundational principle of biblical theology, that one Christian tenet must be consistent with all other tenets of the faith. The deity of Christ presupposes the doctrine of the Trinity, and vice versa.

Modern prophets are notorious for *forth-telling* concepts that attack the historic faith of the Church. The Health and Wealth Gospel is a direct contradiction of such passages as Luke 9:22 and Romans 8:17, 18. The Social Gospel is an assault upon salvation by grace, through faith alone (Ephesians 2:8, 9). The Self-esteem Gospel attacks the gospel of grace, and humility (Romans 12:3; 3:10; 3:23; 6:23). The *proportion of faith* is the objective standard of the Word of God. By the historic faith of the Church (Jude 14), should all prophets be measured.

Another example of a temporary gift is that of apostleship. There are no apostles today, for there is no one who could ever meet the biblical qualifications for that office (Acts 1:21-26; 1 Corinthians 9:1). While there are temporary spiritual gifts, there are permanent gifts. Among the permanent gifts are giving, ruling, and showing mercy.

- **Ministry.** God has ordained that certain individuals be allowed to minister the Word of Truth to others.

- **Teaching and exhortation.** While teaching is addressed to the understanding; exhortation is addressed to the conscience and feelings. Ideally, these are always united.

- **Giving.** This refers to the ability to give with a cheerful spirit to the Lord's work without any ulterior motives (Acts 5:1-11).

- **Ruling.** Not everyone, by temperament, or testimony, should be in leadership positions. The Lord equips those who should lead with wisdom, discernment, and insight.

- **Showing mercy.** While all Christians are called upon to be kind, there are individuals who have unusually tender hearts in order to show great mercy to those who are in need financially, emotionally, or spiritually. These are just some of the spiritual gifts of grace.

Commandments for Christian Conduct: Romans 12:9-12

In a series of time-honored phrases, the Apostle Paul continues to explain what it means to live out the ethics of the righteousness of God. The commandments are presented in trilogy forms.

- *Let love be without dissimulation.* When Paul says that love is to be without hypocrisy, he is teaching that love is to be genuine (1 Peter 1:22). There are those who pretend to love, by having a smile on the lips, but there is hatred in the heart. An invisible sword is drawn to destroy when the opportunity comes (Psalms 57:4). Christian love is more authentic and is reflected in outward expression, according to the terms of 1 Corinthians 13 and Luke 10:25-37. In summary form, biblical love is not an impulse of the feelings as it is a self-giving expression of right attitude, and right actions, at the right time. Such self-giving love is like God's love that has no regard for the worthiness of the recipient, or object of care.

- *Abhor that which is evil.* The Bible teaches that there is a time to love, and there is a time to hate (Eccl. 3:8). In particular, there is a time to hate evil, and injustice. However, there are some people who find it difficult to hate evil. Some Christians need more spiritual iron in their bones.

   They are much too comfortable with an unholy compromise, with irresponsible behavior. Liberal theology has done much to contribute to this present spiritual decline, for many have been taught to accept the unacceptable, and to call evil, good. Today, America finds itself with practicing homosexuals forming churches, and calling themselves Christians. Denominational churches deny the deity of Christ, the virgin birth, and salvation by grace through faith alone. The doctrinal evil that spills forth from the pulpit goes unchallenged. A clarion call needs to be heard, and heeded again, by conservative Christians: *Abhor that which is evil.*

- ***Cleave to that which is good.*** The ground, or soil out of which a righteous hatred of evil grows, is a love for that which is good. *There is a love that hates evil* (S. Lewis Johnson). The heart is to seize on that which is decent and holy in order to perform the will of God.

- ***Be kindly affectioned one to another with brother love; in honor preferring one another.*** One day, during the course of His ministry, the Lord's mother, and His brothers sought Him out to speak to Him. When the announcement came, Christ turned to the present audience and asked, *"Who is my mother? And who are my brethren? And He stretched forth His hand toward His disciples, and said, Behold my mother and my brethren! For whosoever shall do the will of my Father which is in heaven, the same is my brother, and sister, and mother"* (Matthew 12:48-50). In honor, the Lord preferred those who believed in Him with all their hearts.

- ***Not slothful in business,*** [or better, *Not lagging in diligence*]; ***fervent in spirit; serving the Lord.*** There is a natural progression of thought in this trio of exhortations. Christians are to be distinguished by a *diligence* in devotion that does not fall short, or lag behind enthusiasm given to other things in life such as work, or recreation. There is to be a spiritual *fervency,* which is maintained by the ministry of the Word of God (Luke 24:32). A life of diligence, and fervency, will result in *service* for the Lord. One biblical example of all of this is Apollos. His story is told in Acts 18. Apollos was a Jew, who had been born at Alexandria. He was a naturally gifted man who could persuade audiences with his words, and knowledge of the Scriptures. Being instructed in the things of the Lord, Apollos *was fervent in the spirit* to convince others. When Aquilla and Priscilla heard Apollos speak, they two were impressed, but realized that he needed to understand the Word of God more perfectly. After receiving more instruction in the faith, Apollos went forth to serve the Lord more earnestly than ever before. He did not lag behind even the apostles, in his zeal to win souls to the Savior. May all Christians be like Apollos.

There is a wonderful story that involves Sir Winston Churchill. In the early days of World War II, after the fall of France, and after the evacuation of soldiers from Dunkirk, Mr. Churchill went before the English Parliament to explain the situation of the country. Things appeared to be rather desperate. The government was told plainly, that Adolph Hitler was in total control of Western Europe. *"The whole free world,"* said the Prime Minister, *"is now dependent upon England."* Then he paused and said: *"Gentlemen, I find that rather exciting."* Every Christians should find it rather exciting, to be able to serve the Lord.

◆ *Rejoicing in hope; patient in tribulation; continuing instant in prayer.* With these words, the apostle expresses the inner workings of the Christian heart. It is to be a heart filled with joy, patience, and prayer. Joy is not a matter of circumstance, for Christian joy can be found in the midst of tragedy such as disease, or death. Rather, joy is the grasp that one has been given by the Holy Spirit on the meaning of any situation (John 15:11; John 16:21, 22, 24). *"The Christian does not sink under present trials, because he is buoyed up by the hope of future glory and the divine strength which is imparted to him through prayer. Those who are without God in the world are necessarily destitute of hope, for hope belongs only to those who know God"* (Ephesians 2:12 *Romans, Geoffrey B. Wilson*).

Those who know the Lord always have hope, and with hope comes the ability to endure the sufferings of time, all the while, being sustained by prayer. One night long ago, in a cell in the city of Philippi in Macedonia, two men, Paul and Silas, sang songs to the Lord and prayed after being arrested and beaten for their faith. Heaven heard, and rewarded such faith, for later that same night several new names were written down in glory. The Savior gave His servants souls for their labors, and it was sufficient (Acts 16:16-34).

Diligence in Gospel Duties: Romans 12:13-21

As the apostle continues to set forth a series of concrete ethical concepts for Christian believers, it must not be forgotten that the foundation on which these injunctions rest, is doctrine. In Romans 1-11, the great doctrinal truths have been set forth. Then we come to Romans 12:1, and to the transitional word, *therefore*. Paul writes, *"I beseech you therefore brethren."* What does he mean? Paul means that because of certain doctrines, a particular type of behavior is necessitated for the Christian and a principle is established: doctrine is important. Benjamin Breckenridge Warfield wrote, *"What after all is peculiar to Christianity is not the religious sentiment and its working, but its message of salvation; in a word, doctrine. To be indifferent to doctrine is but another way of saying we are indifferent to Christianity"* (*The Light of Systematic Theology*). Christian doctrine naturally leads to a Christian behavior that is both ethical, and practical, as the following injunctions reveal.

- ◆ *Distributing to the necessity of [the] saints.* In the ancient world, the unity between the social classes was not as agreeable as it is today. Generally speaking, people were either rich or poor, with the majority being numbered among the poor. The message, and ministry, of Christ mandated that the rich should look after the needs of those less fortunate (1 Timothy 6:17-19). Specifically, those Christians who had been given generous resources by God were to look out for the needs of other saints. One way to honor this gospel duty was to be hospitable.

- ◆ *Given to hospitality.* Since travel was difficult, and uncomfortable, at this time in history, families who lived great distances apart, would often agree, between themselves, to establish Guest Friendships. The idea was to provide lodging to traveling members who were well known or related. With the passing of time, and the emergence of a new generation, a way was found to continue the cultural exchange by issuing a sign of recognition. Half of a token would be given to one household and half to another. In the course of travel, individuals could then present the token and, if the two halves tallied, or matched, a place of rest was virtually guaranteed.

♦ ***Bless them, which persecute you: bless, and curse not.*** As loving hospitality was to be provided for the saints, so graciousness was to be extended to those who showed no hospitality but open hostility. Now, it would be nice if the persecution of the saints was restricted in administration to those outside the family of faith, but that is not the case. The enemy has come to sow tares among the wheat (Matthew 13:25). Not only does the world hate the Christians (John 15:18), but the world, along with the flesh, and the devil, has come into the Church to persecute the saints (Zecharius 13:6).

As a result, much persecution of the saints comes from other professing Christians. The result in Christendom, as a whole, is great turmoil and division. If there is to be any peace in local assemblies, and local communities then the practice of blessing the perpetrators of persecution must begin. While it is not easy, it is the stated will of God, the example of Christ, (Luke 23:34; Matthew 6:15) and the exhortation of the apostle.

♦ ***Rejoice with them that do rejoice, and weep with them that weep.*** If the believer can endure persecution then surely there is the ability to adjust to the moods and tragedies of others so that there is rejoicing with those who rejoice and weeping with those who weep. Of the two facets of the soul's sensitivity, the second injunction is easier to perform than the first. One of the early church father, Chrysostom (c. 347-407), noted that it was easier to weep with them who weep because nature has prepared the heart to enter into the sorrows of others, but envy stands in the way of rejoicing with those who have been blessed by God. The petulant heart can actually resent the blessings of God on others (John 21:17-22), but the gracious heart will want to honor those whom the Lord has been pleased to honor (Philippians 4:10; 2 John 4; 3 John 3).

♦ ***Be of the same mind one toward another. Mind not high things, but condescend to men of low estate. Be not wise in your own conceits.*** The Law of Selflessness, and Harmony, is brought into view with these apostolic words, as believers are told to be humble. For some, that is very hard to do. The story is told, that D.L. Moody once met a man on the streets, who said to him, *"You know, Mr. Moody, I am a self-made man."* Mr. Moody replied, *"Young man, you have just relieved the Almighty of a great responsibility."* There is room in most of us for less thinking *about high things* and more thinking of humble thoughts (John 1:26, 27; Philippians 2:48).

◆ ***Recompense to no man evil for evil. Provide things honest in the sight of all men.*** When the heart is humble, there will be less inclination to repay, in kind, those who have wounded with their words, and actions. There is such a thing as the Law of Non-hostility. Of course, this does leave the sheep of God open to the preying wolves, both practically, and doctrinally (Matthew 7:15; Mark 10:16; Luke 10:3; Acts 20:29). Those who love, embrace, and defend the doctrines of grace, know something of the hostile nature of wolves. Thomas Erskine said, *"Calvinism is a sheep in wolf's clothing while Arminianism is a wolf in sheep's clothing."* It is true.

Those who have a high view of God and a low view of man by nature, those who embrace salvation by grace through faith alone apart from free will and good works are but lambs in the midst of religious wolves. Nevertheless, when the wolves attack and justice is needed to right any wrongs, the justice is to be administered by the Divine Being who promises to intervene for it is written, *"Vengeance is mine, I will repay, saith the Lord."* Because God will do what is right, the believer is to make gracious provisions for his enemies. If they are hungry, food is to be provided. If they are thirsty, liquid refreshment is to be given. The reason for this is so that the soul of the saint will not be soiled by the filth of the flesh. In the spiritual warfare, evil can only be overcome by doing well to the enemies of the Cross. Oh, may the Lord grant the supernatural strength of the Holy Spirit for this gospel obedience as a love response to saving grace.

> *"Teach me to love thee as thine angels love,*
> *One holy passion filling all my frame—*
> *The baptism of the heaven descended Dove;*
> *My heart an altar, and thy love the flame."*

—Lines from
Spirit of God, Dwell Thou within My Heart
George Croly, 1854

13

Romans 13

A Matter of Honor: Romans 13:1-14

Having spoken of the evil that men do in Romans 12:20, 21, the natural thoughts of the apostle's readers would turn to state (government) sanctioned evil. The early church knew much about undeserved suffering that had its ultimate origin in a sadist form of government. What, then, should be the Christian's attitude in regard to the state? Is the church to be over government, or subordinate to it? The first seven verses of Romans 14 define the believer's duty to the state.

Paul begins his exposition by showing that the state can claim a certain measure of obedience of *every soul* (Romans 13:1) because the power it enjoys has been entrusted with care from God. *For there is no power but of God: the powers that be are ordained of God* (Romans 13:1; Isaiah 10:57; 45:1; Daniel 5:26). Does this mean that the state has absolute power over people without protest? No, for undergirding Paul's position is another principle: the authority of the state is a divinely delegated power, and so it is not an absolute authority, without redress. *"Some have supposed that the right or legitimate authority of human government has its foundation ultimately in 'the consent of the governed,' 'the will of the majority,' or in some imaginary 'social compact' entered into by the forefathers of the race at the origin of social life. It is self-evident, however, that the divine will is the source of all government; and the obligation to obey that will, resting upon all moral agents, the ultimate ground of all obligations to obey human governments"* (A. A. Hodge, *The Confession of Faith*, p. 293).

Because every human government is ultimately subjected to God, the state has no supreme power over the souls of men. When state laws do come into conflict with the laws of God, then it is better to obey

God, rather than men (Study 1 Kings 21:3; Daniel 3:18; 6:12; Mark 12:17; Acts 4:19; Acts 5:29; Hebrews 11:23). While the Christian is to render unto Caesar the things that are Caesar, the things that belong to God must also be honored.

Resisting the Urge to Rebel

Any movement to resist an established form of government should be done with due consideration lest the Christian be found resisting God, and receiving greater judgment (Romans 13:2). Under normal conditions, believers must obey magistrates, who exercise lawful authority in order to promote self-control, and enhance the good of society. If wives are to be obedient to their husbands (Ephesians 5:22), and children are to be obedient to their parents (Ephesians 6:1), then Christian citizens are to obey the state's sovereignty (Romans 13:3).

If there is no general principle of obedience, even for totalitarian regimes, like Rome, then there will be unrestrained anarchy, for it is the natural inclination for every man, to do that which is right in his own eyes (Judg. 21:25).

Over all, the rulers in government do function as the ministers of God, for good (Romans 13:4). And as God's ministers, they have the supreme right to administer capital punishment upon those that do evil (Romans 13:4). As John Murray notes,

"Nothing shows the moral bankruptcy of a people or of a generation more than disregard for the sanctity of human life. And it is this same atrophy of moral fiber that appears in the plea for the abolition of the death penalty. It is the sanctity of life that validates the death penalty for the crime of murder" (Principles of Conduct).

Those who obey the laws of the land, generally have nothing to fear, and are able to be a good witness for God (Romans 13:5). It would be a meaningless message, to tell people to submit to God's rule and reign, while defying the laws of man. Therefore, let the Christian pay his direct taxes, *"tribute to whom tribute is due,"* and even the indirect taxes as necessary, *"custom to whom custom"* all the while showing fear and honor to God. The reason for such honor to all is this: there will be another day of reckoning. One day the saints shall judge the world (1 Corinthians 6:2). In that day, the state shall perish, but the city of God and the citizens of the heavenly kingdom shall remain.

Walking in the Laws of the Lord: Romans 13:8-14

The Christian is not only to render civil obedience to the state, but he is to faithfully fulfill all social obligations to society (Romans 13:8). Unpaid debts should be avoided, for the social stigma they bring to the cause of Christ. The guiding principle of life, in all things, is to be love (Romans 13:10). The second half of the Divine Law, is summed up in the command, *"Thou shalt love thy neighbor as thyself"* (Leviticus 19:18). Therefore, let God's people avoid adultery, murder, stealing, the bearing of false testimony, and covetousness (Romans 13:9).

Having a Holy Unction

As the apostle brings this section to a conclusion, he sets forth once more, several practical reasons why Christians are to obey civil authorities, honor all personal obligations, live righteously before others, and manifest genuine love.

- ♦ **Time is short.** The Christian message has always contained an element of urgency, for death is certain and eternity is real. Therefore, Christians must awaken from any form of spiritual lethargy. Some Christians are asleep doctrinally. They have no idea of the many cults that have arisen to challenge, transform, or deny the historical faith. Other Christians are asleep practically. They no longer care if souls are saved. It seems that the church has forgotten that hell is not just a doctrinal truth, it is a geographical reality.

> *"Must I go and empty handed?*
> *Thus my dear Redeemer meet?*
> *Not one day of service give Him,*
> *Lay no trophy at His feet?"*

- **Salvation is near.** One day, Jesus Christ will come again the second time, for all that believe (Hebrews 9:28). One day, the skies will split open, and reveal the Lord of lords, and the King of kings (Acts 1:11; 1 Thessalonians 4:16). With each year that passes, with each that day that slips by the coming of Christ draws that much nearer. Robert McCheyne, the Scotch preacher, once said to some friends, *"Do you think Christ will come tonight?"* One after another they said, *"I think not."* When all had given this answer, he solemnly noted, *"The Son of Man cometh at an hour when ye think not"* (Luke 12:40).

- **The spiritual warfare is real.** As some put on evil under the cover of darkness, the Christian is to put on the Lord Jesus Christ like a robe of righteousness. And for any that would be tempted to deny the Lordship of Christ, for salvation, and sanctification, attention should be noted that whenever the terms are used in Scripture together, the focus of attention is on the Lordship of Christ (Acts 2:36). Unless there is a fundamental recognition of Jesus as Lord of one's life, there can be no hope for genuine conversion. Christ said, *"Why call ye me Lord and do not the things which I say?"* (Luke 6:46) Those who think they can live without holiness and still see God, fly in the face of the Scriptures (Hebrews 12:14). They have found a heavenly way to go to hell.

The Salvation of St. Augustine

Because the early church took seriously the apostolic exhortations to live a holy life, a man by the name of Augustine (AD 354-430) more easily came to faith one day, when he picked up the Scriptures and read the call of Christ to a life of consecration. Augustine himself has recorded the story of that dramatic moment of conversion.

He writes, *"There was a small garden attached to the house where we lodged... I now found myself driven by the tumult in my breast to take refuge in this garden, where no one could interrupt that fierce struggle in which I was my own contestant, until it came to its conclusion. I probed the hidden depths of my soul and wrung its pitiful secrets from it, and when I gathered them all before the eyes of my heart, a great storm broke within me, bringing with it a great deluge of tears... For I felt that I was still enslaved by my sins, and in my misery I kept crying, How long shall I go on saying 'Tomorrow, tomorrow'? Why not now? Why not make an end of my ugly sins this moment? I kept asking myself these questions, weeping all the while with the most bitter sorrow in my heart, when all at once I heard the singsong voice of a child in a nearby house. Whether it was the voice of a boy or a girl I cannot say, but again and again it repeated the chorus, Take it and read, take it and read. At this I looked up, thinking hard whether there was any kind of game in which children used to chant words like these, but I could not remember ever hearing them before. I stemmed my flood of tears and stood up, telling myself that this could only be God's command to open my book of Scripture and read the first passage on which my eyes should fall...So I hurried back to the place where Alypius was sitting, for when I stood up to move away I had put down the book containing Paul's letters. I seized it and opened it, and in silence I read the first passage on which my eyes fell: [Romans 13:13-14] 'Let us walk honestly, as in the day; not in rioting and drunkenness, not in chambering and wantonness, not in strife and envying. But put ye on the Lord Jesus Christ and make not provision for the flesh, to fulfill the lusts thereof.' I had no wish to read more and no need to do so. For in an instant, as I came to the end of the sentence, it was as though the light of faith flooded into my heart and all the darkness of doubt was dispelled."*

May Augustine's experience be known to all of God's people as they too put on the Lord Jesus Christ, and make no provision for the flesh, to fulfill the lusts thereof.

14

Romans 14

*"A Christian is most free, lord of all and subject to none.
A Christian is a most dutiful servant of all, subject to all."*
—Martin Luther

Freedom of the Christian Man

Six Laws Guiding the Christian Life: Romans 14:1-12

Apart from salvation, there are many issues in life that concern the welfare of the soul, but on which the Scriptures are silent. As a result, there are Christian individuals who have a difficult time discerning what is pleasing to God, and what is not pleasing to Him. The question arises as how to deal with the doubtful things in life. The challenge comes to the Christian, who is strong in the faith, to help those who are weaker. As mature believers consider the merits of those things that concern the weaker believer, several principles must be kept in mind.

First, the love of Christ compels the stronger Christian in the faith, to treat weaker believers with great respect. *"Him that is weak in the faith receive ye, but not to doubtful disputations"* (Romans 14:1). The reception of the weaker believer into the Christian fellowship is to be done in such a way that a spirit of religious superiority is not created. The spirit of the Pharisees of old does not die easily.

Second, the Church fellowship is not to become a debating club. Rather, respect is to be shown to all, and by all. Respect can best be manifested, by honoring the decisions of those who feel they are pleasing God by giving up certain things, or by observing other things. *"For one believeth that he may eat all things* [including swine]:

another, who is weak, eateth herbs [is a vegetarian]." Those who are stronger in the faith, and able to handle the law of liberty, can act in a gracious manner, by refraining from legitimate activities in their presence. The burden of showing graciousness, in doubtful areas, rest upon the stronger Christian, like Paul (Rom 15:1).

Third, the stronger Christian in the faith is to behave in such a way as to encourage the weaker believer to move towards maturity, and liberty in the Lord. This is best done by not being judgmental. *"And let not him which eateth not judge him that eateth: for God hath received him. Who art thou that judgest another man's servant? To his own master he standeth or falleth. Yea, he [the weaker brother] shall be holden up: for God is able to make him stand"* (Romans 14:3b-4).

For purposes of illustration, the relation of master and slave is used, for it would be well known. If a slave is in need of some form of correction, his own master is the one to administer it. In like manner, the servant of God, in doubtful areas, or unregulated matters, is to answer to Him. Much infighting in local assemblies would immediately cease, if Christians would stop trying to regulate the life of others.

Fourth, all Christians are to operate in faith, believing that everything said and done is for the honor of the Lord, and the benefit of others. *"One man esteemeth* [lit. prefers] *one day above another [sabbatarians]; another esteemeth every day alike, Let every man be fully persuaded in his own mind. He that regardeth [lit. observes as sacred] the day, regardeth it unto the Lord; and he that regardeth not the day, to the Lord he doth not regard it. He that eateth, eateth to the Lord, for he giveth God thanks; and he that eateth not, and give God thanks"* (Romans 14:5-6).

Fifth, Christians should be gracious toward each other, for all believers are interdependent. *"For none of us liveth to himself and no man dieth to himself"* (Romans 14:7). Despite differences on doubtful things, there is an essential unity of the body of Christ that relies on all other parts. The Baptists and the Methodist, the Presbyterians and the Lutherans, and all other expressions of the visible body of Christ, still need one another. In times of a major crisis, such as a world war, or a local or national emergency, this interdependency is more clearly seen, as doubtful lines are crossed to embrace and comfort one another. *"Let us not therefore not judge one another any more: but judge this rather, that no man put a stumbling block or an occasion to fall in his brother's way"* (Romans 14:13).

Sixth, at the judgment seat of Christ, all the doubtful things will be sorted out. *"For we shall all stand before the judgment seat of Christ"* (Romans 14:10). It is at the final judgment, that every Christian, strong and weak, shall give an account to God the Son (Romans 14:12; John 5:22). Since there will be a final day of reckoning, since time is short and eternity is real, let Christian charity prevail in non-essential matters.

Romans 14:13-23: Rights and Responsibilities

Having established the fact that every person shall one day kneel to be judged by the Savior, the Scriptures place a prohibition on believers judging one another in an inappropriate manner. The stronger Christian in the faith, should be calm, and quiet, rather than engage in conversation, and behavior that gives offense to a weaker Christian, who has certain qualms about matters on which the Scriptures are silent.

The apostle is not asking believers to do something that he has not done. Paul knows, for example, that there is nothing wrong with Jewish believers eating pork. The Old Testament rules and regulations prohibiting that particular practice have been rescinded. Still, if a person's conscience is violated with the eating of meat, then that individual should refrain from eating it, and the person whose conscience is not violated with the eating of meat, should not be judgmental. The larger principal at stake is this: the strong believer, with his liberty, should not destroy the weaker believer for whom Christ has died.

This passage is not teaching that once a person is saved they can be lost. The doctrine of the security of the believer is not in view here. *"This arresting language is not intended to suggest that any man could actually rob Christ of the fruit of His passion"* (Romans, Geoffrey B. Wilson). Rather, the issue is whether or not the strong believer will recognize their responsibility towards their weaker brethren. (1 Corinthians 8:11) David Brown notes that, *"Whatever tends to make any one violate his conscience tends to the destruction of his soul; and he who helps, whether wittingly or no, to bring about the one is guilty of aiding to accomplish the other."*

Three Truths which will Unite all Christians

Paul is concerned that the liberty of the strong believer not be used in such a way that it can be spoken of in an evil manner (Romans 14:16). While many things are legitimate for the strong Christian, not all things are expedient to perform. There is more to life than being right doctrinally. There are souls for whom Christ has died to sustain, and nurture, in the sphere of sanctification. Spiritual nurturing for the weak, takes place most effectively when the strong believer manifests righteousness, and peace, and joy, in the Holy Spirit. These three things will work to unite all Christians.

There is the righteousness of Christ that is imputed to the believer's account, apart from good works. There is the peace with God, because of no condemnation. And there is the joy of the Holy Spirit, based on the realization that fellowship with the Father is restored. When the strong believer keeps these doctrinal concepts close to the heart, and emphasizes them over personal liberties, heaven and earth will unite to approve.

The Essence of Sin

There is one final major point to observe in this section of scripture: whatsoever is not of faith is sin. While there are many definitions of sin that could be set forth, the summary of sin, is lack of faith. When Adam ate of the forbidden fruit, it was because he had lost faith in the sovereignty of God. When the children of Israel made a golden calf and danced around it in the dark night of the desert, it was because they had lost faith in the sustaining power of God. When Peter sank into the cold waters of the Sea of Galilee and cried out that he was perishing, it was because he had lost faith in the sustaining power of the Lord. When the disciples fled on the day Christ was killed, it was because they had lost faith in the promises, and power of God. *Whatsoever is not of faith is sin.* When a weak believer eats something, says or does something without the faith that is pleasing to the Lord, for that person, it is sin. Therefore, the strong believer must be careful not to insist that a person does something that will violate the conscience.

Summary

Graciousness is to be a mark of every genuine Christian. Spiritual graciousness is manifested, in part, when the strong believer practices the Law of Love, and does not use liberty to offend weaker brethren. Graciousness is manifested when questionable matters are not argued over, but peace is promoted through the remembrance of imputed righteousness, redeeming reconciliation, and the delight of being under the guidance of the Holy Spirit.

15

Romans 15

Romans 15:1-6: Seven Principles and a Prayer

The apostle continues to set forth the obligation of the strong believer toward the weak. Paul has been saying that the weak believer is to be readily received in the fellowship of the local congregation (Romans 14:1). He has argued that special care should be shown toward those who are concerned about questionable non-essential elements of the faith lest peripheral issues overshadow the greater truths of the Christian life. As a strong believer himself, Paul is very sensitive about the weak brethren, in part, because there are always so many of them.

Of course, the reception of the weak brethren into spiritual fellowship must not be construed to mean that they are never be challenged to mature and grow in the grace and knowledge of the Lord Jesus Christ. Growing in gospel grace will lead every believer to enjoy the religious liberties that faith brings. So the weak brethren should be challenged. There is grave danger in showing too much leniency toward those who are weak in understanding the gospel to the point that they become harmful to themselves and to others—as far as truth is concerned. To confirm a person in legalism and prejudices is something that the Savior never did. Time after time the Lord arrested erroneous thinking, but He always confronted individuals at the proper time (Luke 14:16). The proper time for righteous confrontation is when a particular situation demands that something be said or done that more accurately conforms to the perfect will of God. This method of patiently waiting for a precise moment to teach a spiritual subject is in contrast to creating an environment of confrontation with leading questions guaranteed to create a debate among the brethren. That simply must not be done

(Romans 14:1). The strong believers are not to create a false standard of conduct for the weak believer or to engage in theological arguments that are of no profit.

In context, Paul does not seem to worry about the weak believer taking advantage of the strong believer as he does the reverse. Therefore, the apostle has set down point after point to establish the principles to guide the conduct of the strong believer toward the weak. By way of summary review seven great principles may be restated.

- The strong believer is to gently and graciously receive the weak believer who is concerned about questionable matters (Romans 14:1).

- The strong believer is not to belittle, think harshly of, nor pass ultimate judgment upon the weak believer (Romans 14:3, 10).

- The strong believer is never to put before the weak believer any issue or situation that would tempt the weak believer to violate a personal principle and practice of faith (Romans 14:13).

- The strong believer is not to recklessly destroy the value system of someone for whom Christ has died (Romans 14:15).

- The strong believer is to manifest a life of personal faith all the while remembering that, *"If a person be convinced that a thing is contrary to God's law, and yet practices it, he is guilty before God, although it should be found that the thing is lawful"* (*Romans*, Robert Haldane). *"What so ever is not of faith is sin."*

- The strong believer has a moral responsibility to bear the infirmities of the weak believer because of the example of Christ, whose steps must be followed (Romans 15:13). According to prophecy (Psalms 69:9), the Lord Jesus was destined to suffer reproach, and He did. By being unswerving in His loyalty to the will of the Father, Christ attracted the hostility of those who hated God. *"The reproaches of them that reproached thee [Father] fell on me."* And a powerful point is made: if Christ can suffer with the weak, then Christians in the Church can certainly be long-suffering with the weak as well.

- The strong believer is to take the leadership role, in pursuing conversations and a code of conduct that leads to peace, and righteousness, and joy, in the Holy Spirit (Rom 14:19).

The Saint and Selfless Love

To find strength for gospel obedience, in the showing of mercy to the weak believer, the strong believer is to consider not only the sufferings of Christ, but the scriptures as well. *"For whatsoever things were written aforetime were written for our learning, that we through patience and comfort of the Scriptures might have hope"* (Romans 15:4). The hope that comes from a study of the Scriptures is a quiet confidence that a life of love, lived in faith, while being graciousness to the weak brethren, will be rewarded. But the Christian must go to the Scriptures to find this great hope and therein is one of the great tragedies of Christendom.

Unfortunately, many Christians are more than willing to let popular culture in a religious congregation, be it liberal or conservative, set the standard of Christian conduct. That should not be. It is the expressed will of God the Father that the Scriptures guide the practice of the professing saint, not modern society. Paul knows that by studying the Scriptures and following the Savior a life of selfless love will be manifested. For such selfless love Paul prays. *"Now the God of patience and consolation grant you to be like-minded one toward another according to Christ Jesus"* (Romans 15:5).

In this apostolic prayer, two attributes of God the Father are requested to be apparent in the lives of all Christians. There is the attribute of patience, and there is the attribute of comfort. And there is a purpose for these two attributes. As Christians learn to be patient with one another, and exhort one another graciously, a spirit of unity will be created and a cacophony of harmonious love will ascend to heaven. In the throne room of God there will be a wonderful symphony made with one mouth in praise to God, *"even the Father of our Lord Jesus Christ"* (Romans 15:6). *"Behold, how good and how pleasant it is for brethren to dwell together in unity"* (Psalms 133:1).

Three Questions to Consider

To enhance the coming together of Christians in unity to praise God there are three questions that all believers would do well to ask themselves be they weak, or strong, in the faith.

- Does the Bible forbid my doing this? Are there any specific commandments that prohibit this course of conduct? Are there any general commandments that limit this activity?

- Will this activity lead me into temptation and cause me to sin? The Lord instructs His followers to deal radically with any source of temptation to sin (Matthew 5:29, 30).

- Will this activity cause a weaker brother to be offended in a needless manner, and so lead to his spiritual downfall?

By consistently applying these three simple questions, to specific situations on a daily basis, sin will be arrested, the saints will be edified, the body of Christ will be strengthened, and the name of the Lord will be exalted. The weak brethren, who seriously apply these questions to life, will find themselves maturing in the faith, while the strong brethren who are guided by these questions, will be able to bear the infirmities of the weak, according to the will of God, and the prayer of Paul.

Romans 15:7-13: Four Calls for Christian Unity

Having shown that constant worship is the basis for congregational harmony (Romans 15:6), the apostle again exhorts the believers to receive one another. (Romans 15:7) With this exhortation, the discussion on the problem of the *strong* and the *weak* believer (Romans 14:1-15:6) is concluded, but a wider application of the principle of graciousness is desired. Paul is now concerned that harmony exist between Jew and Gentile. There is great drama present. For the first time in history, in a significant way, Jewish believers were uniting with Gentile believers to receive, and honor, the Lord Jesus Christ, as the eternal Son of God, based upon the efficacy of His redeeming work at Calvary.

But tension was high, because many Jews were struggling with their old customs and prejudices. After a lifetime of honoring specific prohibitions, and thinking in a negative way about a whole group of people, it was hard to suddenly reverse habits of the heart, and inbred hatred. For conscientious Jews it was not easy to eat formerly forbidden foods. It was not easy to give up worship on the Sabbath. It was not easy to love historical enemies. Nevertheless, the plan of God called for unity between Jew and Gentiles as the Psalms, (Psalms 18:49; 2 Sam. 22:50; Psalms 117:1) the Law, (Deuteronomy 32:43) and the Prophets anticipated (Isaiah 11:1, 10).

The first quotation from Psalms 18 has reference to the victory of David over the Gentiles whereby he is able to confess to them the source of his power and honor the name of God in their midst. David viewed victory on the field of battle as an opportunity to dispel spiritual darkness and bring light to the Gentiles.

The second quotation from Deuteronomy 32, inviting the Gentiles to share in what God had done for Israel, is also an invitation to enter into the covenant blessings of the same.

The third quotation from Psalms 117 constitutes a messianic summons to all Gentiles to praise the Lord. This psalm anticipated the spread of the gospel to the ends of the earth.

The fourth quotation sets forth the messianic prediction of the lordship of Christ over all the earth, including the Gentile nations. No wonder Paul called upon the Church of Rome to honor the heartbeat of heaven, and to be a harmonious part of the universal people that Christ shall rule and reign over.

The God of Hope

Having established the scriptural and doctrinal foundation for his practical exhortations for unity, the apostle turns to prayer. *"Now the*

God of hope fill you with all joy and peace in believing, that ye may abound in hope, through the power of the God" (Romans 15:13). What a wonderful name for the Lord, *The God of Hope*. Paul commends the believers to the God who is the author of the gospel hope of unity, and to the One who is able to fill them with all spiritual joy, and peace, so that they abound in optimism by the dynamic power of the Holy Spirit.

Gentiles and the Gospel

As Paul begins the lengthy process of bringing his letter to the Church of Rome to a conclusion, he says many wonderful things about the people, for he does not want the believers to think that he views them as being deficient in either knowledge, or Christian practice. Not at all. Rather, the apostle just wants to express confidence, that those who receive his letter *will* understand the doctrine he has expounded, and will *continue* to move to implement the implications of the same by personal application. Therefore, Paul praises the believers for their goodness, and their ability to admonish one another to gospel duties. Finally, the apostle explains that he writes in a forceful or bold manner to them, because he is simply reminding them of spiritual truths that have already been communicated.

It is this *reminding* of the saints of something they had already been taught, which has led some bible scholars to conclude that the Church of Rome was founded by those who had been converted under Paul's ministry (and not Peter's ministry as tradition holds). For Paul to be the original founder of the Church in Rome, would not be too surprising for he was ordained to be, *"the minister of Jesus Christ to the Gentiles, ministering the gospel of God, that the offering up of the Gentiles might be acceptable, being sanctified by the Holy Ghost"* (Romans 15:16).

Though once a Pharisee of the Pharisees, Paul was quite pleased to have a specialized ministry to the Gentiles. Because it was ordained of God, he gloried in his calling (Romans 15:17). Because it was unique, he would not labor where others had labored (Romans 15:20, 21; 1 Corinthians 3:10). And so the years of imprisonment, the physical beatings, the false arrests, and all the other hardships Paul suffered for the Savior were nothing, because they served to make *the Gentiles obedient* to the gospel of Christ (Romans 15:18; Isaiah 52:15). From Jerusalem to Yugoslavia (Illyricum), the sweet story of the Savior was heard, as a single saint went forth to spread the gospel to the ends of the earth. Signs and wonders confirmed his ministry. (Romans 15:19; Acts 19:11)

Apostolic Affection

Because of his great affection for the people of Rome, Paul anticipated a visit to the Church on his way to Spain. Up to this point his missionary labors had prevented his going to Rome (Romans 1:13; 1 Thessalonians 2:17, 18). *"But now, having no more place in these parts, and having a great desire these many years to come unto you; Whensoever I take my journey into Spain, I will come to you"* (Romans 15:23, 24). However, before Paul could start his journey to Spain and be able to stop in Rome, he had to visit Jerusalem. *"But now I go unto Jerusalem to minister to the saints"* (Romans 15:25).

A Ministry of Financial Mercy

The reason Paul had to go to Jerusalem, was to deliver to the Jerusalem church a large offering that had been taken up on behalf of the saints. *For it hath pleased them of Macedonia and Achaia to make a certain contribution for the poor saints which are at Jerusalem* (Romans 15:26). Paul thought this was not only a *good* thing for the Gentile believers to do for their Jewish brethren but the *right* response for having received the gospel (Romans 15:27). Time and again in the course of his teaching, Paul will return to an interesting theme, that material possessions have no comparison to eternal values being communicated or partaken of (Romans 11:17; 1 Corinthians 9:11). To Paul, it is *right,* that those who have ministered spiritual things be supported by those with carnal things. So, after performing a ministry of financial mercy, the apostle planed to resume his missionary labors, and go to Rome, on his way to Spain.

What Paul did not realize, was that God had different plans for him. Oh, Paul would go to Jerusalem. He would turn over the money he had received for the poor. And he would leave the city for Rome—

but not the way he had planned. Paul did not know that he would be arrested in the Holy City.

16

Romans 16

Romans 16:1-27: Sincere Salutations

Having set forth the nature (Romans 15:14), power (Romans 15:19a), and extent (Romans 15:19b) of his ministry, the apostle begins the final portion of the epistle with salutations to many individuals in the Church of Rome. Only five or six are Jews (Aquila and Prisca, Andronicus, Junias, Herodion, and maybe Mary).

First Series: Salutation *to* Specific Saints

- **Andronicus** (*andronni'cus; conquering man*), was Paul's relative, who shared a prison sentence with the apostle (Romans 15:7).

- **Amplias** (*am'pleas; enlarged*), a common name among the slaves of Rome, was an early Christian companion of Paul, who was fondly thought of in the Lord (Romans 16:8).

- **Apelles** (*apel'leze; called*), was an *approved* Christian in Rome whom Paul greeted (Romans 16:10). His faith had been proven to be genuine by some specific trial of faith (James 1:12).

- **Aquilla** (*ac'quilah; eagle*), was a Jewish man, born in Pontus. For a time he lived with his wife Priscilla in Rome (Romans 16:3). He settled in Corinth, where he worked as a tentmaker. Because he was of the same occupation, Paul lodged with him (Acts 18:13). When the apostle began his travels to Syria, Aquila and Priscilla traveled with him from Corinth to Ephesus (Acts 18:18, 19). At Ephesus the devout couple met Apollos, and instructed him more fully in the Christian faith (Acts 18:26).

- **Aristobulus** (*aristobu'lus; best advising; best counselor*) was a Christian in Rome. Paul greeted his household, including any Christian slaves (Romans 16:10; 1 Corinthians 1:2-6; 3:1). Tradition presents Aristobulus as being a brother of Barnabas. He was ordained a bishop, and ministered in Britain, where he died.

- **Asyncritus** (*asin'critus; incomparable* or, *unlike*) was a Christian in Rome, whom Paul greeted in the Lord, prior to his visit to the great city (Romans 16:14). He was probably a slave.

- **Epaenetus** (*epen'etus; praiseworthy*), was one of the first to be converted to Christ from Achaia (Romans 16:5). Achaia (*akah'yah, lit. Asia*), was a province of Rome, in NW Greece. In 140 BC the Romans divided Greece into two provinces: Peloponnesus, and Macedonia. When writing to the Church at Rome, Epaenetus was greeted by Paul, and described as his beloved.

- **Hermas** (*her'mas*), was a Christian who resided in Rome. (Romans 16:14) He was probably a slave.

- **Hermes** (*her'mees; gain, refuge*), was a Christian in Rome, to whom Paul wrote (Romans 16:14). He was probably a slave.

- **Herodion** (*hero'deon*), was a Christian at Rome, a Jewish kinsman of Paul (Romans 16:11).

- **Julia** (*ju'leah*), is the feminine of Julius. Julia was a woman who was a disciple at the city of Rome (Romans 16:15).

- **Judea** (*jude'ah*), was a desolate and barren region, W of the Jordan, and S of Samaria. Jerusalem was its capitol.

- **Junia** was a certain disciple at the city of Rome, AD 60, who became a Christian before Paul, and suffered imprisonment for the Savior (Romans 16:7). The labors and sufferings of Junia and Andronicus, were recognized among the original Twelve Apostles.

- **Macedonia** (*masedo'neeah*), refers to a country N of Greece. Its main cities were Amphipolis, Apollonia, Beria, Neapolis, Philippi, and Thessalonica.

- **Mary,** was an unknown lady of great grace who labored on behalf of the apostle Paul (Romans 16:6).

- **Narcissus** (*narsis' us*; a well-known flower), was a member of the Church in Rome to whom Paul sent special greetings (Romans 16:11).

- **Nereus** (*ne' reus; a lamp*), is the name of a Roman Christian, to whom Paul sent greetings, AD 60. He may have been servant of the emperor of Rome (Romans 16:15). His sister is not named.

- **Olympas** (*olim'pas; heavenly*), was a prominent believer in the house church at Rome (Romans 16:15).

- **Patrobas** (*pat'robas; life of his father*), was a Christian in the city of Rome, to whom Paul sent a greeting (Romans 16:14). He was probably a slave.

- **Persis** (*pur'sis; that cuts* or, *divides, a horseman*), was a beloved Christian lady in Rome, to whom Paul sent greetings (Romans 16:12). She gave much spiritual labor for the cause of Christ.

- **Phebe, Phoebe** (*fe' be; radiant*), was a Christian lady who was part of the church at Cenchrea (Romans 16:1). Cenchrea (*sen'kreah; pulverized, granular*) refers to a harbor of Corinth located about 8 miles E of the city. Phebe, the servant [lit. *deaconess*], made her home there. Paul commended or introduced her favorably to the Church of Rome. The apostle wanted the saints there to assist *"her in whatsoever business she hath need of you: for she has been a succour* [comfort] *of many, and myself also"* (Romans 16:2).

- **Philologogus** (*filol'ogus; fond of talk*), was a Christian disciple in Rome to whom Paul sent greetings (Romans 16:15). He may have been the husband of Julia.

- **Phlegon** (*fle'gon; burning*), was a Christian disciple at the church in Rome to whom Paul sent greetings. He was probably a slave.

- **Priscilla** (*pris'sil'lah; ancient, little old woman*), with her Christian Jewish husband Aquila, met Paul in the city of Corinth, when the emperor Claudius ordered all the Jews to leave Rome in AD 49. Paul honors not only their friendship, but also their personal courage, in spreading the gospel of redeeming grace. They were *helpers in Christ Jesus, Who have for my life laid down their own necks* (Romans 16:3, 4).

- **Rufus** (*ru' fus; red*), was one included by Paul among those in Rome, to whom he sent special greetings (Romans 16:13). His mother was also honored, as being a spiritual mother to Paul. Another man by this name was the brother of Alexander, and the son of Simon the Cyrenian, whom the Jews forced to help bear the cross of Christ on His way to Calvary (Mark 15:21).

- **Urbane** (*ur' bane; of the city, polite*), was also a popular slave name. Urbane is recognized as *our* (Romans 16:9) rather than *my* (Rome. 16:3) *helper in Christ* [or fellow worker] which suggests that his spiritual gifts were widely recognized and used.

- **Stachys** (*sta'kis; an ear* [of corn]), was a disciple, in the Church of Rome. Paul sent him personal greetings (Romans 16:9).

- **Tryphaena** (*trifenah; delicate*), and **Tryphosa** (*trifo'sah, dainty*), were two Christian woman of Rome, to whom Paul sent a special salutation for their service for the Savior (Romans 16:12).

Second Series: Salutations *from* Specific Saints

- **Erastus** (*eras'tus; beloved*), was the treasurer [chamberlain] of the city (perhaps Corinth cf. 2 Timothy 4:20). He was one of the first converts to Christianity (Romans 16:23).

- **Gaius** (*gah'yus*), was a resident of the city of Corinth, whom Paul baptized (1 Corinthians 1:14). Christians assembled in the home of Gaius (Romans 16:23).

- **Jason** (*ja' sun; healing*), provided for the needs of Paul and Silas in Thessalonica. When a mob wanted to hurt Paul, but could not find him, they dragged Jason before the ruler, who released him (Acts 17:59).

- **Lucius** (*lushi' us*, Lat. for *Lucius*, surnamed the Cyrenain), was one of the prophets and teachers who ministered at Antioch. In the year AD 45, moved by the Holy Spirit, he ordained Barnabas and Paul to the work of the ministry (Acts 13:1; Romans 16:21).

- **Quartus** (*quar'tus; a fourth*), refers to a Christian from the city of Corinth who sent greetings by way of Paul to Rome.

- **Sosipater** (*sosip'atur; savior of his father*), was a kinsman of Paul who sent greetings by the letter of Paul to the church at Rome (Romans 16:21; note Acts 20:4).

- **Tertius** (*tur'sheus; third*), was a disciple who acted as an amanuensis [secretary] to the Apostle Paul in the writing of *The Epistle to the Romans* (Romans 16:22) He may the same as Titius Justus of Acts 18:7.

- **Timothy** (*tim'othy; beloved of God*), was taught the Law of God by his mother and grandmother (1 Timothy 1:5; 3:15). His mother was a Jewess and his father was a Greek (Acts 16:13). Timothy was converted at Lystra when Paul made his first visit there (Acts 14:6; 2 Timothy 1:5). The apostle Paul wanted Timothy to journey with him on his missionary work. After he was circumcised by the apostle, Timothy was set apart by the laying on of hands (1 Timothy 4:14; 2 Timothy 1:6; 4:5). He traveled with Luke and Silvanus to Phillippi (Acts 16:12), where he was entrusted with the care of a church. Timothy appears at Berea, later uniting with Paul at Athens. From Athens, Timothy was sent to Thessalonica (1 Thessalonians 3:2). He returned to Athens. His name is associated with Paul's who wrote to the city of

Thessalonica (1 Thessalonians 1:1; 2 Thessalonians 1:1) and to the Church of Rome (Romans 16:21). Timothy was also with Paul when the apostle wrote the Epistles to the Philippians, to the Colossians, and to Philemon (Philippians 1:1; Colossians 1:1; Philippians 1). Paul left Timothy at Ephesus to oversee the care for the church (2 Timothy 1:4).

Six Separate Topics

Woven into fabric of the apostle's concluding comments are six special topics that are worthy of brief consideration.

- **Home churches** (Romans 16:5). When the New Testament expression of the Church first met to worship, they generally did so in private homes. Such a physical setting allowed for a less formal leadership structure. A forum was provided for an active participation by all with emphasis on the priesthood of believers. Relationships were emphasized and nurtured by singing of songs, apostolic doctrine, teaching, communion, prayer, testimonies, exhortations, and expressions of affection (Acts 2:42; 1 Corinthians 12:611; Romans 16:16). The institutional church that exists today emerged with the passage of time. The local assembly of believers is generally characterized today by a formal structure (i.e. a building, legal incorporation and staff) and a paid clergy (Pastors, etc.).

- **The need for verbal and physical affection** (Romans 16: 16). A spirit of gratitude, along with verbal and physical expressions of love, should be part of the Christian fellowship. Notice how often Paul refers to someone as my beloved, my helper etc.

- **Church Discipline** (Romans 16:17, 18; Matthew 18:15-17). While church discipline is certainly commanded by the Scriptures, it must be something more than a religious judicial process against immorality, and doctrinal error. Church discipline is to take place within the context of a loving, and caring, pastoral environment.

It is to be undergirded by instruction in righteousness, and permeated by gentleness, and humility, on the part of those who dare to administer discipline. (study Matthew 7:15; 28:20; John 21:15-17; Galatians 6:1; 2 Timothy 2:14-26; Titus 2; Hebrews 13:17; 1 Corinthians 5:1-13; 2 Corinthians 2:5-11; 2 Thessalonians 3:6, 14-15; Titus 1:10-14; 3:9-11).

- **The defeat of Satan** (Romans 16:20). The Christian is wise to acknowledge the reality of Satan, take his opposition seriously, and understand his various strategies. There is a spiritual warfare and every Christian is part of it. However, Christ has already won the ultimate victory over the greatest enemy of heaven and earth. (Hebrews 2:14) Satan is a strong creature, but he is not divine. He is neither omniscient, nor omnipotent, nor is he omnipresent. Moreover, His ultimate destiny is the Lake of Fire (Revelation 20:10).

- **Doxology** (Romans 16:25-27).

The Epistle to the Romans comes to an end with a doxology that also serves as a summary of the message that Paul preached in love. In this closing paragraph, we have a great doctrinal declaration: God, the only true God, has power to establish those who believe in Him, and receive Him as their God. Paul says that God establishes them according to my Gospel, and the preaching of Jesus Christ. Paul, like all other God ordained, God-sent ministers, preached the Gospel of Jesus Christ – and the Gospel is the death, burial, and resurrection of Jesus according to the Scriptures.

Writing to the Corinthian believers, Paul said:

"Moreover brethren, I declare unto you the Gospel which I preached unto you, which also ye have received, and wherein ye stand: By which ye are saved, if ye keep in memory what I preached unto you, unless you have believed in vain. For I delivered unto first of all that which I also received, how that Christ died for our sins according to the Scriptures; and that He was buried, and that He rose again the third day according to the Scriptures (1 Corinthians

15:14). Paul had a singular subject: *The death, the burial, the resurrection of Jesus according to the Scriptures"* (*Romans*, Oliver B. Greene).

It is the gospel that calls forth the greatest praises from the souls of the saints who love the Savior, and value His redemptive work at Calvary. And what a privilege it is to be used of God to tell the greatest story ever told. It is the story of Jesus and His love.

There is a wonderful old story about how Christ returned to heaven after the ordeal of Calvary, and after His resurrection. The marks of His great sufferings were still visible. An angel approached the Lord, and said to him, *"You must have suffered terribly for men down there."* Jesus said simply enough, *"I did. Do they all know about what you did for them?"* asked the angel.

"No", responded the Lord, *"Not yet. Only a few know so far. Well,"* said the angel, *"what have you done that the rest of mankind might know?"*

And Jesus replied, *"I have asked Peter and James, and John, and the rest of the disciples and their converts, to make it their business to share with others and they in turn with still others, until the fartherest man, on the widest circle of the globe, has heard the gospel."*

The angel looked skeptical, for he knew all too well the frailty of fallen humanity. *"Oh",* he said, *"but what if Peter and James and John and others forget? What if they grow weary in well doing? What if they grow tired of telling the story? What then? Do you not have other plans?"*

And Jesus answered, *"I have no other plans. I'm counting on them."*

- **The revelation of the mystery** (Romans 16:25). Allowing *Scripture* to interpret *Scripture*, the *revelation of the mystery* is made manifest.

    "For this cause I Paul, the prisoner of Jesus Christ for you Gentiles, if ye have heard of the dispensation of the grace of God which is given me to youward: How that by revelation He made known unto me the mystery; (as I wrote afore in few words, whereby, when ye read, ye may understand my

knowledge in the mystery of Christ) which in other ages was not made known unto the sons of men, as it is now revealed unto His holy apostles and prophets by the Spirit; that the Gentiles should be fellow heirs, and of the same body, and partakers of His promise in Christ by the Gospel: whereof I was made a minister, according to the gift of the grace of God given unto me by the effectual working of His power. Unto me, who am less than the least of all saints, is this grace given, that I should preach among the Gentiles the unsearchable riches of Christ; and to make all men see what is the fellowship of the mystery, which from the beginning of the world hath been hid in God, who created all things by Jesus Christ: to the intent that now unto the principalities and powers in heavenly places might be known by the Church the manifold wisdom of God, according to the eternal purpose which He purposed in Christ Jesus our Lord: in whom we have boldness and access with confidence by the faith of Him" (Ephesians 3:1-12 ; Colossians 1:26ff).

What a wonderful truth it is that God loves Gentiles as well as Jews. God loves the nations, as He has loved Israel. In matchless grace, the gospel goes forth, calling souls to salvation. No wonder Paul says, and all who love Christ says with him,

*"To God only wise, be glory
through Jesus Christ, for ever.
Amen."*

A Final Note

Please write…

Dear Reader,

If the Lord has set your soul free from a system of salvation by works, or from the fear of not being found justified and righteous before God, please write to me. I would love to hear from you, and would like to encourage you in your walk with the Lord. Address your correspondence to:

Dr. Stanford E. Murrell,
5357 Indigo Crossing Drive
Viera, Florida 32955

E-mail: stanfordmurrell@yahoo.com

Website: www.stanmurrell.org

Appendix I

General Comments and Personal Application from

The Epistle to the Romans

General Comments and Personal Application from Romans 1

1. As Paul was a servant of Jesus Christ, and called of God (Romans 1:1), so is every Christian. Every saint has been saved to serve. Therefore, let each believer find a place of usefulness in the body of Christ without delay (Romans 12:4-18).

2. What God has promised He will perform. His word can be trusted (Romans 1:2). Rely fully upon what God said.

3. Paul was a man of prayer (Romans 1:8-9), and so provides a proper example of spiritual leadership to spiritual leaders. Pray, pastors, pray.

4. Comfort for Christians should be able to be found in the sweet fellowship of the Church (Rom 1:12). There is no need to seek the friendship of the world, the flesh, or the devil.

5. As the gospel is lived, the demands of an ethical life must not be compromised even in the face of death. The Christian must never be ashamed of Christ (Romans 1:16).

6. Because the foundation of the Christian life is faith, it will be tested. Every Christian will have their faith tried, in order to prove what sort it is. In days of prosperity, or in days of adversity, *"the just shall live by faith"* (Romans 1:17).

7. The wrath of God should hold no fear to those who are godly, and righteous, and who follow after the truth. But the ungodly should learn to tremble before the anger of a holy God (Romans 1:18).

8. Because it is easy for the heart to become defiled, those things that pollute, and then saturate the soul with the filth of the flesh must be avoided at all cost. God will give individuals up to uncleanness (Romans1: 24), and vile affections (Romans 1:26).

9. Sexual sins bring the most sever judgment (Romans 1:26-28). Sexual sins are by nature the most addictive and lead to other manifestations of evil (Romans 1:29-30).

10. There is a self-test to see whether or not salvation has come to the soul. Several questions can be answered. *"Do I practice any of the evils that are listed in Romans 1:23-31?" "Do I know intellectually the judgment of God will take place, but do not care to stop my secret sins?" "Am I really pleased with those who have abandoned themselves to all forms of wickedness?" "Do I take part in the sins of others vicariously, through inappropriate mediums?"*

General Comments and Personal Application from Romans 2

1. What we excuse in ourselves, we tend to judge harshly in others. There is a Dutch proverb that says, *"He who compares himself with another person is generally easy on himself."* But it is wrong to be this way (Romans 2:1).

2. There is one judgment that no person shall ever escape, and that is the judgment of God (Romans 2:2). What can be done? First, flee to Calvary, and hide behind the Cross-of Christ. Second, confess all known sin. Third, ask forgiveness. Fourth, if possible, make restitution. Finally, by the grace of God begin to live a new and clean life.

3. While the sinner must be warned that he is storing up judgment by being impenitent (Romans 2:5) the Christian is free to sing, *"Jesus paid it all, all to Him I owe, Sin has left a crimson stain, He washed it white as snow."*

4. While good works do not save the soul, neither are they to be neglected. *"For not the hearers of the law are just before God, but the doers of the law shall be justified"* (Romans 2:13).

5. Because the conscience can be changed for good or bad (Romans 2:15), it must be instructed by the Bible. Only then shall behavior be found pleasing to the Lord.

6. The Christian must keep in mind, that not only does God remember overt actions but the Lord will reveal the secrets of the heart as well. Though some important things may remain undiscovered by men in time, it is not so with the Lord. (Psalms 139; Hebrews 4:13) The omniscience of the Lord is not all negative or fearful. There can be comfort in the Divine omniscience, reflected in the fact that even before we speak, God knows if we truly love Him (John 21:17).

7. The Word commends self-examination (Romans 2:17-23). The solution to natural pollution is discovered in Psalms 51.

8. No professing Christian should ever put their ultimate trust in baptism, church membership or any other external or physical form. Salvation consists of having a heart that has been circumcised of sin by faith in Christ (Romans 2:28-29).

9. Every Christian should be careful of being a religious hypocrite, and no better than the legalistic Jews of old (Romans 2:22-24).

10. Outward forms and ceremonies may impress men and earn their praise, but God's standards are more holy and higher. Nothing less than a life of holiness will please Him.

11. Are you a Christian? To answer this question is to pass judgment upon oneself. When the heart begins to pass judgment upon itself, there is hope of being a Christian. When the heart finds a new longing for holiness, there is hope of being truly converted. *"Not all Jews are Jews"* and, *"not all Christians are Christians."* Are you a Christian? If not, would you like to be?

If the answer is, "Yes," then right now call upon the name of the Lord. You might want to pray a simple prayer: *"Lord, I know that I am a sinner. I need a Savior. I need Christ. I ask that Christ will save me right now from all my sin. I believe that Jesus is the Son of God. I believe that He died for my sins at Calvary. I believe that He was buried and that He arose again from the dead on the third day. I believe that He is coming again. Father, I want to be saved from the power and pollution of my sins. I believe in Jesus Christ as my Lord and Savior, and I want to follow Him all the days of my life. Thank you for the gift of salvation. Amen."*

If you have prayed this prayer from your heart and have received Christ as personal Savior, please write to the author, or to Mt. Zion ministries and let them know that Christ has become your personal Savior. They will rejoice with you in this matter, and send you some material to help you grow in your faith.

General Comments and Personal Application from Romans 3

1. Like the Jews of old, Christians must realize they too have now been entrusted with the gospel. (Romans 3:1) This privilege gives church members an advantage over others (Romans 3:2), which should be valued, and protected.

2. Humility should characterize God's people (Romans 3:9, 10). The story is told of a minister who arrived in his new parish. He was told by some well-meaning members, *"Your work here will be easy, for we are all good people."* The next Sunday the wise pastor took as his text 1 Timothy 1:15. *"This is a faithful saying, and worthy of all acceptation, that Christ Jesus came into the world to save sinners; of whom I am chief."*

3. It is the declaration of Scripture, and the testimony of time, that men talk too much at times. There is a constant self-justification of those things that are indefensible. It is far better to acknowledge our guilt before God (Romans 3:19). Perhaps then He will be pleased to show mercy.

4. The Old Testament is not to be lightly regarded. The concept that the Old Testament is for the Jews and the New Testament is for the Church is an unworthy proposition. The Old, and the New Testaments, are actually one (Romans 3:21, 22).

5. It should never be thought that there is salvation apart from redemption through the blood of Christ (Romans 8:24, 25). The Christian community should make this message crystal clear.

6. The wrath of God against sin must never be minimized in personal work. When the plan of salvation is presented, the wrath of God is to be pressed. Then a wrath removing Sacrifice, in the Person of Jesus Christ, can be presented (Romans 3:25). Against the black drop of sin shines the love of God (John 3:16).

7. The Christian should be careful never to boast (Romans 3:27). Faith in the grace of God, excludes all human merit, and basis on which to glory, in one's will, decision baptism, etc.

8. Only in Christ, is there to be any boasting. Let us join the redeemed in heaven that cast their crowns before the throne, by saying, *"Thou art worthy, O Lord, to receive glory and honor and glory and power: for thou hast created all things, and for thy pleasure they are and were created"* (Revelation 3:10, 11).

General Comments and Personal Application from Romans 4

1. Faith pleases God (Romans 4:1). Therefore, seek to increase your faith, as well as grace, and knowledge.

2. The life of David is often sanitized in its presentation. And yet, if ever a man received righteousness from God, without having earned it, it was David (Romans 4:6-7). Study his life afresh, with this concept in mind.

3. God delights to give grace gifts. In particular, God takes pleasure in saving sinners (study Isaiah 1:18; Ezek. 18:23, 32; 33:11; Hosea 11:8; Matthew 1:21; 11:28-30; John 3:16; 7:37; Revelation 22:17). Nevertheless, the signs and seals of salvation are not to be neglected (Romans 4:11).

4. Because God is no respecter of persons, He has many souls, from many nations—which eliminates racial prejudice. The

family of God is one family, as it crosses racial boundaries (Romans 4:16-18; Eph. 3:14, 15).

5. Hope has been called a quiet confidence in God. Abraham has such hope and so must we. (Romans 4:8; Hebrews 6:19, 20; 11:1).

6. Agrippa told Paul that he had almost persuaded him to become a Christian (Acts 26:28). In contrast Abraham was fully persuaded that what God had promised, He would be able to perform. Every Christian is either like Agrippa, or like Abraham, almost persuaded or altogether persuaded.

General Comments and Personal Application from Romans 5

1. As the heart searches for peace with God, it must be directed back to the Person of our Lord Jesus Christ (Romans 5:1). There is no substitute for a right relationship with Christ. Christian, always look to the root of righteousness, when trying to produce fruit.

2. In the struggle for sanctification, the Christian must always remember that *"past sins are forgiven, present access to the throne of grace is assured, and future glory is guaranteed"* (Dr. William Hendriksen).

3. One attitude towards tribulation is to glory in it. In order to do this, a dramatic adjustment must be made in one's thinking, to accept the proposition that tribulation produces spiritual fruit (Romans 5:3-5 see also 1 Corinthians 4:11-13; 15:30-32; 2 Corinthians 11:24-32).

4. For those who are struggling with the presence of addictive sins, there is much hope to be found in Romans 5:6-11. The person enslaved by a habitual sin, knows all about being *"without strength"* (Romans 5:6). What can be done? Part of the answer is to remember Romans 5:8 and believe Romans 5:10. *"We shall be saved by His life."* It is a Divine promise. You shall yet be saved!

5. Four times in Romans 5, the phrase *"much more"* is used (5:9, 15, 17, 20). There is a reason. Paul was filled with Divine optimism that the issue of sin would not frustrate the plan of God to save, and sanctify sinners. In moments of spiritual depression, a rereading of Romans 5 brings much encouragement.

General Comments and Personal Application from Romans 6

"The doctrine of justification without works, so far from leading to licentiousness, furnishes the most powerful motive to obedience to God. They who receive the doctrine of justification by the righteousness of God, have the fullest and most awful sense of the obligation which the holy law of God enforces on His creatures, and of the extent and purity of that law connected with the most profound sentiment of the evil of sin. Every new view that believers take of the Gospel of their salvation is calculated to impress on their minds a hatred of sin, and a desire to flee from it. In the doctrine of Christ crucified, they perceive that God, who is holy and just, pardons nothing without an atonement, and manifests His hatred of sin by the plan which He adopts for the salvation of sinners. The extent of the evil of sin is exhibited in the dignity and glory of Him by whom it has been expiated, the depth of His humiliation, and the greatness of His sufferings. The obligation of the law of God also derives unutterable force from the purity of its precept as well as from the awfulness of its sanction."

In the death of Jesus Christ the eyes of believers are directed to the Spirit of sanctification, whom God hath sent forth; for in dying Jesus Christ has obtained for His people the inexhaustible graces of the Holy Spirit. This leads them to renounce the spirit of the world, and submit to the direction and guidance of the Spirit from on high. They feel the honour of their communion with Jesus Christ, being His brethren and joint heirs, the members of His body, those for whom He shed His blood, and whom He hath redeemed at so astonishing a price.

They behold the peace, which He has made between God and them, which imposes on them the duty of never disturbing that blessed reconciliation, but, on the contrary, of rendering the most profound obedience to the Divine law. They discover the most powerful motives to humility; for the death of Jesus Christ is a mirror, in which they behold the vileness and indignity of their natural corruption, and perceive that they have nothing in themselves wherewith to satisfy Divine justice for their sins. His death, placing before their eyes their original condition, leads them to cry out before God, "O Lord, righteousness belongeth unto Thee; but unto us confusion of face."

Robert Haldane

General Comments and Personal Application from Romans 7

Are you struggling with some particular sin? Are you constantly fighting an area of weakness that will lead to eternal death if not arrested and killed? (Revelation 7:8) Are you in bondage to something that produces shame when succumbed to? (Romans 6:21) Do you really want to gain the victory after so long a time? That is good. The fact that you still long to be free from the pollution of indwelling sin speaks well of the state of your soul.

By faith begin afresh to believe what God wants you to know (Romans 6:3, 6:16, and 7:1).

- You have died in Christ.

- You are married to a new Master, Jesus Christ the Righteous One.

- This marital union will produce the fruit of a new spiritual life.

- Christ loves you with an everlasting love and will not let you go.

- The victory is yours because union with Christ is yours.

Receive these truths by faith, and then go forward in the freedom of your vital relationship to the Lord to serve in the newness of life. The Christian life is not to be a life of bondage, but that of freedom.

If you can say, *"Wretched man that I am! Who shall deliver me from the body of this death?"* you should also be able to say, *"I thank God through Jesus Christ our Lord!"* (Romans 7:24, 25)

General Comments and Personal Application from Romans 8

1. There is great comfort in knowing that, *"There is therefore now no condemnation for those who are in Christ Jesus"* (Rom 8:1).

   > *"I hear the Accuser roar*
   > *Of ills that I have done;*
   > *I know them well*
   > *and a thousand more—*
   > *Jehovah findeth none."*

2. Any person can know that they are truly converted by the words of Romans 8:5. If the one absorbing interest is the kingdom of God, it is a sign of salvation.

3. To know that one is loved by God is priceless. Little children like to sing, *"Jesus loves me this I know, for the Bible tells me so."* Adults can read what the Bible says, as per Romans 8:28 and 1 John 4:19, and sing, *"We love God because He first loved us."*

4. All questions wondering if prayers being heard by God are answered by Romans 8:26, 27.

5. While not ever Christian is rich, according to the wealth of this world, every believer is an heir to a spiritual fortune (Romans 8:17, 18).

6. The chief end of man has always been to know God, and enjoy Him forever, by acts of gospel obedience (Rom 8:14).

7. Of all the people in the world, the Christian has the right to be most hopeful (Romans 8:15-19, 35-39).

General Comments and Personal Application from Romans Chapter 9

1. Great doctrines raise great objections and tremendous hostility (Romans 9:19). The best response to hostility is to stay close to the Scriptures (Romans 9:20-33).

2. The Lord is a promise making and a promise keeping God.

Gracious Predictions and Promises Glorious Fulfillment

Genesis 3:15	Romans 16:20
Genesis 12:3	Galatians 3:8,9
Genesis 17:7	Acts 2:38,39
Genesis 18:10,14	Romans 9:9
Genesis 22:15-18	Hebrews 6:13,14
Genesis 29:35	Romans 2:28,29
Exodus 12:13; Leviticus 17:11	Hebrews 9:22
Numbers 21:8	John 3:14,15
Numbers 24:17	Revelation 22:16
Deuteronomy 18:15,18	Acts 3:22
2 Samuel 7:12,13	Luke 1:31-33
Psalms 2:7,8	Ephesians 1:22
Psalms 8:4	Hebrews 2:6-8
Psalms 16:10	Acts 13:35
Psalms 22:1	Matthew 27:46
Psalms 68:18	Ephesians 4:8
Psalms 69:20,21	Matthew 27:34
Psalms 110:1	Matthew 22:44
Psalms 118:22,23	Acts 4:11; Matthew 21:42
Isaiah 7:14	Matthew 1:23
Isaiah 9:1,2	Matthew 4:12-16
Isaiah 9:6	Luke 2:11
Isaiah 10:22	Romans 9:27
Isaiah 28:16	Romans 9:33; 10:11; 1 Peter 2:6,8
Isaiah 53	Matthew 8:17
Isaiah 59:20, 21	Romans 11:26, 27
Isaiah 61:1	Luke 4:18,19
Jeremiah 23:5	Luke 1:32,33
Jeremiah 31:31-34	Hebrews 8:8-12
Daniel 2:34, 35, 44	Matthew 28:18
Daniel 7:13,14	Matthew 26:64

- Daniel 9:24-27   Romans 3:21,22
- Joel 2:28,29   Acts 2:17f
- Amos 9:11-15   Acts 15:16-18
- Micah 5:2   Matthew 2:6
- Haggai 2:6-9   Hebrews 12:26
- Zechariah 3:8, 9   Hebrews 10:12-14
- Zechariah 6:12, 13   Hebrews 6:20-7:3
- Zechariah 9:9   John 12:15
- Zechariah 11:12   Matthew 26:15
- Zechariah 12:10   John 19:37
- Malachi 3:1f.   Matthew 11:10

3. The doctrine of election is designed to humble the soul, by teaching that salvation is not of works (Romans 9:11), but according to sovereign grace, and mercy. (Romans 9:15) It is God who ordains all things that shall come to pass, including the conversion of the soul.

> *"Ere into being I was brought,*
> *Thine eye did see, and in Thy thought,*
> *my life in all its perfect plan*
> *was ordered ere my days began."*

4. The doctrine of reprobation is as clearly set forth in Scripture as the doctrine of divine election. Dr. William Hendriksen has notes that, *"Reprobation is God's eternal purpose to pass by certain specific individuals in the bestowment of special grace, ordaining them to everlasting punishment for their sin"* (Romans 9:13, 17, 18, 21, 22; 1 Peter 2:8). While no one should ever teach more than the Word of God warrants, neither should the difficult doctrines be obscured. The God of love is also the God of justice and He is sovereign in all His ways.

5. Why God has chosen to elect some to salvation, and not all, is a great mystery. That God should choose to save some is according to great mercy. All that can be said in the final analysis is that *"The secret things belong to the Lord our God, but the things revealed belong to us and to our children forever"* (Deuteronomy 29:29). Before the

holy God there is to be a holy hush, and a humble bowing for *"He doeth all things well."*

General Comments and Personal Application from Romans 10

1. Prayer should be made to God that souls are to be saved in all nations, including the nation of Israel (Romans 10:1; Psalms 122:6).

2. A soul winner's heart should be cultivated at all times (Proverbs 11:30).

3. God has accomplished those things that are impossible for sinners to accomplish, in the area of salvation, from the penalty and power of sin. In the sight of God the spiritual struggle is over (Psalms 16:10; Acts 2:27; Romans 4:25; 1 Corinthians 15:20, 55-57; Revelation 1:17, 18). The saint can rest in a definite redemption accomplished, and applied (John 1:14; Romans 10:6, 7).

4. There is no contradiction between divine sovereignty and human responsibility. Israel, like all people, was, and is, responsible for rejecting God (Romans 10:14-21).

General Comments and Personal Application from Romans 11

1. The fact that God has not, and cannot, cast off the people of the covenant, should be a source of comfort to every Christian. (Romans 11:1-2).

2. Though labor in the Lord's vineyard may grow difficult, no Christian labors alone. God has a large remnant *"according to the election of grace"* (Romans 11:3-5). Someone has said, *"I grow weary in the Lord's work, but I never grow weary of it."*

3. Every believer must live out the ethics of the Christian life according to the principle of grace. The salvation, sanctification, and service of every saint, is to be done in the sphere of undeserved favor, freely bestowed (Romans 11:6).

4. A study of the Old Testament must be maintained (Romans 11:8-10). There is an essential unity between the Old Testament and the New. Whenever a point of doctrine needed illustration, or clarification, Paul always appealed to the Old Testament Scriptures [*study Scriptures Interpreting Scriptures*].

5. The sins of the saints are treated differently from the sins of the unconverted. While unbelievers perish in their transgressions, the children of God are sustained by the work of Christ at the cross of Calvary. His blood cleanses from all sin. Christians may stumble, but they shall not ultimately fall from grace (Romans 11:11-12).

6. There is a sanctified form of pride (Romans 11:13). While self-exaltation is wrong, self-recognition of the grace of God is not sinful (1 Corinthians 9:16; 2 Corinthians 9:15).

7. Every effort should be made, by every legitimate means, to bring souls to the Savior. (Romans 11:14)

8. It is wrong to give a false sense of security to those who reject Jesus as Lord. No hope is to be extended to any racial group or nationality that they are God's chosen people, apart from faith in Christ (Romans 11:15; Romans 10:12, 13).

9. The root supports the fruit, more than the fruit supports the root (Romans 11:18). Ministers of the gospel, and gospel ministries, labor for eternal matters while they are sustained by temporal gifts.

10. Romans 11:36 summaries *"the grand truth, which lies at the foundation of all religion. All things are of God, for He is the Author of all; His will is the origin of all existence. All things are through Him, for all things are created by Him as the grand agent. All things are likewise to Him, for all things tend to His glory as their final end"* (Robert Haldane, *Romans*).

General Comments and Personal Application from Romans 12

1. In a formal act—in private or in public—consecrate your body to the Lord for His service (Romans 12:1).

2. Study the Bible (Psalms 119), and read good Christian literature (Romans 12:2).

3. Seek to be more humble, by arresting all thoughts of pride (Romans 12:3; 12:16; Study Genesis 14:13, 14 with Genesis 3).

4. Make a commitment to be a more loving, and kind person (Romans 12:9, 10).

5. Serve the Lord more seriously and faithfully (Romans 12:12).

6. Find a way to give something to those who are in need (Romans 12:13).

7. Pray for those who have persecuted you, to be blessed (Romans 12:14).

8. Be sensitive to the sorrows and sufferings of others with sincerity (Romans 12:15).

9. Do not seek to repay reprehensible behavior with reprehensible behavior (Romans 12:17).

10. Do not seek personal revenge (Romans 12:19).

11. Do not be surprised when those who have hurt you, and violated every facet of the Christian life prosper. Instead, pity them, in light of Psalms 73, and Romans 12:19, and then show them mercy (Romans 12:20). They will need it.

12. Overcome acts of evil with acts of good (Romans 12:21).

General Comments and Personal Application from Romans 13

1. Submit willingly, and as unto the Lord, to all civil governments (Romans 13:1).

2. Remember that civil forms of punishment are justified, including capital punishment (Romans 13:4).

3. Pay all legitimate taxes (Romans 13:6).

4. Give all due honors to those who deserve them in every sphere of life (Romans 13:7).

5. Avoid debt (Romans 13:8).

6. Keep the Moral Law of God, summarized in the Ten Commandments (Romans 13:9).

7. Maintain a sense of spiritual urgency about the Lord's work (Romans 13:11, 12).

8. Walk honestly in the sight of all, and cease from a lifestyle of immorality (Romans 13:13).

9. Do not make any secret provisions for sinful conduct (Romans 13:14).

General Comments and Personal Application from Romans 14

1. Receive the believer who has scruples in non-essential areas, into the fellowship of the Church without quarreling with them (Romans 14:1).

2. Do not judge other Christians in matters that are not relevant to salvation, or sanctification (Romans 14:3).

3. Remember that there is a day of ultimate accountability for each person before God (Romans 14:9-12).

4. Love the weaker brother or sister in the faith enough not to engage in legitimate behavior they find offensive (Romans 14:15-17).

5. Make peace a primary goal of the Christian life (Romans 14:19).

6. Do all things according to faith for *"whatsoever is not of faith is sin"* (Romans 14:23).

General Comments and Personal Application from Romans 15

1. The Christian who is strong in the faith, and can handle Christian liberties, must bear the infirmities of the weak, in order to help them grow in the Lord (Romans 15:1).

2. The Christian is not to live to please himself but to edify, and encourage others. (Romans 15:2-3).

3. Remember that all things that have been written in the Old Testament have been written to guide the conduct of the New Testament believer (Romans 15:4).

4. Seek to be like the Lord, by showing great patience with others (Romans 15:5).

5. Christians are to remember their essential unity in Christ (Romans 15:7-13).

6. Christians are to glory only *"through Jesus Christ"* and then only *"in those things which pertain unto God"* (Romans 15:17). These are the limits of glory.

7. Christians are to pray earnestly one for another (Romans 15:30).

General Comments and Personal Application from Romans 16

1. Hospitality is to be shown to other Christians (Romans 16:1-2).

2. Honor is to be shown to those who labor in the Lord (Romans 16:3-15).
3. Outward affection is to be shown to other Christians (Romans 16:16).
4. Church discipline is to be maintained within the Church among the members (Romans 16:17).
5. Christians are to seek a good reputation through gospel obedience to the faith (Romans 16:19).

Made in the USA
Middletown, DE
09 January 2022